e Court System

OF THE UNITED STATES

and all federal statutes, after decision by federal courts of appeal and state supreme courts. Hears argument in about 170 cases each year.

MW00425954

Created by state constitutions, by the Ninth and Tenth Amendments, states retain all powers not granted to federal government. Appointed by governor (1/3) or elected by people of state (2/3) for varying terms.

(discretionary review) each year;

30 percent from state courts

Direct appeal from decisions holding U.S. laws unconstitutional

STATE SUPREME COURTS
Fifty states and the District of Columbia. Decides questions of law on briefs and oral argument.

AREAS OF STRESS
1. A single federal judge may enjoin a pending state prosecution or state official, if a clear showing of irreparable harm.
2. A single federal judge may grant habeas corpus relief to a state prisoner, after the prisoner has exhausted his state remedies.

3. Federal courts may abstain from deciding how the state courts would interpret a state statute. May certify specific questions to state supreme court.

INTERMEDIATE COURTS OF APPEAL
Discretionary review; in 24 states.

STATE SUPERIOR COURTS
All cases, criminal and civil; trials with or without jury. One in each county, or similar geographic area. Jurisdiction: law and equity; state constitution; statutes, common law; also federal Constitution (including most of Bill of Rights) and statutes. Limited by the supremacy, commerce, full faith and credit, and equal protection and due process clauses of the Fourteenth Amendment.

SPECIALIZED COURTS
Probate, Domestic Relations, Juvenile

STATE LOCAL AGENCIES
Industrial accidents, zoning boards, licensing boards, etc.

DISTRICT COURTS
Small towns, a justice of the peace; large urban centers, a municipal or district court. Jurisdiction: petty crimes, traffic offenses, small claims. No jury.

THE WAYS
OF A JUDGE

By Frank M. Coffin

Witness for AID (1964)
The Ways of a Judge:
Reflections from the
Federal Appellate Bench (1980)

THE WAYS
OF A JUDGE

*Reflections from the
Federal Appellate Bench*

FRANK M. COFFIN

HOUGHTON MIFFLIN COMPANY BOSTON

1980

*Library of Congress Cataloging
in Publication Data*
Coffin, Frank Morey.
The ways of a judge.
Includes index.
1. Appellate courts — United States.
2. Judges — United States.   3. Judicial process —
United States.   I. Title.
KF8750.C63   347.73'24   80-20179
ISBN 0-395-29461-4

Printed in the United States of America

V 10 9 8 7 6 5 4 3 2 1

FOR MY TWO RUTHS —
My mother, Ruth Morey Coffin
My wife, Ruth Ulrich Coffin

Acknowledgments

ORDINARILY, a debtor's disclosure of his obligations reveals liabilities. An author's acknowledgments, however, are a sly way of indicating assets, the revelation being pardonable because others are credited as the source of wisdom. Yet for some strange reason the author also attempts to absolve his creditors of deficiencies. Since this book is about my life and work as an appellate judge, and since what I am and how I work are in no small part shaped by my acknowledgees, they cannot have it both ways; they have contributed to both sides of the balance sheet. True, they are not responsible for what I have written, only for my being the sort of person who could pen such thoughts.

In the broadest sense, I am indebted to several waves of mentors and peers during the several turns my vocation has taken. There are the lawyers, clients, and judges of my youthful practice of the law; the electorate, media, political leaders, and office-holders of my days in politics and in Congress, particularly Edmund S. Muskie, my early coworker and senatorial judgeship sponsor; and fellow bureaucrats of the civil and foreign service from my time in the executive branch.

Most directly and immediately my benefactors have been my associates on the United States Court of Appeals for the First Circuit — my own former chief judge, Bailey Aldrich, who delicately presided over my apprenticeship years and still tidies up the loose ends; my former colleague Edward M. McEntee, who set an example of fairness and humility; and my present colleagues, Levin H. Campbell and Hugh H. Bownes, whose dedication to our work and deep friendship make life on our particular bench stimulating, satisfying, and pleasant.

No coworker is in the same category as my faithful, unflappable, and competent secretary of nearly a quarter-century, Mignonne Bouvier. She has aided me with congressional mail and speeches, with the task of helping administer an executive agency, and, now, with a decade and a half of judging. Another pillar of strength, contributing immeasurably to the smooth functioning of our circuit, is the clerk of our court, Dana H. Gallup.

As much of this book reveals, ranking high among my creditors are my present and former law clerks, some thirty-four. All of them, consciously and unconsciously, by intellect, character, and personality, have contributed to my judicial growth and personal happiness. I cannot begin to itemize my indebtedness here, but it would be unfair not to note the help my former clerk William C. Kelly, Jr., has rendered me, beginning with the encouragement he gave in his clerkship year, 1971–1972, continuing with his suggestions for readings over the years, and his sensitive review of Part III.

I have also had the good fortune to be placed in the hands of my editor, Anita McClellan. She has brought to this enterprise not only expected editorial expertise and encouragement but insight and creative concepts that have proven fruitful. For example, whatever sense of immediacy and participation is conveyed in these pages is largely attributable to Anita's reactions to an early draft. At the penultimate stage, where rewriting and meeting final deadlines were simultaneously pursued, I could not have had a more understanding or good-humored amanuensis than Clara Klein.

Finally, my family has given me the type of unostentatious

support that I needed. I was blessed still to have my mother always eager to hear of progress, my wife not only to protect my privacy but to apply her astringent (literally, "tending to draw together or constrict tissue") critical sense to my sometimes overambitious prose. My children and their spouses, Dan Kurtz and Nancy, Kris Engman and Douglas, Meredith, and Susan, have, particularly during our summer holidays together, granted the boon of leaving me alone without a sense of guilt and have never questioned my sense in pursuing this venture.

FMC

South Portland
Maine

Contents

II. WORK WAYS

I
A SEPARATE WAY

Chapter 1

On Judging Judges

DURING THE PAST decade and a half of judging federal appeals, I have tried, not always successfully, to keep my ruminating self at enough distance from my operating self so that the former could observe the latter with some sense of perspective. My habit was to make notes about the process of judging, some of the stubborn problems, some of the approaches that worked, some of the benchmarks of craftsmanship, as I came to recognize them. Whenever the spirit moved and time allowed — in an airplane, hotel room, or restaurant, even on the bench — I would scribble on tickets, menus, court docket lists, even baggage checks. In my own way I was, it turns out, following Thoreau's advice: "Know your own bone; gnaw at it, bury it, unearth it, and gnaw it still."

What I have to say, the bone I have been gnawing and burying, centers on the importance of understanding judges, particularly appellate judges. Today, one living in these United States cannot read a newspaper or listen to a newscast without realizing that judges are affecting human life more deeply at more points than ever before in our history. Rights and duties, liberties and servitudes, privileges and punishments, are defined ever more minutely in state and federal courts throughout the land. At all levels of sophistication, citizens are asking questions: Why must we entrust justice to the wisdom, mercy, and objectivity of this small

and elite group, the judges? Isn't there something undemocratic about this? If they must judge us, how can we
tell who is good, and why, from who isn't and why not?
Even if we know, is there anything we can do about it? This
kind of question, from those of high and low stations, from
disappointed litigants to columnists and even Presidents,
has made me want to try to help interested citizens take a
deeper, sharper, and more penetrating look at this delicate
business of judging.

While such large questions are aimed at judges of all
courts and levels, appellate judges exist in a special limbo.
Trial judges, after all, are on the firing line. Their conduct in
presiding over trials, their every decision and jury instruction are visible and audible to all. But appellate judges, ex-
cepting only the justices of the Supreme Court of the United
States, are often no more visible or comprehensible to the
citizen than the vapor-inhaling priestesses at the Oracle of
Delphi. The judges sit in a phalanx behind their elevated
bench, listen to argument, ask a few questions, and, weeks or
months later, issue an opinion. Exactly what goes on, if anything, between argument and decision is veiled in mystery.

The judges of the highest courts of the states and of the
federal courts of appeal number fewer than 500, fewer than
the members of Congress. Because the Supreme Court can
review only a small number of cases, it is these few hundred
who exercise critical and usually final authority over most of
the significant state and federal lawsuits and have much to
say about the direction the development of law takes. This
community of top judicial decision-makers is obviously
worth the citizen's acquaintance, but it remains largely hidden from public view and intelligent appraisal compared
with legislators and bureaucrats, the other two kinds of
policy-making officials. As a society, we are fairly well settled in our minds as to what to expect from, and how to
evaluate, both legislators and public executives. But even
after two centuries of national existence, citizens are still
caught up in a quandary about the role of judges. Let us

briefly consider common perceptions of the three branches.

Life in the Congress is a heady existence. A senator or congressional representative makes headlines, cross-examines the great, takes study trips to all corners of the world, feels involved and sometimes important in the great issues of the times, inexorably grows in both stature and influence with each re-election, and increasingly enjoys the attention of the media, the cooperation of peers and the bureaucracy, and the touching loyalty of people back home who feel well served. But for all this a heavy price is paid: most obviously, a bifurcated life — between home and the Capitol, between public and private life; the frustrations of having to scatter one's energies, of never being able to know very much about anything, of having always to read on the run; and the haunting specter of the next election. Variety, breadth, respect, and influence on the one hand; lack of time, depth, privacy, security, and serenity on the other. Only Faust could appreciate the trade.

It is on these embattled and battling figures that we must rely to achieve security and stability, to promote the social good, to forge unity out of diversity, enlightened nationalism and even internationalism out of parochialism. Whether they are state or federal lawmakers, they exist to serve the majority in two ways. Most often they serve by faithfully interpreting and following majority opinion. But those who render greatest service also help to develop and guide that opinion.

In either case the special qualities demanded are intuition, the ability to remember the past and yet sense the shape of things to come, and the manifold skills of communication with a constituency, party, state, committees, and the nation at large. One does not ask of a legislator: Is he or she brilliant? * Is he an expert? Is he systematic and well organized?

---

* The time has come for me to try to confront the Genie of Gender, which, once let out of the bottle, threatens to he-she a text to distraction. An almost exclusively male preserve until recently, the American judiciary — and the entire legal profession — is on the way to being humanly inclusive. Rather,

Is he objective? But, rather: Where does he stand? Does he work for the people? How effectively does he foresee, understand, and discuss issues? Can he ferret out common interests and mobilize diverse groups to support socially valuable goals?

The executive branch official is called on to be a circuit breaker for a whole series of currents in order to make the administrative process work. Internally he draws first on subordinates, clears laterally with equals, proposes to superiors, then, armed with an agency position, ventures forth to obtain clearance from other affected departments, and finally faces the Office of Management and Budget and the White House. Once he has done all this, he must still sell the proposal to Congress. At the end of the road are the delegation of responsibility to regional and field officials to work with the local governments, individuals, groups, institutions, and countries, and, finally, operations.

The executive lacks the visibility, the independence, and the wide range of influence of the legislator, but he possesses other strengths. Perhaps most significant is a limited and thus sharpened focus on only one kind of government activity. Although the administrator is busy, even harassed, with all too little time for creative thinking, the actions he is called on to perform lie within a manageable field of expertise. Within that field, even though he may be a quite invisible middle-level official, his authority and responsibility can be enormous when compared even with those of the captains of commerce and industry. Moreover, the government executive has incredibly vast intellectual resources to command: he can draw on departmental specialists for studies and reports, bring experts from all parts of the country to Washington for discussions, hire consultants, and commission outside studies.

---

however, than trying mechanically to alternate masculine and feminine pronouns and possessives, I shall use the masculine referent, unself-consciously, as, I hope, the reader will accept it.

The executive branch civil servant's function is to do, to carry out, to operate. His expertise is summoned in the translation of the President's program into new legislation, in explaining and defending it to Congress, in formulating regulations, and in devising the institutions and procedures to carry out the program that has been legislated. One does not ask of the bureaucrat whether he senses the mood of the people or can discuss issues publicly in an effective way, but whether he is competent in his field, knows the arts of bureaucracy, and can get things done. Through his expertise rather than his intuition he, too, serves the perceived will of the majority.

The appellate judge lacks the broad-ranging influence of the legislator and the specific levers of power of the executive. And he possesses almost no visibility. The appellate judge's immediate audience are his colleagues who sat with him when an appeal was argued. A slightly wider audience are the lawyers and parties in the litigation. Later, the audience may include a few more judges, lawyers, and law professors who someday will read his opinion. Reaction, favorable or unfavorable, is rare, confined to a law review comment, a reference in another court's opinion, or possibly an affirmance or reversal by the Supreme Court, months or even years after the work is done. Unlike the trial judge, whose decisions often place him uncomfortably in the headlines, editorials, and cartoons, the appellate judge is generally a media cipher.

To the remoteness of the appellate judge's chambers is added the insulation imposed on all judges by their code of ethics. Since about 1970, both the federal and state judiciary have austerely revised the standards of conduct expected of judges in activities and associations outside the courtroom. I can remember the time when judges commonly served on boards of directors of banks, businesses, and industries; arbitrated all kinds of disputes outside court; headed up fund drives; and publicly maintained their partisan political ties.

The feeling was that because a judge was eminent, he should be exploited.

Today the ethic is that just because the judiciary is so precious, it should be jealously conserved for its own work. So judges have accepted standards requiring them to sever any employment relationship with businesses, to refuse to solicit funds even for the best of causes, to limit their organizational affiliations to those charitable and civic groups which are not notably litigious and to programs aimed at the improvement of the administration of justice, to be wary about the sponsorship of any awards or ceremonials tendered in their honor, never to hear a case involving a corporation in which they own even a dollar's worth of stock, and never, never to contribute to, participate in, or attend a function of any political party.

All this, and much more, is a monastic prescription far more stringent than that imposed on or accepted by any other group of public servants. In this gregarious, extroverted American society, the fact that judges pursue a separate way is not always appreciated. Such separateness, much of it fashioned by Congress, has nevertheless not compensated for what, in the congressional view, is the unforgivable gift of life tenure. The Congress passes law after law affecting courts, adding immensely to their responsibilities, often with little effort to solicit the judiciary's views. Sometimes, when the judiciary is consulted, the response may be considered by the Congress to be overly formal, begrudging, and uncooperative. What is very clear is that these two branches of the federal government have not discovered how to communicate with each other in a regular and useful way compatible with the dignity and independence of each. Perhaps this is part of the price we pay for separation of powers.

In a superficial sense, the appellate judge falls heir to the negative facets of the work of the other two branches without their saving graces. Although he patrols the same broad spectrum of national problems as the representative or senator, his focus is generally not on policy but on some alleged (and usually hidden) defect of statute or regulation. He may be considering some smoldering (or flaming) public issue, but often his basis for decision is some unavoidable technical point. Even when cases require judges to dig deep into a functional field, unlike the administrators they cannot remain long enough to become experts; they must move on to the next case.

Yet the very narrowness of focus of a judge is itself a saving grace. It is what keeps his job manageable. He has the opportunity to dig deep into a problem, invest all his energy and ability for (with some exceptions) as much time as it takes to come up with an answer. More than the work of those in either of the other branches, his work product reflects his own personal involvement from start to finish. Then, too, the appellate judge operates within a discipline that, while it constrains him most of the time and in most cases, allows him some freedom of judgment. Meeting the professional challenge to his capacity to make a disciplined decision and the additional professional-plus-philosophic challenge to exercise his freedom responsibly are the most profound rewards for a judge. Finally, the appellate judge knows that he will eventually be dealing with the most vexing and stimulating issues of the day; the business of the courts is no longer, if it ever was, a backwater.

The function of the judge is of a quite different order from the functions of the legislator and administrator. The judge has the ancient task of settling disputes between specific individuals, groups, or institutions — a field we could call private law. He is also vested with a wide range of responsibility in the field of public law: he interprets the laws passed by the legislature and the regulations issued by executive agencies, and monitors the conduct of government agencies, public institutions, and even private individuals and groups in the light of the Constitution. When a judge interprets and

applies a law to specific facts, he is, of course, carrying out
the will of the majority as manifested through its elected
representatives. Not its will as precisely expressed, for legislatures cannot foresee every problem, and courts must fill in
the gaps. But in so interpreting, he is acting in a sense as a
specially convened, narrowly concentrated, amending legislature. When, however, a judge enjoins a government agency
or official from enforcing a law because it violates the Constitution, he does not decide on the basis of what the majority wishes, or would wish if the problem were presented to
it. He does not decide on this basis because the Founding Fathers and those who ratified the Constitution and its Bill of
Rights so long ago decided that limitations should be placed
on government (that is, the majority) and that certain rights
of individuals should be protected (that is, despite the
wishes of the majority).

One is not so sure of the qualities to be expected of judges.
Of course, some are obvious: Has the judge mastered the disciplines of his craft? Is he hard-working? Does the judge consistently strive to be fair and impartial? Does he have a
judicial temperament? Beyond these there is no clear consensus. For example, should the judge, like the legislator, be
expected to apply his sense of the mood of the country, or
what he thinks the sense should be? Is this nonlegal kind of
consideration simply none of a judge's business? Or is it possible that the resolution of some questions, like those involving due process, equal protection, capital punishment, abortion, free speech, cannot escape being influenced by the
moral values of judges? In other words, is the judge in a
dilemma where his moral values will have an effect, whether
by his action or his refusal to act? To take another example,
should the judge, like the bureaucrat, be expected to have
any expertise in administering programs and institutions?
This would seem to call for a clear *no*, but it may be that in
an era in which litigation brings broad-based challenges to
institutions and seeks long-range remedies, judges should

welcome all of the administrative wisdom they can attract. Unlike discussions about legislators and bureaucrats, discussions concerning contemporary judges and the appellate courts, whose decisions loom so large on the current scene, are magnetized by the very basic questions of judicial role and function in today's complex society. It is therefore my hope that this book may shed some light on the standards by which judges should be judged — both the conventional ones relating to the quality of a judge's work and the newer and less certain ones relating to how a judge should approach whatever area of free choice is vouchsafed him.

There may have been a time when we drew comfort from the image of the judge as a kindly Olympian who looked exactly like Learned Hand, Benjamin Cardozo, or Oliver Wendell Holmes, Jr., and radiated wisdom, pithily expressed. The myth of the omniscient judge — accentuated by that vestige of a more decorous era, the robe — has ceased to be a reliable source of strength. Indeed, perhaps because the aura of perfect wisdom and justice is nourished by our mythology, leading us to idealize judges, especially deceased ones, we feel let down by particular decisions that do not accord with our sense of law, justice, or sound governmental policy. Both the mystical reverence for the judge figure and the crossfires of criticism from misconception are extreme reactions, far removed from a healthy, realistic perspective based on what can and what cannot reasonably be expected of judges. If some of this mystique is encouraged by the judiciary itself, it is, I believe, a mistake. Today, all of our institutions are under tension, and to expect an unquestioning faith in judges is to expect the citizenry to bring to the last decades of the twentieth century the habits of mind of the sixteenth. More to the point, searching inquiry into the truth about the judging process, particularly about the way in which appellate courts reach decisions, is devoutly to be desired, for it is in my view no less worthy of respect, and at bottom far more reassuring, than heroic myth.

Much has been written about the judging process.
Teachers of law of varied insights and schools of thought,
from Christopher Columbus Langdell, who ascended to the
deanship of the Harvard Law School in 1870, to a thriving
pride of contemporary young academic lions, have contributed much to both sharpening and deepening the consciousness of judges as to their roles and available choices. Beyond
these, casting long shadows of influence, are the philosophers, beginning with Plato and Aristotle, continuing with
such as Locke, Mill, Bentham, Kant, and Rousseau, and a
growing host of their intellectual progeny. Historians, biog-
raphers, political scientists, reporters have added to the
shelves.

Yet it is surprising that, midst all the diagnosticians and
pathologists, the subject — the judge — is all too rarely
found. Comprehensive and sustained commentary on the
judging process does not flow easily from judicial pens. The
small but magisterial series of lectures by then Chief Judge
Cardozo, published over a half-century ago as *The Nature of
the Judicial Process*,[1] remains the paradigm of judicial self-
analysis. Other judges, like Holmes, Hand, and Frankfurter,
have contributed insights into the process in volumes of letters, lectures, speeches, essays, and journals. Judge Jerome
Frank's *Law and the Modern Mind*,[2] a seminal tract challenging much of conventional wisdom about judging, was issued
in 1930. Since midcentury, a number of gifted judges have
written about substantive problems of importance in the
law, with occasional shorter pieces about some aspect of the
judicial process itself. But, for the most part, judges in recent times have largely left to others the writing about their
craft and calling.[3]

There are ample reasons for this. One is that the judge's
code of ethics precludes his writing about what he knows
best — the steps he took in arriving at his last or his most
widely known decision — for that decision must be judged
solely by what he or his court wrote to justify and explain it.

Barred from backstage reporting, the would-be judicial essayist faces the hard fact that judging is infinitely complex. It does not lend itself to an authoritative how-it-is-done book. To aspire to say anything fresh and sensible about judging evokes Judge Learned Hand's prescription that

> it is as important to a judge called upon to pass on a question of constitutional law, to have at least a bowing acquaintance with Acton and Maitland, with Thucydides, Gibbon and Carlyle, with Homer, Dante, Shakespeare and Milton, with Machiavelli, Montaigne and Rabelais, with Plato, Bacon, Hume and Kant, as with the books which have been specifically written on the subject.[4]

Even if he felt so formidably equipped, a judge would face another ineluctable enemy, time — or, rather, the lack of it. Induced by new sensitivity to individual rights arising from both the Constitution and a host of recent statutes, by new procedural devices such as class actions, and by the pressures of modern living, the volume of trials and appeals in state and federal courts has, as we shall see, mushroomed in the last fifteen years. It is not astonishing that judges today are seldom given to the kind of commodious reflections on the meaning of their vocation that distinguished Holmes, Hand, and Cardozo.*

There is one other restraint. Judges are almost always doing something in middle life that, as young lawyers, they never planned to do. Unlike his European counterpart, an American lawyer cannot set his cap to be a judge, take the proper university courses, serve an apprenticeship in minor courts, and work his way up the judicial bureaucracy. No matter how prescient he may be, he simply cannot foretell the happy conjunction of the planets that could bring him to

---

*The perceptive reader will wonder how it was that this particular author-judge could find the time to produce this work. The first half of the answer is that the substance is not so much a product of time-consuming study and research as it is of years of fermentation, of reflection on experience. The second half is that over a period of several years I simply gave this effort my top extrajudicial priority, devoting to it weekends, evenings, and vacations.

the favorable attention of a governor, senator, President, selection commission, or, if the post is elective, to a spot on a
political party's ticket during a favorable election year. So it
is still largely true that in the United States most judges don
their robes in midcareer and, when their contemporaries are
beginning to think of retirement, are still engaged in the
humbling task of learning their new vocation. Small wonder, then, that judges hesitate to "go public" about their life
and work.

But even though work is pressing and complex and time is
limited, it is useful for each generation of judges to try to
reinterpret their ways of work. For the work changes with
the times, the ways change, even the basic roles of judges
may change, and with the changes comes a need for ensuring that people understand what is happening so that their
ultimate, intuitive judgment of judges be informed, sensitive, and sound.

This is a personal document. I do not claim to speak for all
judges, all appellate judges, or even all federal appellate
judges. I write only of my own work ways and thought ways,
but I hope to reflect basic values widely held.

We shall try to get a good close-up glimpse of what happens at each stage of decision-making. Attempting this poses
something of a dilemma. If I discussed the real behind-the-
scenes colloquies among clerks and judges and the bargaining among judges in actual decided cases, I would, as I have
noted, be guilty of a breach of ethical standards. On the
other hand, if I were to content myself with listing the significant contributions of each phase of the process, as in a text-
book, I would be sacrificing all the life and color that make
the work of an appellate judge a constant adventure. One
might as well ask a ballet dancer to explain his or her art
solely in terms of plane geometry.

I have therefore occasionally resorted to my "judge's journal," which I have kept intermittently over the years whenever I felt that a judicial experience was worth recording.

More important, I have devised three illustrative cases. Two are basically fiction, but each issue and its context are borrowed from similar situations in actual cases; if there is any differentiating principle, it is that the real situations were more bizarre. My third case is not fiction but rather the public record of superseded history. It is borrowed from what we wrote as law — before the Supreme Court changed the law.

The three cases will, if all goes well, serve several ends. They will reveal what kinds of actions occur at each stage of the appellate decision process. They will also illustrate the several functions performed by judicial review: the simple correction of error; the allied exercise of supervisory power over subordinate officials; the assurance of continuity of doctrine; the guiding of evolving doctrine; and the monitoring of relationships between the institutions of government and the individual. And they will also show the kinds of litigation coming before the courts, varying from the traditional to the technological; the broad areas of agreement of judges of differing philosophies; and what happens when a case lands in an area where judges are free to give vent to their deeply held convictions.

The first case is a criminal appeal presenting both legal and factual issues, typical of many. The second is an appeal from an agency decision of a complex nature and involving a massive record, raising broad procedural and factual questions characteristic of a high-technology age. The third is an appeal by a prisoner from an adverse decision of a district court, raising fundamental questions about the meaning of the Constitution.

I hope that readers will accept my invitation to come behind the bench and spend some time in an appellate judge's chambers. I welcome as well lawyers, professors, and even judges. If these pages stimulate other commentary and sharing of experience, so much the better.

Chapter 2

The Appellate Idea
in History

THE OPPORTUNITY to take one's case to "a higher court" as a matter of right is one of the foundation stones of both our state and federal court systems. It fits in with our most seasoned folk wisdom that a human being vested with the responsibility of passing judgment is never so wise, so pure, so alert as to make a "second opinion" redundant. Furthermore, with courts in every city throughout the fifty states, often differing in their views of the law, there must be a way for some court or courts higher than the others to settle what the law is or should be.

Probably most Americans, if they think at all about the matter, assume that every country and legal system of any sophistication has a right of appeal serving the same functions. A look at how the appellate idea has fared in other countries from remotest times to the present is both illuminating and disquieting. It tells us that there is nothing new under the sun, including the idea of appeal. It also tells us that by no means has the idea been deemed vital by all civilizations; there are great voids in history when even the most law-conscious countries seemingly made little provision for effective appeals. Then the idea painfully emerges once again; the wheel is reinvented. And where judicial review of lower court decisions is provided for, the purposes to be served may have been — and may be — quite different from those served by our appellate review. On reflection this is not surprising, since the role of judge in most other countries differs considerably from that in the United States. It is a good idea, early in our effort to understand judges, to know how our kind of judge differs from others, and how that kind evolved.

The appellate tradition dates back some 4000 to 6000 years to several highly developed civilizations in that fecund area of the world we call the Near East.[1] The earliest concept of a judge is perhaps that of a tribal leader, such as the feisty characters depicted in the Book of Judges in the Old Testament. They could and did make war, love, and laws as the need arose. More typically, the judge was not the supreme ruler but a key minister of state, in whom were combined both judicial and high-level administrative duties. The course of appeal was to the monarch in the most rudimentary appellate systems.

By the Fourth Dynasty in Egypt (2900–2750 B.C.), the chief judge was also the chief minister of the pharaoh, from whose divine authority all law and justice came. He wore the image of Maat, the goddess of justice, on a gold collar. We know that there was a structured appellate system because administrative officials acted as local judges and the chief judge presided over a group of top officials who served as a supreme central court, the pharaoh himself being the final recourse on appeal. Further, there is a record of an appeal in a land title case dating from the reign of Ramses II, around 1300 B.C. One Mes sued Khay for wrongfully obtaining a title through fraudulent documents. Papyrus records preserve the written arguments, or briefs, of the parties and a summary of the testimony — an uncannily close approximation to the record on appeal of a contemporary land title case.

Meanwhile, Sumeria was living out its long span, enjoying the first extensive code of laws in history, that of Ur-Engur,

precursor of Hammurabi. One feature seems worthy of contemporary emulation: every case was first submitted to a
public arbitrator, who tried to bring about an amicable settlement. Priests sat as judges in the temples, but professional judges presided over a superior appellate court.[2] By
2100 B.C., the youthful Hammurabi had vanquished Sumeria
and brought it within the Babylonian hegemony. Under his
leadership, the administration of justice passed from the
priestly class to professional secular judges, clerks, notaries.
The Code of Hammurabi itself, well preserved on a diorite
cylinder, consists of some 285 laws organized by subject
matter, and ranging from the barbaric to the enlightened.
The appellate process was advanced. In towns and villages,
the mayor and a court of elders decided cases, the proceedings being summarized on clay tablets. In Babylon, a chief
magistrate presided over a court of appeals staffed by "the
King's Judges." A final appeal might in some cases be taken
to the king himself.[3]

Pausing to survey the vast domain that was briefly Persia,
we note again that the king was *the* supreme court. Below
him was a seven-member High Court of Justice, and then
local courts, with priests gradually yielding to laymen and
even laywomen as judges.

Although our view of appellate apparatus in the ancient
Egyptian, Sumerian, Babylonian, and Persian civilizations
resembles that of a snapshot, capturing one moment in time,
we are able to trace more of an evolution in the Hebraic
legal system. Delegation of the justice function from tribal
leader to a hierarchy of local courts took place early in the
Mosaic period, around 1200 B.C. The process is encapsulated
and perhaps telescoped in Exodus. Moses had been fully occupied settling arguments among his people, hearing their
plaints from dawn to dusk. His father-in-law, Jethro, came
to visit him, and, sizing up the situation, told Moses that he
wore out both himself and everyone else. "You must," said
Jethro, "instruct them in the statutes and laws, and teach

them how they must behave . . . But you must search for capable, God-fearing men among all the people . . . and appoint them over the people. They shall sit as a permanent court for the people; they must refer difficult cases to you but decide simple cases themselves."[4]

As specialization of function took place, the Hebrew judicial system developed into a three-tiered structure. In every village, faithful to the mandate recorded in Deuteronomy 16:18, courts of three elders were appointed, their traditional locus being the city gate. By perhaps 300 B.C., there had developed the finely orchestrated network of sanhedrins ("sitting within council"). The larger cities had Little Sanhedrins of twenty-three members. And Josaphat (or Jehoshaphat) had created in Jerusalem a court of priests, Levites (a tribe that supplied the court officers), and heads of families. This Great Sanhedrin, of seventy or seventy-two, the court of first instance for the inhabitants of Jerusalem, was the court of appeal for all others and appointed the lesser tribunals. With the passage of time, there were professional secular judges at all levels, the lineal descendants of those first appointed by Moses.* Large schools of religious law furnished recruits, each of whom served an apprenticeship as one of a judge's several juniors and ultimately succeeded to any vacancy. If a judge proved capable, he would move up, eventually to the supreme court.[5]

At this juncture, where ancient civilization left off and modern civilization began, we might expect the appellate systems of these great civilizations to have continued on their way to perfection, or at least to have bequeathed their institutions to others. But with the demise of the Egyptian

---

* The list of qualifications demanded of a judge in the criminal courts was strict. In addition to having full-blooded Jewish parentage, a judge had to have "an impressive physique," be a great scholar of the law, be forty years old, though "very old age was a disqualification." "One who had no children, or was extreme in his temperament, either too harsh or too kindhearted, was also disqualified." (Rabbi Meyer Waxman, "Civil and Criminal Procedure of Jewish Courts," in *Studies in Jewish Jurisprudence*, edited by Edward M. Gershfield [New York: Hermon Press, 1971], vol. 1, p. 194.)

and Mesopotamian societies, much of their depositories and rich libraries disappeared, and their processes and institutions proved to be without progeny. As for Hebraic jurisprudence, it did not disappear. It followed every Jewish community throughout the Diaspora, the courts being allowed great sway by civil authorities to the extent that the Middle Ages saw Jewish judicial influence rival that of the original Palestinian courts.[6] But this tradition was internal, not associated with any centralized nation-state.

Two other venerable civilizations, those of the Chinese and the Hindus, do not seem to have made room for a layered justice-dispensing process. Confucius, a judge among his many other roles, lived about 500 B.C. and placed his stamp ineradicably on Chinese life up to modern times — a span of some two and a half millennia. His concept was that of the wise ruler who, taking all human particulars into account, would arbitrate a face-saving compromise acceptable to all. In a deep and benevolent sense he envisaged a government of men, not of laws. His key official for each province or village was a magistrate or governor in whom was vested all authority — executive, legislative, and judicial — with the emperor in Peking holding over him an appellate power in the form of the fatal silken cord, which, in case of bad judgment or misfortune, commanded suicide.

Lao Tse, Confucius' teacher, had distrusted intellectuals and professed a yearning for as little regulation by law as possible, trusting in spontaneity and simplicity. This proved to be a durable theme in Chinese thought. Law was to play a minor role. Differences were settled not by disputants standing on rights but by their seeking to re-establish harmony. Self-blame was a common response and solvent to a conflict. Mediation was far to be preferred to a lawsuit. And supporting these deep-seated attitudes was a traditionally maladroit organization of judicial administration — an untrained judge from another province, corrupt clerks, vexing delay, and humiliation. The seventh-century emperor K'ang Hsi is said to have articulated a doctrinal defense for this state of

affairs, saying, "Law suits would tend to increase to a fright-
ful amount, if people were not afraid of the tribunals, and if
they felt confident of always finding in them ready and perfect justice . . . I desire, therefore, that those who have recourse to the tribunals should be treated without any pity,
and in such a manner that they shall be disgusted with law,
and tremble to appear before a magistrate."[7]

The early development of the Hindu legal system is
largely lost in the mists of time, at least to me. But I pick up
the trail shortly after Alexander's retreat and death, late in
the fourth century B.C., when India came into the skilled and
fortunate hands of Chandragupta. Justice was meted out by
village headmen or councils (panchayats). An inferior and
superior court system served districts and provinces, with a
royal council at the capital as a supreme court. The king
himself, as we have noted elsewhere, was the court of last
appeal.[8] By 270 B.C. the personal involvement of the monarch was brought to a high level by Chandragupta's grand-
son Asoka, whose Rock Edict VI, inscribed on stone, proclaimed: "Complainants may report to me the concerns of
the people at any time, whether I am at dinner or in the
harem or in my carriage or in my garden . . . and any dispute or fraud shall be brought forthwith to my notice." Here
again is, apparently, the ruler-judge of first and last resort.

A more extreme contrast with this kind of autocratic justice cannot be imagined than that of the Greeks in their
golden years. Innovative in art, architecture, philosophy,
and drama, they also launched the first thoroughgoing democratic experiment in government. They left no room for any
complaint about an elitist or undemocratic judiciary. As
early as 594 B.C., Solon began cutting back on the adjudicative powers of the archons, the principal magistrates, allowing appeal to the people's courts.[9] Moreover, it was said,
Solon was deliberately so obscure in wording his laws that
litigants were forced to seek the aid of the popular courts in
interpreting those laws.[10]

By Pericles' time, beginning in 462 B.C., the conservative

Senate of the Areopagus, which had sought to make itself
supreme, was stripped of many of its powers and restricted
to trying cases of arson and homicide. As for other types of
cases, public arbitrators were first resorted to in an effort to
relieve the overcrowded dockets, but, failing satisfaction, the
losing party could appeal to fellow citizens assembled as a
court.[11]

The popular courts, several of them in session every day,
constituted the *heliaea*, or supreme court. They were
manned from a jury list of some 6000, approximately a seventh of Attica's enfranchised citizenry. The juries in specific
cases varied from 201 to 2500 and decided all questions,
whether of law or of fact. Almost any issue of politics or administration, as well as private justice, was fodder for decision. The parties would be allotted time by the water clock,
witness statements would be read, arguments would be
made (often from texts written by professional "speechwrit-
ers" like Demosthenes), and, without further ado, the jury of
hundreds or thousands would vote. There being no higher
source of justice than the people, there was no appeal, even
though a Socrates be condemned to death by a plurality of
only 60 in a jury of 501.

Every citizen's turn to serve on a jury came around about
every three years. By the time of Pericles, jurors received sizable compensation; jury duty therefore must have been a
major industry. While this was a day of the common man,
the common man at the apogee of Athenian civilization was,
compared with other times and places, uncommon. For a
couple of centuries this system apparently worked well, with
this remarkable, extroverted, theatergoing, market-shop-
ping-and-talking, assembly-filling, jury-serving populace.
The secret may have been that all shared a common stock of
experience, values, and aspirations. Gradually, however, the
lack of juridical memory, the inability of unguided and untrained juries to decide like cases by the same principles, the
absence of any sense of the importance of precedents, so

eroded respect for the law that even a man of such social consciousness as Plato despaired of a career in public service.[12]

So precipitate was the exit of Greece from stage center that in 338 B.C., only nine years after Plato's death, Greece yielded to Philip of Macedon, beginning twenty-one hundred years of subjugation. Two hundred years after Plato's death, both Greece and Macedonia became provinces of Rome, at the very beginning of Rome's signal contributions to the concept of government by laws. In the days of the republic, the Roman legal apparatus was something of a carbon copy of that of Greece. There were no professional magistrates or principles of judicial direction. Juries, sometimes numbering in the thousands of citizens, were entrusted with deciding both facts and law, intermingling popular feeling and clemency as they saw fit; there was no right of appeal. The key role was that of the orator, whose knowledge of law was far less important than his efficacy in appealing to the jurors.

In the early days of the Roman Empire, at the beginning of our era, under Augustus, the lineaments of a professional legal system began to appear. The office of praetor was created — a full-time secular adjudicator, divorced from any duties of administration. Jurisconsults, who had been mere soothsayers or augurs, became skilled legal counselors, so much so that Augustus decreed that the written opinions of some jurisconsults were to carry the authority of his office — a significant step across the threshold toward the development of legal doctrine. Schools sprang up to train advocates: celebrated professors attracted students from all the empire and the provinces. Jurists began to think and write systematically; they were the first in history to approach law as a rigorous intellectual discipline. A century after Augustus, the emperor Hadrian gathered a cadre of jurists about him and commissioned them to replace the annual pronouncements of praetors with a Perpetual Edict to guide all future judges.

During the ensuing century, scholars brought Roman jurisprudence to its height — ironically, just as Roman administration and civilization were deteriorating. The Goths
besieged Rome, leaving Justinian in Byzantium as the heri-
tor of Roman law. He more than adequately lived up to the
challenge, commissioning seventeen Byzantine Greeks to
gather, organize, and condense all juristic writings into a
permanent, usable Digest. All of this enriched both Church
or canon law, later civil law systems, and even, ultimately,
English law. The right of appeal became the prized right of
any Roman citizen. We know from Paul that any Roman citizen, anywhere in the empire, if charged with any offense
meriting death or imprisonment, could claim an appeal to
the emperor.[13]

Then came that crepuscular era in the western world
known as the Dark Ages. Because of the fragmentation and
uncertainty of authority, the reign of law disappeared. The
environment posed no incentive for study or teaching of law.
Such law as existed was in the nature of "rules of social behavior" applicable to certain regions. A competent court
would have been hard to find. Even if such were to be found,
there would have been no will or capacity to enforce a de-
cree. The goal of dispute settlement was to restore a community to peaceful coexistence rather than to achieve a "just"
solution. The means were supernatural and nonrational.[14]
The Druids administered the Keltic legal system, such as it
was, with absolute power, even to designating human sacri-
fices. The only approximation to appellate review was the
legendary gold collar, which the Irish judge Morann wore.
When his judgment was just, it would expand; when it was
not, it would contract and choke him. In Scandinavia, as in
Greece and republican Rome, early justice was unalloyed
democracy. At a given phase of the moon, all the free men,
the Al-ting, met near the Hill of Laws. One man, old or
clever or both, a "law-speaker," would propose and expound
a decision, and the multitude would shout approval or dis-

approval. Montesquieu writes revealingly of such methods of dispute resolution in medieval France as trial by boiling water[15] and judicial combat, in which a litigant might choose a champion to fight for him, the champion's diligence heightened by the threat of having his hand cut off if he lost the battle.[16]

The resolution achieved by judicial combat being likely to be final (that is, resulting in the death of one party), said Montesquieu, "an appeal, such as is established by the Roman and Canon laws, that is, to a superior court in order to rejudge the proceedings of an inferior, was a thing unknown in France."[17] Indeed, the notion of an appeal, like other decision processes, was a challenge to arms, and what came to be called the appeal of false judgment required a vassal who felt himself aggrieved by a judgment to challenge the sentence as unjust and malicious and to fight the peers constituting the court convoked by the lord.[18] Even in those benighted days the principle was accepted that "justice delayed is justice denied." And so, if a vassal simply could not obtain any decision, he would, with some risk to himself or his property if he lost, bring the appeal of default of justice before a lord paramount, whose court might then deal with the case.[19] Strangely enough, England observed the same practices in this era. "Appeal" also meant a criminal prosecution, to be resolved through trial by battle, based on the belief that Providence would give victory to the deserving. By the thirteenth century, appeal meant a way of getting a review, but, as in France, only at the price of accusing a judge of malfeasance or a jury of perjury.

With the first stirrings of the Renaissance in Europe came a widespread yearning for a return from the anarchical, the arbitrary, and the supernatural to a secular rule of reason and law.[20] The ingredients were at hand — canon law and the bedrock of Roman law. The Church's courts had been, perhaps, the only centripetal force during the Dark Ages, setting the one standard of enlightened practice. Trial by battle

was forbidden. The appellate process provided the structure
for the development of doctrine. The Opinions of the Sacra
Romana Rota, the supreme tribunal of the entire Christian
world, spanned over six centuries. When finally gathered
and collated by the monk Gratian in 1140, canon law
emerged as a discrete and palpable legal system. At the very
same time, as Montesquieu tells us, "upon the discovery of
Justinian's digest towards the year 1137, the Roman law
seemed to rise out of its ashes."[21] Not, apparently, without
some deliberate help from its friends, for Montesquieu adds,
"St. Louis [Louis IX, whose long reign stretched from 1226
to 1270], in order to give a distaste of the French jurisprudence, caused the books of the Roman law to be translated;
by which means they were made known to the lawyers of
those times."[22]

So it happened on the continent of Europe that, without
any emergence of a dominant centralizing secular power,
the spirit, style, and content of the Roman-canon legal tradition became widely disseminated. The chief agents of this
revolutionary movement were the universities, starting with
Bologna but penetrating even Scandinavia and the British
Isles.[23] In France, St. Louis not only let in the winds of
change on basic attitudes and customs; he put his own im-
print on justice as a goal of society. He bade his officials
throughout the realm to receive in writing and to examine
grievances, and would himself, says Joinville, "sit against a
tree in the wood of Vincennes . . . And all those who had
any cause in hand came and spoke to him without hin-
drance." More to the point of our inquiry, Louis established
in his palace, now the Palace of Justice, the first Curia Regis,
or court of appeal, for the kingdom.[24]

Across the English Channel, quite different forces had
been at work. Before the Norman Conquest there was no
central court or law common to the entire country; three
bodies of customary law were broadly identified — Mercian,
Danish, and West Saxon. The critical contribution of the

Conquest to English law was a strong central ruler.[25] Indeed, by the time of Magna Carta, centralized royal justice had become so important to all classes that the net effect of the new charter was to make it "clear that the future of English law is with royal justice, and that therefore there will be a law common to the whole of England."[26] As the thirteenth century unfolded, there grew up around the king the beginnings of a regular court; prior to the early 1200s the king had been absent for so much of the time that no such court could perform with any continuity.[27] But, as was the case in France at this time, one could ask for a review of a decision only at the price of accusing a judge of malfeasance or a jury of perjury. By the fourteenth century, however, the idea of challenging a judgment without impugning the judge had taken root and led to what was called a writ of error, specifying particular errors appearing on the record of a case. Employing this writ of error, the court that had been the closest to the king, even accompanying him on travels, King's Bench, began to exercise review authority over other courts, including the other royal courts at Westminster, Common Pleas and Exchequer.[28] The central position of the king and, compared to Europe generally, what William Holdsworth has called "the precocious growth of the state" in England led to an early resistance to canon law and ecclesiastical judges. By the end of the thirteenth century, common law courts were no longer staffed partly by churchmen but by common lawyers who had made their career at the bar.[29] Their training being intensely practice-oriented, shaped by the jurisdictional and procedural peculiarities of the various courts of the realm, there was no need, incentive, or time for university education in the elegant rationality of Roman law.[30]

By the fourteenth century, England was well launched on the sea of common law, and France on that of civil law. Each was to be the exemplar for dozens of nations following suit. Their diverging experiences as they approached modern times have had much to do with shaping the role of judges and the functions of appeal in the vast domains each has influenced.

As France began to rediscover the Code of Justinian, and as the concepts of Roman and canon law were adopted by the baronies and became a nationalizing force, so in England the various writs by which the king authorized his subjects to seek remedy led to the complex network of royal courts. The source and genius of the civil law were the codes, statutes, and the doctrinal writings of jurists; those of English law lay in rules of procedure and jurisdiction.[31]

Then as now the rule governing any case under civil law pre-existed in the codes; the task of a judge was merely to find the right principle and interpret it. The system was a closed one, sufficient for any need. Under common law, the principles governing decision of any case were found in the articulated reasoning justifying the decision in similar cases. The system was open in that the resolution of the instant case might not be compelled by any prior decision or statute but might indeed be a new rule, arrived at by the method of common law reasoning.[32]

The principle distilled from a case decided by a "superior" court, in the common law tradition, was binding precedent on "inferior" courts. A decision by a court in civil law countries was not binding on other judges even in similar cases. The only basis for decision remained legislation or scholarly doctrine. The function of a reviewing court was to watch over the correct application of legislation; sometimes such a court could only set aside a lower court decision and not announce a positive holding of its own.[33] The key figures in civil law systems were — and are — the legislator and the treatise-writer. The central figure in common law systems was, and remains, the judge.

All of these differences were implicit in the rival systems. Insofar as the roles of judges and functions of appellate review are concerned, the disparities were accentuated by the revolutionary changes taking place at the end of the eighteenth century. In *fin-de-siècle* France, the Parlements, or top appellate courts of the kingdom, although the center of opposition to authoritarian government, at the same time stubbornly resisted various reforms proposed by the king and his ministers.[34] The pent-up venom stimulated by this "aristocracy of the robe" was vented during and after the French Revolution in the care taken to isolate and restrict the judiciary. "The emphasis on separation of powers," wrote Professor Merryman, "led to a separate system of administrative courts, inhibited the adoption of judicial review of legislation, and limited the judge to a relatively minor role in the legal process."[35]

This reaction was not experienced in either England or America. There had been more of a social evolution, with vastly less trauma, in England; in the English colonies in America the rigors of feudalism had never been deeply felt. Moreover, as Professor Merryman noted:

> in the United States and England . . . there was a different kind of judicial tradition, one in which judges had often been a progressive force on the side of the individual against the abuse of power by the ruler, and had played an important part in the centralization of governmental power and the destruction of feudalism. The fear of judicial lawmaking and of judicial interference in administration did not exist. On the contrary, the power of the judges to shape the development of the common law was a familiar and welcome institution. The judiciary was not a target of the American Revolution in the way that it was in France.[36]

Another judge-conditioning attitude shared by the American colonists themselves was their inheritance of the notion of judicial power to review legislation, something completely alien to conventional civil law. It had been asserted most forcefully by Sir Edward Coke as chief justice of England in 1609 in his celebrated dictum in Bonham's Case: "For when an Act of Parliament is against common right and reason, or repugnant, or impossible to be performed, the common law will control it and adjudge such Act to be void." Even the Glorious Revolution of 1688, which established the principle of parliamentary supremacy and also the supremacy of statutory law in England, had the opposite effect in America. For while in England it took away from the judges all control over the validity of legislation, in America it empowered colonial judges to disregard any local legislation not in conformity with English law, and, later, judges of newly independent American states to hold null and void laws contrary to the new state charters or constitutions.[37]

We have seen the early civilizations of the Near East develop a structured appellate system, with secular professional judges, a permanent record of proceedings, and the possibility of a final appeal to the sovereign's clemency, which the world was not to see again for 2000 years. Farther east, in China, the goal was not justice for litigants but peace and harmony for the community. In classical Greece, there was no appeal from the popular courts; the people could do no wrong. Imperial Rome gradually restored the appellate idea. It was nourished and sustained for centuries within the Church during the Dark Ages, when appeals elsewhere in Europe were exercises in supplicating the supernatural or demonstrating the truth-serving function of brute force.

Finally, civilized forms once again emerged in France and Britain. The role of judges and the purposes of appeal took their shape from the basic mold of either the civil or the common law. Though the civil law idea of reducing all law to codes held attraction for many in the United States during the first half of the nineteenth century, we have remained a common law country. This story, now spanning seven centuries, of the diverging paths of common and civil law has some relevance to the basic concern of this book: judging judges. Not a little criticism of American judges springs from assumptions that are valid in a civil law system, where the law is totally the creature of the legislature:

judges exist merely to locate the applicable law; they are not to "make" law; their rulings need not be followed in any other case. I suspect that many Americans would subscribe enthusiastically to all these tenets, without realizing that what they were yearning for was a civil law system. But our forebears crossed this bridge sometime back in the 1200s.

This is not to say that our fate has been totally prefigured. The story of the development and workings of our own appellate system is well worth the telling. I harbor the conviction that our present appellate system, as it is embodied in the highest courts of the states and in the federal courts of appeal, represents an achievement affecting the diverse population of a continent-wide nation, sustained and improving over time, that has no equal today or in ages past in terms of utility and breadth of review, accessibility to the populace, and structure of deliberation.

Chapter 3

The Appellate Idea
in the United States

THE HISTORICAL MILESTONES

Our Colonial Inheritance

For nearly half the time we and our forebears have spent on this continent, we were part of England. Our inheritance from the mother country in legal and judicial systems, values, and tradition has been a rich one. We imported such articles of faith as allegiance to the supremacy of law, the determination of controversies by resort to an orderly and rational system, and the overarching concept of due process. Being such believers, we were also uncommonly litigious. Moreover, for centuries we, or, rather, those who had gone before us, had participated regularly and intimately in the business of law administration, taking part in the dispensing of justice almost as a matter of daily routine.[1] Perhaps most significantly, we were inevitably and deeply shaped by the fact that during the long era of our colonizing experience, the judiciary in England had come to occupy a position of eminence and power unmatched in any other western country.[2]

In terms of our inquiry into the appellate process, we think first of the royal courts of Westminster — King's Bench, Common Pleas, and the Exchequer — which had long had their own galaxies of lesser courts, separate procedures, and appellate systems. Yet strangely enough, the major practical contribution of England may well have been not these vaunted high royal courts, but the ancient and intricate network of local courts for boroughs, manors, hundreds (divisions of counties), and counties, in which the humblest citizen participated. It was the ways of these familiar courts that were widely adopted in the colonies, where travel to a distant city was out of the question.[3]

The colonists, however, in setting up their local courts, could be more rational than the feudal inheritance of England permitted. Not only could they avoid such antique lumber as manorial courts but, thanks in large part to an early ordinance of the able colonial governor, Edmund Andros of Massachusetts Bay, the concept of one centralized superior court to which lower courts all through the colony could appeal became a widely accepted model.[4] The outlet for most of their causes, though, lay in the first instance with the local justice of the peace. Very often this official was a layman, whose views understandably would not be accepted as final by disputative colonists.[5] The English model of review of such courts was the relatively broad and unrestricted appeal to the Court of Quarter Sessions of the Justices of the Peace.[6] And so, being thoroughly at home with ready access to such review, the colonists came to view wide-ranging, easily accessible appeal as something to which all had a right. Indeed, they carried this to such an extreme that in Massachusetts litigants had the opportunity on appeal to have a second jury pass once again on factual questions.[7]

These uniquely American colonial practices and attitudes — an uncomplicated layer of local courts, a centralized review authority given to a "superior" court charged not only with seeing that justice is done between the parties but with supervising the lower courts and seeing that "the right rule" was applied, easy access to the broad review stemming from England's justice of the peace courts, and awareness of the excesses to which litigiousness and a passion for juries could lead — preconditioned debate and deeply influenced decision in forming both our state and federal judicial systems.

The Constitutional Convention

Perhaps the most notable, if least noted, by-product of the colonial experience was that in the Constitutional Convention the judiciary article came in for relatively little debate. This would seem, in a body otherwise not inarticulate or phlegmatic, mute evidence of agreement on basic principles. The Virginia Plan, for example, which came to be used as the basis for the work of the Convention, embodied the concept of inferior and superior courts with a power of superintendence through appeal in the latter.[8] Also, so deeply felt had been the colonists' experience with royal judges serving at the king's pleasure that, despite their ardent democratic principles, the provision giving federal judges life tenure — during "good behavior" — was speedily and unanimously adopted.[9]

If it could be said that there were major issues concerning the judiciary discussed at the Convention, one was whether members of the judiciary should serve with the executive in a Council of Revision with power to veto newly enacted legislation considered unwise. The Convention refused so to use the judiciary for extrajudicial purposes.[10] Indeed, time and time again, it repulsed efforts to make the judiciary dependent on the legislative branch. It seems that the Founding Fathers were determined to protect the integrity and separateness of the judiciary, but, once that was accomplished, to entrust great tasks to it; for when at last they expressly proclaimed the supremacy of the Constitution and laws "in pursuance thereof" in the judiciary article, it was the judges who were singled out as "the ultimate arbiters of enforcement and enforceability."[11]

The Judiciary Act of 1789

So the Constitution sallied forth for the ordeal of ratification. Although the great drama of ratification and the implied price exacted by an important minority of the states[12] — the Bill of Rights — have taken the limelight in history, our interest in the shaping of the appellate system in the United States takes us to the Judiciary Act of 1789. This lesser-known piece of legislation was signed into law the day before the final vote on the Bill of Rights. While the focus of the latter was on vital rights and liberties, that of the former was on the practical, prosaic features of structure and function best suited to help the judiciary of the new nation emerge from its chrysalis. Each has proven its worth.

It is remarkable in retrospect that both the basic frame and the necessary furniture of the federal judicial establishment could be assembled, considered, and made part of the law of the land in five months, during the same period in which the Congress was creating the Bill of Rights. The major structural features of the act were a bottom tier of separate juridical entities — federal district courts having jurisdiction in civil and criminal cases — and three higher-level circuit courts, having both original and appellate jurisdiction.[13] These circuit courts were a venture in eclectic improvisation. Having two levels of jurisdiction, with power to review decisions of district judges, their decisions in many matters not being reviewable by the Supreme Court, these courts — the vital middle level of the system — had no personnel of their own. Instead, each circuit court was manned by two justices of the Supreme Court and a district judge, a direct borrowing from the old English practice that sent the judges from Westminster out on circuit, where they would sit with local judges.[14]

For the time being this device was thought to be well calculated to meet any imagined appellate need, without exacerbating those who feared and would fight against any sizable cadre of national judges. Indeed, the drafters of the act, although Federalist in sympathy, were keenly aware of the depth of anti-Federalist concern that had been evident both at the Constitutional Convention and during the debates over ratification. Accordingly, they took pains not only to create minimally intrusive "national" circuit courts containing one locally oriented district judge and to limit the district courts' jurisdiction, but also to provide that state laws would be regarded as the "rules of decision" for trials in federal courts.

The new middle tier, the circuit courts with borrowed judges and justices, soon revealed its flaws. Circuit riding by the justices was unimaginably onerous. All but one lived far from Washington, to which they came for two court sessions a year. In addition, as circuit judges, they were obligated to hold twenty-eight courts a year — this in a time when the trip from Boston to Philadelphia took almost three weeks.[15] Some relief was provided when only one justice was required to sit on a circuit court. But, as commentators have noted, "this was at the cost of establishing a precedent of a two-judge court — creating a problem of split decisions, and exaggerating the problem of district judges reviewing, on the circuit court, their own decisions."[16]

For almost exactly a century this structure, despite its inadequacy, endured without important change. More districts and circuits were created, and in 1869 Congress did at last appoint the first exclusive circuit judges, nine of them, one for each circuit. By 1890, the country's population had reached 64 million, the justices of the Supreme Court had exhausted themselves trying to fulfill their duties on circuit, and their backlog had grown to about four years' accumulation of cases. For fourteen years the Congress had fussed with the problem, to no avail.

The Evarts Act

Finally, in 1890, an appellate court reform bill, having been passed in the House, came before the Senate. The manager of the bill was Senator William Evarts, who had been a leader of the American bar, lead counsel defending Andrew Johnson in the Senate impeachment trial, and most recently secretary of state under President Rutherford B. Hayes. The bill recommended adding nine circuit judgeships to the existing nine, one for each circuit, and the establishment of circuit courts of appeal, to be manned by one district judge, two circuit judges, and, when feasible, one Supreme Court justice. Mercifully, the bill at last barred a district judge from sitting in review of his own decision. It was the underlying idea that a great portion of litigation would end at this strengthened middle level, thus relieving the Supreme Court.

Perhaps the most effective provision introduced the notion of removing the burden from the Supreme Court of having to hear every appeal. Instead, the Supreme Court was given the very considerable privilege of selecting those cases for appeal which it thought significant and refusing others. This kind of review at the Court's discretion is referred to by lawyers as review by writ of certiorari, such being the name of the document that is used to order a lower court to send a record of a case to a higher court.

When we reflect that the addition of a middle tier to the federal court system was the only noteworthy alteration in court structure accomplished in a century, it is surprising to learn that the debate on the Evarts bill was rather perfunctory. Perhaps the fourteen years of abortive consideration of the problem had prepared the way or wearied antagonists. In any event, debate did not center on the bill's proposals so much as on a proposal, advanced by the minority report and sponsored by the chairman of the Judiciary Committee, Senator George F. Edmunds, that the Supreme Court's workload problem be solved by allowing the Court to sit in "quorums" of three.[17]

The supposed virtue of this arrangement would be a three-fold increase in the ordinary citizen's chances of having his case heard by the Supreme Court. This was an idea whose time never came. Today, anyone acquainted with the wide divisions of opinions among the nine justices would realize that the law of the land, if allowed to be made by a panel of three, would ricochet back and forth between competing values and principles, depending on the composition of the panel.

The minority proposal was never advanced with much enthusiasm. What lay behind it was soon revealed — a deep-seated reluctance to appoint more judges, the basic distrust of life-tenured judges, which has found voice in every generation. Senator George G. Vest of Missouri led the charge. His words would find many modern sympathizers:

> . . . When you put a man into an office with a life tenure, you . . . put him on a sort of pedestal above the rest of the people, he then thinks that leisure is the first element of his new position. You may take the hardest-working lawyer in this country and make a Federal judge of him and he will quit, unless it has become the practice of a whole lifetime, unless he is over 50 years old and work has become a necessity, as it does with any man in any pursuit after that time. If he is a young man, with the passions and appetites and ambitions and instincts incidental to the years before fifty, the chances are largely in the majority that he will immediately become a dilettante.[18]

Evarts did not deem it necessary to answer this jeremiad. Soon the quorum proposal received minute and deft examination, the lethal scalpel being wielded with the utmost suavity and courtesy. The Evarts bill passed its crucial Senate test by a 44 to 6 vote.[19]

The major outlines of the American federal appellate system had now been etched. The state systems had had a parallel development.* Succeeding years were to produce legislation creating two more circuits, more circuit judgeships, and, in 1925, another Supreme Court rescue mission, when, in legislation drafted by the justices themselves — "the Judges' Bill" — the Court's mandatory appellate jurisdiction over decisions of state supreme courts and circuit courts of appeal was drastically reduced, most appeals now being subject only to the discretionary review of certiorari.

THE STATE-FEDERAL APPELLATE SYSTEM TODAY

The contemporary American appellate system is really two systems, state and federal, equal in dignity and importance, coexisting in a symbiotic relationship. They differ in the ease of access afforded the citizenry, the number of judges and volume of litigation, and the nature of cases adjudicated. They also overlap. To the extent that they deal with similar issues, both tension and accommodation accompany the relationship. As we shall later see, leadership in various fields of the law shifts from one to the other.

I have tried, at the risk of oversimplifying, to reflect the most salient facets — the hierarchy of state and federal courts, the subject matter of their jurisdictions, their interrelationship, the nature of review — in one chart, presented inside the front cover of this book.† More quantitative data as to numbers of judges and cases in the sibling systems follow in tabular form.

At the peak of these two systems, except for the very pinnacle — the Supreme Court of the United States with its

---

* Indeed the report of the House Committee on the Judiciary claimed that its proposed bill "simplifies the whole judicial establishment by modeling the system largely after the systems in the several States." (Report no. 1296, Fifty-first Congress, first session, April 7, 1890, p. 4.)

† I first used this chart in attempting to explain the American judicial system to young European lawyers at the Salzburg Seminar of American Studies in 1974. Law professors have since found this useful, and users have suggested various improvements. More could be made, but I feel that the chart has reached its capacity to absorb confusion.

nine justices — are fewer than 500 top appellate judges: 132
on the federal courts of appeals and 352 on the supreme
courts of the fifty states.* This comes down to one federal
appellate judge for 1.7 million people and one state supreme
court justice for 625,000.

The cases arising in a state court revolve about the ordinances of towns and cities, the statutes and common law of
the state, and the regulations of its public agencies. To federal courts is given review of the many federal agencies,
disputes involving federal statutes, and other questions of
federal law. There is overlap between the two systems, for
state courts, like federal courts, have frequent occasion to interpret and apply the federal Constitution, and federal
courts still interpret and apply state law in cases between
citizens of different states.

*A profile of the two judicial establishments is the following:

	States	Federal
Judges on courts of last resort (except Supreme Court)	352	132
Judges on intermediate appellate courts	463	—
Judges on trial courts of general jurisdiction	6,043	516
Judges on courts of limited jurisdiction (petty crimes; traffic; domestic relations; juveniles; probate; etc.)	18,075	U.S. bankruptcy judges 232
		U.S. magistrates 176 Full time 311 Part time
Total Number of Judges	24,933	1,367

To these totals should be added the invaluable services of "senior," or
retired, judges who continue to carry on judicial work. In the federal system, for example, some 140 give more than half their time to such work.

Federal judgeship statistics are taken from the 1978 Annual Report of the
Director of the Administrative Office of the United States Courts, Washington, D.C., pp. 18–19, and reflect the status as of June 30, 1978. The statistics
for state judges were provided by the National Center for State Courts, Wil-
liamsburg, Virginia, and reflect the status as it was estimated for 1976. (Letter of June 25, 1979, to author from Alice L. O'Donnell, Director, Division of
Inter-Judicial Affairs and Information Services, Federal Judicial Center,
Washington, D.C.)

As this dual system has evolved, the following objectives appear to have been served: to encourage immediacy of adjudication and diversity at the local level; to give prompt access to a court of general jurisdiction; to afford a federal forum in all parts of the country; through state and federal appellate courts, to correct errors and injustice, to provide for the continuity and stability of the law while allowing for its orderly evolution; and to provide a supreme vehicle to assure uniformity throughout the land on important issues and to be the authentic voice for interpreting the Constitution.

The flow of litigation through these two court systems yields the following soundings. The federal trial courts' filings amounted in the year ending December 31, 1979, to some 192,575 new cases.[20] This is an inconsequential number when compared with the litigation entering the state systems. In 1976, the estimated totals for new cases filed in trial courts were as follows:

Civil cases	12,158,054	14 percent
Criminal cases	11,284,898	13 percent
Traffic cases	64,829,871	72 percent
Juvenile cases	1,222,724	1 percent
	89,495,547[21]	

This is truly astounding: almost one out of every two people is involved in a lawsuit each year. Even if traffic and juvenile cases are taken out of the calculus, the result still indicates that one out of ten Americans is in civil or criminal litigation in state courts each year.

At the appellate level, the federal courts of appeal received 21,680 cases in 1979.[22] In other words, although every disappointed litigant has a right to at least one appeal, less than one case in ten is sought to be reviewed. To these must be added about 3000 reviews of federal agency decisions.[23] The attrition on appeal in state courts is much greater than in the federal courts, understandably so, because of the over-whelming number and petty nature of many of the causes. In 1976, 78,058 appeals were filed with the intermediate courts of appeal in twenty-four states, and 47,030 appeals were filed with courts of last resort.[24] With state and federal trial courts processing something in the neighborhood of 90 million lawsuits a year, and with state and federal appellate courts according full appellate review to 150,000 appeals, this country's justice system must surely be unrivaled in its ease of access to a large, widespread, and heterogeneous population.

Yet these figures invite a query: Why wouldn't anyone who lost a case in a trial court want to take advantage of his right to have at least one review by a higher court? To an-swer this, we must delve into the process of "taking an ap-peal." After the jury has returned its verdict or the judge or agency has issued a decision, the unhappy litigant discusses with his lawyer his chances of winning on appeal or of being worse off, the benefits or drawbacks of the delay inherent in any appeal, and the costs of the appeal itself. If the decision is to pursue the appeal, one must file a notice of appeal within a strict time limit, pay a docket fee to the appellate court, and begin the process of assembling the "record."

The record on appeal, the only source of factual knowledge that the appellate court is permitted to have about the case, consists of the various motions and pleadings filed in court, the exhibits introduced at trial, and, most important, a tran-script of testimony. If the trial extends over several days, the transcript alone will cost over a thousand dollars — a meas-urable depressant to appeals. Another chilling force is the future prospect or immediate reality of attorney's fees, for the attorney is not idle during this period of gestation. His job is scrupulously to identify the issues he wishes to raise, designate the parts of the record that will be relevant to the issues on appeal, review all of the testimony and all of the exhibits, and do exhaustive legal research so that his written argument to the court will be as commanding as possible. All of this takes time, and each hour of such work costs the client from $75 to $200 or more.

In the light of these risks and burdens, one is tempted to reverse the inquiry and wonder why anyone in his right mind appeals. The answers are as diverse as human motives generally: the client can afford it; the principle is important; the case is worth the Supreme Court's attention even if the immediate appeal fails; it is obvious that the trial court erred; the client is simply angry, stubborn, or proud; any delay gained is worth the price; an appeal preserves one's bargaining position for possible settlement; if one has been convicted of a crime and is out on bail, there is no doubt that being at liberty during appeal justifies the cost.

To these reasons may be added a systemic one attributable to our view of the rights of an indigent to a meaningful appeal: both state and federal governments finance the appeals of indigent criminal defendants as well as many cases in which a prisoner is seeking his release through a writ of habeas corpus. In such cases, the government pays for the transcript and even compensates the attorney. Therefore, the great majority of criminal cases resulting in conviction are appealed; it costs the client nothing, and the attorney risks facing his client's charges of incompetence if he does not fight to the bitter end. Once in a while, however, the result is that an indigent prisoner is given his freedom because the attorney his government gave him convinced a court that his rights had been violated. I stress "once in a while" to counter the public's impression that appellate courts free criminal appellants on a wholesale basis. I know of no other country that has gone to such lengths to institutionalize government-supported defenses and appeals by accused and convicted persons.

Whether this observation goes any distance toward explaining why, despite the costs, anyone appeals is really irrelevant. The fact is that appeals in both state and federal

systems have increased exponentially during the 1960s and
1970s. The three memorable generalizations that can be
made about this era are that never before have the courts
been so productive, never before has the quantity of new
cases so steadily increased, and never before have there been
so many novel and complex cases presented. The result, of
course, is that, despite productivity twice or three times that
of their predecessors, judges face ever greater backlogs of
pending cases.

An irreducible minimum of statistics tells the story. In
1960, new filings of cases in the federal district courts were
about 90,000;[25] in 1979, as we have seen, filings had reached
192,575, a doubling of traffic. In 1960, the appeals reaching
the federal courts of appeals were 3899; in 1979, they were
21,680, more than a fivefold increase. The First Circuit Court
of Appeals, on which I sit, the smallest in the federal system,
entertained 154 appeals in 1960; in 1979, still the only court
of appeals with no more than three judges, we processed no
fewer than 666 appeals — a fourfold increase.[26]

Not only has there been this metastasis of litigation, particularly in the appellate sector, but the complexity of the
cases has increased during the 1960s and 1970s. The main-
stay of the federal appellate caseload used to be straight
criminal appeals, civil cases involving state law, reviews of a
few federal agencies, and "federal" questions revolving
about some nationally applicable statutes. Today, even the
traditional kind of case, such as a criminal prosecution,
requires much more sophisticated analysis because of the
developments in constitutional law relating to the rights of
the accused. The discovery of new ways to provide remedies
from existing law has produced whole categories of cases
largely unknown in the past — civil rights cases challenging
official authority, petitions of prisoners challenging prison
conditions, class actions in which hundreds or thousands of
people are plaintiffs or defendants, consumer suits based on
defective products. Another source of new cases is the con-

tinuing stream of new consumer-oriented federal statutes
and new agencies like the Environmental Protection Agency
and the Occupational Safety and Health Administration,
which themselves account for a considerable appellate caseload.

Here is today's profile of the federal appellate caseload,[27]
which I have annotated to show how new are the legal issues
or how they have changed:

Number of Appeals	Percent of Total	Source of Appeal	Comment
1991	10	Suits in contract and tort between citizens of different states ("diversity jurisdiction").	This is the last fastness of conventional adjudication. And Congress is in the process of abolishing this kind of jurisdiction for federal courts.
5211	25	Cases involving federal statutes, or the United States as plaintiff or defendant.	Traditional litigation in form, but new statutes such as Truth in Lending, Freedom of Information, Occupational Safety have changed the landscape.
4100	20	Criminal cases.	Standard fare, but subject to a host of new interpretations in civil liberties since the mid-1960s.

46

A SEPARATE WAY

Number of Appeals	Percent of Total	Source of Appeal	Comment
3000	14	Federal agency orders.	"Old Faithfuls" such as National Labor Relations Board, Internal Revenue Service, but controversy-spawning new agencies such as Environmental Protection Agency, Nuclear Regulatory Commission.
2753	14	Prisoner cases: habeas corpus — to seek release from confinement; and prisoner petitions — to seek improvement in conditions of confinement.	Habeas corpus (about 1000 cases) is traditional; prisoner petitions (a form of civil rights suits) date from the late 1960s and present new issues.
2227	11	Civil rights appeals against both federal and state governments and officials.	Born in the 1960s, matured in the 1970s — the new breed. Often in the form of large class action lawsuits.

So far we have been looking at the system at the intake end of the tunnel, seeing how appeals get on the docket of appellate courts, what they cost, why appeals are taken, and what the traffic is, in quantity, complexity, and novelty. What happens when the new case on appeal and the appellate court at last come into contact with each other? This depends somewhat on the size and organization of the court. As is shown in the accompanying map and table, the eleven federal circuits vary in size from the vast expanses of the Ninth Circuit, stretching from Arizona to Alaska and from Montana to Guam; the sprawling Fifth, reaching from Jacksonville to Houston; and the super-urban Second, comprising all of New York, Vermont, and Connecticut; to our own tiny First Circuit, harboring the rest of New England and, illogically, Puerto Rico. The courts of appeal reflect the wide discrepancies in area, size of population, numbers of district judges (from twenty-three to seventy or eighty), in the formality and complexity of their ways of doing business. The differences in procedure between the twenty-six-judge Ninth Circuit Court of Appeals and our own First Circuit Court of Appeals, up to now a three-judge court, are enormous in terms of size of staff, numbers of committees, prescribed procedures, meetings, and paperwork. Yet both courts go about the essential work of judging in much the same way.

The first step taken by an appellate court in dealing with new cases on its docket is to try to reduce the oral argument calendar to manageable proportions. The appeals are subjected to preliminary screening to see if there are frivolous cases, cases not within the jurisdiction of the appellate courts, or cases that can be disposed of on the basis of written arguments alone. These sometimes amount to a substantial percentage of all cases, much to the discomfiture of lawyers and litigants, who understandably want the chance to talk face to face with those who hold in their hands the litigants' fate. Sometimes, in complicated cases, conferences are held to arrange a schedule for the compilation of a record and the filing of briefs by all the parties. Then at last the

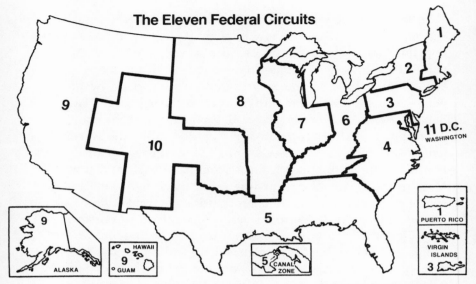

The Eleven Federal Circuits

Circuit	States Included	Federal Judges	
		Appellate	District
1st	Maine, New Hampshire, Massachusetts, Rhode Island, Puerto Rico	4	23
2nd	New York, Connecticut, Vermont	11	50
3rd	Pennsylvania, New Jersey, Delaware, Virgin Islands	10	50
4th	Virginia, West Virginia, Maryland, North Carolina, South Carolina	10	44
5th	Texas, Louisiana, Mississippi, Alabama, Georgia, Florida, Canal Zone	26	110
6th	Michigan, Ohio, Kentucky, Tennessee	11	51
7th	Illinois, Indiana, Wisconsin	9	36
8th	Missouri, Iowa, Minnesota, North Dakota, South Dakota, Nebraska, Arkansas	9	35
9th	California, Alaska, Hawaii, Washington, Oregon, Idaho, Montana, Arizona, Nevada, Guam	23	75
10th	Colorado, Kansas, Oklahoma, New Mexico, Utah, Wyoming	8	27
D.C.	District of Columbia	11	15
(Status as of October 20, 1978, with passage of 1978 Omnibus Judgeship Bill.)			

Legislation before Congress would create a new Fifth Circuit composed of Louisiana, Mississippi, and Texas, and a new Eleventh Circuit composed of Alabama, Florida, and Georgia.

written arguments, or briefs, of the parties are filed, oral arguments of the lawyers are heard by a panel of judges of the court, and, by the process we shall soon examine, a decision is delivered in the form of a printed opinion. The total elapsed time from the filing of the record to decision averages eight months,[28] although the individual circuits vary widely, from 4.4 months to 13.8 months.

The results of this prolonged, complex, costly process are neither across-the-board reversals nor a rubber stamp of approval for most lower court and agency decisions. Year in and year out, the average rate of reversals has been around 17 or 18 percent, with courts of appeals varying from as low a reversal rate as 11.6 percent up to 23.3 percent. This kind of statistic tells only part of the story. The appellate courts exert much of their influence in ways other than simple reversals. Often, part or all of the decision below will not be reversed but only vacated and sent back to the trial court or agency for further consideration, evidence, findings, and justification. Sometimes no decision below is changed but is merely interpreted, narrowed, or broadened. Or the appellate court will indulge in giving views that are termed "dicta," not needed for decision but deserving careful study by trial judges, prosecutors, agency counsel, and private lawyers. The appellate court, in announcing a new rule or principle, whether deriving it from case law, the Constitution, or its own reservoir of supervisory power over the lower courts in its jurisdiction, may not apply it to the case at hand but may choose to proclaim its application to all cases arising in the future.

This is not the end of the appellate road. The litigant who has been disappointed either by a state supreme court or a federal court of appeals has one more chance. There is always the United States Supreme Court. Each year there are between 3800 and 4000 requests for review by litigants. Each year the Court, because of the limits on its time and energies, accepts and decides only 300 to 500 cases — from 7

to 13 percent of the requests, a very small proportion of all
the appeals decided in the state and lower federal courts.
Year after year the number of full-scale opinions has remained about the same — 135 to 150. There have been, in
addition, some 200 short, less discursive per curiam (literally, "for the court") opinions. A rough idea of what to expect when the Supreme Court decides to take an appeal by
granting a writ of certiorari is revealed by the fate of 208
such actions in the 1977 term (October 1976 to June 1977):
reversals — ninety-one; judgments vacated — eighty-five; af-
firmances — only thirty-two.[29]

Small though the annual harvest of Supreme Court opinions may be, these are the cases that determine the direction
of contemporary American jurisprudence on the moving
edge of the law. Yet though this be true, it is equally true
that for most litigants and most issues most of the time the
law is made by the nearly 500 state and federal appellate
judges presiding over the twin-towered establishment we
have just silhouetted. Even this brief survey of the size and
structure of that system and the volume and complexity of
litigation flowing through it is concrete evidence of a remarkable national experience in building an institution.
Though rooted in centuries of history, the American view of
courts, judges, and the appellate process has proven to be
distinctive and valuable. To the essence and genius of that
process we now turn.

Chapter 4

The Elements of
Deciding Appeals

Up to this point we have treated our subject, the appellate process, as a remote and unidentified phenomenon. We have traced its ups and downs through history. We have viewed it in the United States through a wide-angle lens, noting its use by multitudes, its rapid growth, and the increasing complexity of the grist for its mill. But we have not yet troubled to fix clearly in mind what "it" is. So we have one more long view to take before we join a judge in chambers, that of the elements of deciding appeals that make it a unique decision process.

We shall pursue the quintessence of the appellate process in the original sense of that ungainly Latinate word. A product of ancient and medieval philosophy, "quintessence" meant the fifth and highest essence after the four mundane ones — earth, air, fire, and water. It was thought to be the substance of the heavenly bodies. This may connote something of the mystical, but for me it means asking a different set of questions about appellate decision-making than what are the steps, sources, forms, and modes. Such seem surface inquiries. In the hope that we may focus on what is special about deciding appeals, I have identified nine critical features that set apart how we appellate judges go about our business.[1] Taken together, they form a distinctive profile.

A TRADITION OF INDEPENDENCE
AND OBJECTIVITY

The prerequisite quality is objectivity. This, after all, is the judge's reason for being. His legislative counterpart is first and foremost an advocate. His executive counterpart is primarily an implementer. Decision serving those ends is not necessarily objective. But the judge's task is to adjudicate, to apply appropriate principles in accordance with legal discipline to facts that have been properly determined in accordance with that discipline. The judge is not trying to advance any cause, his party, his company, or himself. He is not trying to accumulate credit for promotion or to curry favor with individuals or groups. Even in states where judges are elected, there is the security of the term, often the bulwark of a law that, barring serious problems, makes a judge's re-election likely, and, in any event, the expectation of all that the judicial tradition of objectivity will be respected.

THE FOCUS OF A PRIOR
HEAT-TESTED DECISION

Deciding an appeal is not a matter of approaching a problem as if for the first time. It is determining whether another, earlier, carefully structured decision should be upheld. That earlier decision, if by a court, is already the full-bodied product of a formal adversary hearing, held with all the garnishments of due process; if by an agency, it is the product of either such an adversary hearing or a rule-making proceeding in which the responsible official must invite and respond to public comments. Such a decision ought to be more likely to be just than the great mass of decisions that govern us in our everyday living, because the latter are made unilaterally, spontaneously, and perhaps emotionally by someone temporarily in charge of our fate, without organized forethought, testing, standards, or apprehension of review.

Even a structured lower court decision, however, can be in error. A jury can be carried away by passion or prejudice. A judge can make mistakes in rulings. (I hasten to confess that the fact that we rely on appellate judges to correct error carries no implication that they are wiser. Higher courts are "right" because they are "superior," not superior because they are right.) Apart from presenting an opportunity to correct mistakes, an appeal frequently provides an occasion for a desired change in legal doctrine. In such a case, one cannot say that the trial court has erred in applying conventional law; the appellate court's action in reversing is in pursuance not of its error-correcting function but of its lawmaking function.

At the same time, so much has been invested in the first decision that intuition tells us it should not be too easily discounted. There is no public policy for preferring a second decision that differs from the first only because the second decider weighs the evidence differently. Nor does what hindsight reveals to be a mistake by the trial judge, but one that has not significantly infected the final result, count enough in the scales of justice to warrant a second trial. There must, therefore, be conscious and controlled deference to the decision of the lower court. By the same token, both sense and fairness dictate that the same ground rules govern the decision-making process in both arenas. Unlike a congressional committee, a government department head, or a business executive, an appellate court may not consider every last piece of information that comes to its attention. It is restricted in two ways: it must confine itself to the factual record established in the trial court or administrative agency, and it must generally recognize only those legal issues which were raised in the trial court.

While being so limited may be thought to shackle a reviewing court, the limitations are a source of strength. The raw materials for appellate deliberation are already fixed, assembled, and focused. Unlike other decision-makers, appellate courts cannot worry over whether there is a need for more or better information. There is some advantage in having a target that has stopped moving.

RELIANCE ON STRUCTURED ADVOCACY
BY ADVERSARIES

Our common law court processes differ from the decisional processes of many other institutions in that they rely heavily on the contributions of the parties to a lawsuit. A basic tenet of our system is the paradox that out of the hammer-and-anvil confrontation of opposing advocates, each of whom seeks only victory, both a true view of facts and an informed view of the law will emerge.

Reliance on adversaries, of course, is only one way of assuring that all sides of an issue will be considered and tested. In the executive branch, important decisions are subjected to the most convoluted vertical and horizontal staff, office, bureau, department, interagency, and Office of Management and Budget clearances. Somewhere along the line it is reasonable to expect that all points of view will have been considered. Decision-making in the Congress relies on infusions from both adversaries and staff. Indeed, to the extent a bill is controversial, the committee members themselves will display their colors as adversaries; the partisan division will produce majority and minority reports and endure through debate on the floor. On the other hand, many pieces of legislation do not provoke partisan stands. As to these, it is fair to observe that as partisan schism diminishes, greater reliance is placed on the committee staff for analysis and drafting.

Although reliance on advocacy by adversaries is not peculiar to the American judiciary, adherence to a formal structure for that advocacy is unique. The structure is dual, covering both written and oral argument. Here again there are subtle differences among the three branches. The executive branch, feeding on its own remorseless river of paperwork, places its primary reliance on the written word. In the Congress, as we have seen, the harried members do not begin to have time to read committee reports; they have no alternative but to rely mainly on the spoken word of staff and trusted colleagues. Judges, particularly appellate judges, rely most of the time on the written word, yet the spoken word plays a critical role often enough to be considered a significant part of effective advocacy.

The two instruments of appellate advocacy, the written argument or brief* and the oral argument, are themselves institutions shaped by insistent and long-enduring convention. Books on both have been written, courses given, and clinical experience featured in the law schools. The result is that courts are not merely receptacles of the urgings and points of view of the parties; the parties, through their trained counsel, participate in shaping the issues, in collecting all relevant information, and in organizing its presentation. In competent hands, briefs and oral arguments have undergone in their preparation a great deal of conscious and unconscious selectivity and editing. They can be tools of extraordinary efficiency, enabling an appellate court, after investing only several hours of reading briefs and no more than an hour of listening to argument, to comprehend the essential facts, legal authorities, and issues of a case that may have taken a month or more to try in the court below.

THE CONVENTIONS AFFECTING DECISION

Decision in any field must reckon with its own constraints. In commerce, cost is a remarkable clarifier of thought, keep-

---

* "Brief" belies the reality, since a lawyer's brief is usually anything but. Just as the great arks of summer mansions in turn-of-the-century Newport continue to be called cottages, so do the book-sized compendia of facts, law, and argument submitted these days to American appellate courts brazenly carry the name once reserved for a slip of paper listing a few cases. The English barrister would hand this slip up to milord on the bench so that the latter could, if curious, send a bailiff for a case and read it.

ing flights of fancy to reasonable altitudes. In large bureaucracies, the jealously guarded boundary between competing
fiefdoms deeply influences what may or may not be done. In
legislative halls, the sixth sense of the seasoned politician
tells him what is negotiable and what is not, what his constituents will tolerate and what they will not. These constraints, while real and even compelling, are on the whole
less sharply limned by convention and less overtly intrusive
than the constraints confining judicial decisions.

In the judicial process, these conventions or disciplines of
decision are felt at several levels. They chart the bases of
decision — the rules of evidence determining what facts may
be considered, and the Constitution, statutes, and decided
cases identifying what legal principles may be applied. They
provide a series of rules that, like guards at a palace gate,
select those cases which may properly come before courts in
general and appellate courts in particular. They give lawyers
and judges an arsenal of methods of legal analysis, some of
which are recognizable as common sense and others that
must seem to the layman to be ancient and occult mysteries.
Finally, there is the underlying discipline of aspiration, the
goal of determining a party's rights or liabilities in a way
that is at once consistent with earlier cases (so that the result is quite expectable, not a rude surprise), with current
decisions affecting others who are similarly situated (so that
a party may be, and feel to be, fairly treated), and also
with a rational and responsive evolvement of the law.

As we shall see, the total effect of these conventions of the
law is to limit the freedom of a judge or court across much
of the spectrum of decision. But at the same time they make
tolerable and manageable a life of decision-making. And
lying just beyond the area of restraint lies a smaller un-
charted area of freedom, with quite enough challenge to
one's reservoir of philosophy and wisdom.

THE CONSTRAINT OF WRITING

A remarkably effective device for detecting fissures in accuracy and logic is the reduction to writing of the results of one's thought processes. The custom of American courts of embodying decision in a written opinion setting forth facts, law, logic, and policy is not the least of their strengths. Somehow, a decision mulled over in one's head or talked about in conference looks different when dressed up in written words and sent out into the sunlight. Sometimes the passage of time or a new way of looking at the issue makes us realize that an opinion will simply not do, and back we go to the drawing board. Or we may be in the very middle of an opinion, struggling to reflect the reasoning all judges have agreed on, only to realize that it simply "won't write." The act of writing tells us what was wrong with the act of thinking.

One can canvass other kinds of deciders who come to mind and find few who accompany their routine decisions with written explanations. If explanations there are, they are likely to be incomplete, informal, oral, and perhaps meant to be forgotten. Or, if in writing, there is little guarantee that they reveal the real reason for decision. A legislature may vote down a tax increase, invoking impressive economic data; one may suspect that the prospect of an impending election had more to do with the result. A chief executive may announce a policy decision and marshal sophisticated reasons in support; in reality he may have been reacting to interest groups or congressional pressures.

What makes the "in writing" tradition a demanding one for appellate courts is that judges do not write on a clean slate. Prior decisions in other cases of different degrees of similarity demand to be reconciled with, or distinguished from, the present one. If results differ, the court must explain why. While conscientious and competent judges may disagree, the rigors of dealing honestly with facts, of recognizing and respectably treating precedent, and of reasoning logically, reduce the occasions for differences and narrow the gulf of such as remain.

A COLLEGIAL DECISION

Every important appellate court decision is made by a group of equals. This fact reflects the shrewd judgment of the architects of our state and federal judicial systems that an appellate judge is no wiser than a trial judge. His only claim to superior judgment lies in numbers; three, five, seven, or nine heads are usually better than one.

This element of collegiality is not unique. As the very word implies, the governance of colleges and universities relies heavily on faculties. Boards of directors, committees, commissions, and legislative bodies act collegially. But there are differences. An appellate court is a small "college." The members may differ in seniority, but each holds rank equal to the others. Most important, almost everything an appellate judge is called on to do he must do with his colleagues. He does not practice a specialty in his own chambers, joining his peers only to make top policy decisions. Virtually all decisions are made by a panel of at least three.

There is intimacy, continuity, and dynamism in the relations among judges, at least on the smaller courts.* They do not come together just to vote. They interact with each other, influence each other, and have each other in mind almost from the time they first read briefs for the next session of court. In a sense, the relationship among judges who differ in their values and views is a bargaining one, yet it is a

---

*I am sensitive to the fact that my portrayal of the workings of collegiality is informed and limited by my own happy experience in the First Circuit. I realize that relationships on some larger courts may be characterized by more distance, differences, and tension than those I describe. Nevertheless, if what I depict is more often aspiration than actuality, there is, I think, some merit in holding up a goal for the kind of judicial collegiality we have experienced.

continuing negotiation, where each player lays his cards on the table just as soon as he discovers what cards he has. There is, on a serene court, no suggestion that anyone seeks to manipulate anyone else.

In short, there is a difference between arriving at a yes or no decision through majority vote and working up an opinion on a close case so that three or more judges of different sensitivities, values, and backgrounds can join not only in the result, but in the rationale, tone, nuances, and reservations. Although the task of building toward a unanimous opinion, or even of carpentering a majority, demands a certain amount of sacrifice of ego and substantive concession, collegiality has its solid satisfactions. One quickly realizes that he is not the only source of useful insights. He learns to rejoice when he sees an opinion he has written measurably strengthened by the suggestion of one of his colleagues. Then, too, decisions are sometimes unpleasant, hard, risky, controversial, when the public and the press are hot and quick in their criticism. On such occasions, the comfort of collegiality is a pearl of no little worth.

THE INTENSITY OF
INDIVIDUAL INVOLVEMENT

One of the paradoxes about appellate courts is that there can coexist the kind of intimate collegiality I have sketched and a profound, almost antique individualism. Indeed, perhaps the collegiality is the more enduring because it feeds on, cherishes, and respects the individualism nourished by appellate courts. In any case I make so bold as to say that in this supertechnical, industrialized, computerized, organized age, appellate courts are among the last redoubts of individual work.

While reliance on machines and staff proliferates apace in corporations, legislatures, and executive bureaucracies, the appellate judge still lives and works in his chamber with his law clerks. Although, unlike his predecessor, he can no longer write the first draft of every opinion, he is, as we shall see, in the very heart of creation of every opinion at every stage.

The kind of individualism I refer to is not the individualism of style, flair, or color, though these, happily, are not absent. Rather, every work product of an appellate court, a judicial opinion, bears the individual trademarks of, and is freighted with, the personal scrutiny and reflection of each member to a greater extent than that of any other collegial body. An appellate court's work is the least delegable of that of any major public institution. That this is so is made manifest by the concern of the bar and the Congress that judicial involvement not be diluted by too much reliance on central staff attorneys or parajudicial officers. This is not to say that this preindustrial stronghold is beyond assault. Computer-assisted legal research, elaborate memoried typewriters, word-processing equipment, and machines that can instantaneously reproduce a draft opinion in the chambers of one's colleagues have already made their entry on the scene.

THE BUFFERS OF TIME AND DISTANCE

Just as Einstein managed to marry time and space, so do we, as we join the two in paying homage to the invaluable appellate virtue they make possible, perspective. By "time" I mean the proposition that an appellate opinion is issued when it is ready, not before. One of the attributes of our times, or, we might say, one of the wounds of the age, is the remorseless press of deadlines that is brought to bear on virtually all decision-making. And, of course, promptness in deciding is a standard by which we measure the performance of a trial court. Perhaps there is no better way to point up the difference between the functions of trial and appellate courts than by noting that whereas a judge may give ten seconds thought to a ruling admitting a document at trial, an appellate court will take perhaps two months to decide whether the ruling was error or not.

Appellate courts are not immune from the pressures to decide promptly, but there is rarely such a thing as a mandatory deadline. If a court has trouble in developing a consensus, it waits until it has a majority — until each judge in the fullness of his reflections and the freedom of his conscience takes his final stand. The process allows scope for maturation, the slow, subconscious germination of thought. Again, what a quaint concept: to come to decision when all are ready.

The perspective of distance is not that of a maturer view, but that of a view unclouded by the anxieties, concerns, and passions of those who may be caught up in local feeling or know too much about parochial issues or people. I know that sometimes I look back on a decision our appellate court has made and feel that we may have been so caught up that we lacked perspective. How precious, therefore, it is that we are buffered as well as we are, with our judges coming from various states, their chambers scattered widely in the circuit, and that a certain "ripening time" of several weeks or months elapses between the decision below and the hearing of the appeal.

GRADUATED DECISION-MAKING

At the risk of overemphasis I would say that *the* genius of appellate decision-making is this final quality: a prolonged, graduated, and incremental process of deciding. Here is yet another paradox: the quality of decision is enhanced by prolonged indecisiveness.

Deciding and decisiveness usually go hand in hand. This holds true of commerce and industry. Schools of business administration teach the rational, efficient, expeditious making of executive decisions. The government executive sits at the top of the most sophisticated option-testing apparatus yet devised to aid decision-making. Legislators live lives of constant decision, informed by their deepest values, party position and tradition, intuition, and whatever information is at hand. The more aspiring the politician, the more "decisive" he must be and appear. "I don't know" and "I'll have to think about that" make poor banners in a parade.

Judges, particularly, are expected to "know the law." It is true that establishing what the facts are may take some time and the help of a jury, yet once this is done, a judge should have little trouble and need less time in applying the law to the facts and reaching a decision. This expectation is, in fact, realized in large numbers of cases that are either not appealed or should not be. But by definition an "appeal" is a protest by a party after a full-scale hearing, with the assistance of lawyers, before a trial judge and jury or an administrative agency. One would not expect such tribunals and processes often to produce decisions that are blatantly wrong. Nor would one expect a prudent person to appeal a decision that is incontestably right. Most of the time these expectations are realized. This leaves as the grist for appeal those cases where the trial judge or agency head had difficulty in coming to a decision, where error, though it may be significant, is not egregious but hidden and subtle, and where appellate judges apply a different perspective from the trial judge in guiding the evolution of the law.

Perhaps there are appellate judges who, on hearing the essential facts of such a case, can confidently announce a sound decision without pause. I have seen professors in the classroom so respond; also panelists, lecturers, and cocktail-party pundits. But I am thankful that nothing said under such circumstances affects the rights of parties. Judges do have their share of excellent talkers. The best of them are called brilliant. Brilliance, however, seems to me more associated with the pyrotechnics of speech and writing; as the word suggests, it has to do with how thoughts can be made to shine and sparkle. Sound decision, on the other hand, is more than result; it is an edifice made up of rationale, tone, and direction. It is faithful to the past, settles the present, and foreshadows the future. Such a decision is rarely made quickly.

I see decision-making as neither a process that results in an early conviction based on instant exposure to competing briefs nor one in which the judge keeps an open mind through briefs, discussion in chambers, argument, and conference, and then summons up the will to decide. I see the process, rather, as a series of shifting biases. It is much like tracing the source of a river, following various minor tributaries, which are found to rise in swamps, returning to the channel, which narrows as one goes upstream.

One reads a good brief from the appellant; the position seems reasonable. But a good brief from appellee, bolstered perhaps by a trial judge's opinion, seems incontrovertible. Discussion with the law clerks in chambers casts doubt on any tentative position. Any such doubt may be demolished by oral argument, only to give rise to a new bias, which in turn may be shaken by the postargument conference among the judges. As research and writing reveal new problems, the tentative disposition of the panel of judges may appear wrong. The opinion is written and circulated, producing reactions from the other judges, which again change the thrust, the rationale, or even the result. Only when the process has ended can one say that the decision has been made, after as many as seven turns in the road. The guarantee of a judge's impartiality lies not in suspending judgment throughout the process but in recognizing that each successive judgment is tentative, fragile, and likely to be modified or set aside as a consequence of deepened insight. The nonlawyer looks on the judge as a model of decisiveness. The truth is more likely that the appellate judge in a difficult case is committed to the unpleasant state of prolonged indecisiveness.

II
WORK WAYS

Chapter 5

Place and Patterns of Work

THE CHAMBERS COMMUNITY

Senators, congressional representatives, company presidents, generals, admirals, cabinet officers, even the President of the United States, do most of their work in offices. Professors and members of the clergy have studies. Judges have chambers. I suspect that the time-honored English designation signals a hope to preserve something of the serenity, dignity, and grace associated with more leisurely and reflective times. There is some substance to the hope. A judge's quarters should not be a pressure point, a rallying place for press conferences, or a command post for hectic tactical brainstorming sessions.

Entering my chambers, we find ourselves in the middle room of three. This would be a reception room if ever we had to receive anyone, but we seldom do. It is the exclusive domain of my secretary. There are case files here and a set of state statutes, a tax treatise, the United States Code (containing all of the United States statutes), a treatise on federal procedure, and looseleaf notebooks containing several years' opinions.

To the right is my office, with real credentials as a chamber, since it boasts a fireplace. Its prior occupant was the last judge appointed from my state to serve on my court before I was appointed, but he had stepped down in 1941, a quarter-century before I succeeded him. I can recall, when in the late 1940s I was a young law clerk to the federal district judge whose chambers were next door, stepping from my little cubicle into this room, then overlaid with dust and cobwebs and serving chiefly as storage space for mimeograph paper. Of course I had no idea that this would someday be my chief work place. Most of the wall is sheathed with books: 440 volumes of Supreme Court Reports and 270 volumes of reports from the federal courts of appeals, the latter spanning my time of judicial service. On one side of our suite is "the library," or clerks' quarters. Here, in a room no larger than 400 square feet, entirely surrounded with bookshelves, three vigorous young clerks live and work. Fortunately, they thrive on propinquity. Around them are over 600 volumes of federal district court reports, almost 600 volumes of circuit court reports, various indices, digests, treatises on administrative law, federal procedure, patent law, admiralty, labor, evidence, bankruptcy, and the Restatement of the Law. All in all, about 2500 books.

The importance of law clerks to the work and life of a judge cannot be stressed too much, particularly since the contemporary role of law clerk is so little understood. Law clerks have existed for over a hundred years, since Chief Justice Horace Gray of the Supreme Judicial Court of Massachusetts began in 1875 the practice of annually choosing a fresh law school graduate to help in chambers. Justice Oliver Wendell Holmes, Jr., succeeding Gray, continued the practice. The future Justice Felix Frankfurter, while a professor at Harvard Law School, undertook to pick out bright young third-year students and send them on to Washington to serve as clerks to various justices. Karl Llewellyn, of the Columbia Law School, twenty years ago, wrote, "I should be inclined to rate it as Frankfurter's greatest contribution to our law that his vision, energy, and persuasiveness turned this two-judge idiosyncrasy into what shows high possibility of becoming a pervasive American legal institution."[1] Pervasive indeed has this institution become, there being over a thousand law clerks serving federal judges, and more in the state courts.

A century ago, it may well have been that law clerks were kept busy and useful by checking citations, correcting galley proofs of opinions, running errands, and preparing memoranda on specific questions of law. Even today, there are judges who largely confine clerks to this range of narrowly defined tasks. But I suspect that judges increasingly are reposing larger responsibilities in their clerks, expecting them not merely to draft a memorandum of law on the major legal issues in an appeal but, after discussions with the judge, to organize and present the facts and to discuss the issues in some sensible order. Under this broader charter, the clerk's contribution is not a disembodied analysis of a refined legal issue; it is a prototype or aspirant opinion that reflects a sifting of the raw facts in the record, an ordering of priorities, and a discussion of the controlling law in the factual context that gives it point and purpose.

This means that the judge, instead of laboriously poring over briefs and the record to compose a succinct narration of the essential facts, is able to devote his attention to such things as whether an essential fact is missing or has been under- or overstressed and whether too many facts have been included. Of course, he is able more quickly to come to grips with determining if the legal discussion is as he wishes. In short, as a result of the preparatory work of clerks, the judge's critical and judgmental faculties are released for action at a stage when the development of the opinion has ripened and the issues needing decision have been pinpointed. This also means that those critical faculties can be brought to bear on more issues in more cases.

It is the need to cope with caseload pressures that leaves no alternative, in most instances, to the kind of intensive utilization of law clerks that I have described. As we have seen, the decade between the late 1960s and the late 1970s saw the appellate caseload in most federal and state courts at least doubled, with very few additional judges made available to deal with the increase. Moreover, the increase was not merely quantitative; it was qualitatively characterized by the variety, novelty, and difficulty of the new flood of appeals, partly because of the continuing development of constitutional doctrine and partly because of the proliferation of statutes, state and federal.

Some idea of the pressures of time begins to emerge when we realize that the typical federal appeals judge will return to his chambers after a week of hearing argument with from eight to twelve opinions to draft. Perhaps three or four will be insubstantial, easily disposed of. Four or five will be of middling difficulty, where, although the law may be clear, the application is in doubt. Lengthy agency proceedings or trial transcripts must be digested. There will also be several cases that will demand the judge's best thinking on a novel legal issue. Even when, with good fortune, the judge will have two uninterrupted weeks in chambers, during the third week he must read thirty or forty sets of new briefs for the next sitting of his court. The week after that, he is once again back in the courtroom. During his time in chambers, in addition to doing the thinking, research, writing, and editing of his eight or twelve new opinions, he must also continue any unfinished business, write critiques of his colleagues' opinions, respond to their suggestions and criticisms, tend to the daily flow of administrative duties, and try to catch up on his professional reading. A yearly output of ninety or even more formal opinions by a judge, in addition to less formal memoranda opinions and orders, not by any means a rarity, is perhaps three times the output of most judges in the early 1960s.

I doubt that any appellate judge relishes either the extent of these pressures or the role these pressures have created for him — that of the opinion architect-editor. I suspect that each opinion-writing judge would prefer doing every step of the process himself. When every last word in an opinion is the judge's own, there is no doubt about his authorship. When, however, words, organization, and selection were initially another's work, the way one knows that he has made that opinion his own is more subtle and ineffable. It grows out of a near-total immersion in the briefs, record, choices to be made, nuances of tone to be delicately sounded.

The process of creative collaboration between a judge and his law clerks is suggestive of the interaction between the master and his apprentices in a Renaissance artist's studio. Novelist Irving Stone describes the master's studio, or *bottega*, of the Florentine painter Domenico Ghirlandaio as it was at the time the young Michelangelo had been apprenticed to learn the art of painting:

> Michelangelo had to learn from whatever task each man had at hand. No secrets were kept from him. Ghirlandaio created the over-design, the composition within each panel and the harmonious relation of one panel to the many others. He did most of the important portraits, but the hundred other were distributed throughout the studio, sometimes several men working on a single figure and on a one-day spread of plaster.[2]

It is obvious that in such a bottega the master contributed much to his apprentices, and it does not require much reflection to understand that the apprentices contributed to their master. Nor is it too fanciful to say that the same kind of contribution is made by law clerks to their judge. They bring to chambers their recent exposure to excellent professors in demanding schools of law from all parts of the country. They are questioning, articulate, idealistic. They provide the judge with a continuing seminar that cannot fail to keep his mind open and his mental juices flowing. I have often said that having the pleasure of their company is one of a judge's most refreshing fringe benefits.

My own work ways involve, as the succeeding chapters will reveal, an intimate and many-faceted relationship with my clerks during all stages of the decision process except those that take place physically in court or in conference. It is, therefore, not surprising that I invest a large amount of time in recruiting each year's team of clerks.

Every year, I receive over 200 applications. Nearly all are from very superior students, with excellent grades, positions of responsibility in their law schools, the credit of having published some legal writing, and a record of interesting summer employment. After obtaining faculty letters of appraisal and reading samples of the applicants' legal writing, I arrange for the top ten or dozen to come for an interview. During the process, many will have been offered and will have accepted clerkships with other judges who reached the decision stage earlier.* I ultimately choose, never being dissatisfied with those who come, now well over thirty in number, but knowing that I have turned down or have missed seeing many excellent prospects.

The clerks' undergraduate majors have varied from mathematics to philosophy. They come from schools all over the country. I try to promote variety by resisting taking clerks from the same school two years in a row. Since a clerk's work for me requires high productivity in research, writing, and editing, I generally take someone with experience as an officer of a law journal. I suppose that in this kind of competition, where almost each "finalist" is superb in every category, I inevitably look for spark or brightness of spirit that

---

* The gradual advancing of the time for hiring decisions is a matter of concern within the judge–law school–law clerk communities. The chaotic condition of the hiring process — the lack of any consensus as to when offers should be made, the making of hiring decisions at ever earlier dates — ill serves all those concerned: the law schools, the judges, and particularly the harassed second-year law students, each of whom must somehow concoct a decent writing sample, draft and make multiple mailings of a detailed curriculum vitae, and get to know professors well enough to ask them for letters of reference while he is in the very middle of the rigors of his second-year instruction.

engages me, that makes me sit up a bit and relish the prospect of a year's company with the source of that spark. Sometimes I detect this attribute from the larger interests of the applicant, sometimes from perceptive letters from professors, and I am attracted to students who seem sincerely bent on trying to contribute something to their fellow humans. But at the same time I distrust those who are very sure of themselves and whose sureness is reflected in too hard a polish in their speech. I know that probably I have let slip extraordinary clerkship possibilities just because I couldn't sense the something extra that I continue to look for and, happily, continue to find.

Even more important than the "something extra" is a something basic, a trait of character that is independent of talent, personality, and intellect — trustworthiness. A chambers community is nourished in an atmosphere of assured confidentiality. In an era when the public's right to know is asserted in regard to nearly every institution, it may seem archaic to value confidentiality for judicial chambers. But I see no valid public purpose served by disclosure of what goes on between judges or between a judge and his law clerks. Unlike the case of a legislator or an administrator, there is no reason to discover which way a judge votes or why, because the published opinion of the court sets forth the facts, assumptions, reasoning, and conclusions by which alone that opinion is to be tested. On the other hand, disclosure out of context of the informal communications, crossfire, negotiations, and concessions leading up to the final opinion could not fail to give a distorted view of the highly creative, tentative, and experimental process of developing a collegial decision. The apprehension by a judge that his every remark, be it deliberate or random, cerebral or emotional, tentative or final, could someday gain public currency would be a corrosive force. So my first admonition and plea to my clerks is that what goes on in chambers of any serious and professional import remains a matter of confidence for their lifetime. So far, to my knowledge, this request has been heeded.

THE NERVE CENTER

While the chambers of an appellate court may comprise the brain cells of that court, the source of all activating impulses — the nerve center — is the office of the clerk of the court. To the extent that the word *clerk* conjures up the image of a petty functionary performing mechanical chores, it is completely inappropriate. The office of clerk in all courts is of critical and increasing importance in improving procedures to receive, keep track of, and expedite all proceedings.

Our clerk's office, like its court, is still small, employing only seven persons at this writing. As is true of the court itself, the virtues of smallness are appreciated. Our systems of record-keeping are both manageable and comprehensible, and we look on our clerk, a trained lawyer, as a repository of wisdom and knowledge in the arcane areas of jurisdiction and procedure. Much of our workload, consisting of cases and questions other than those in our formal docket, arises from our clerk's preliminary scanning of each new appeal to see if all the jurisdictional and procedural requirements have been met.

Problems identified by the clerk are referred to another resource, our staff attorneys' office. This is a small office of four attorneys who do the legal research on the issues of a procedural and jurisdictional nature, emergency motions, and, indeed, the whole range of what I shall later describe as "windowsill" matters. The staff attorneys also look over appeals in order to recommend to the judges what cases may be taken "on submission," that is, without the benefit of oral argument. They also draft memoranda that can serve as the basis for disposing of some motions and appeals. This central staff attorney position is a relatively new career position in appellate courts but has already proven its worth. The danger that judges will delegate too much of their discretionary function to these officials is one that should always be kept in view, but I have seen no evidence that excessive delegation has, in fact, occurred.

Completing the resources at the nerve center is our central library, which serves not only our court but the large metropolitan district court for the District of Massachusetts and members of the bar generally. An appropriate contemporary symbol of the nerve center is our computer terminal for use in legal research. If we can identify our problem with the appropriate words (and have a little bit of luck), we can retrieve in a few instants the names of cases throughout the country that bear on the issue.

THE WINDOWSILL WORKLOAD

Let us imagine that it is midsummer and that the clerks I have had for the past year are leaving and those I chose a year ago have now finished law school and are reporting for duty. The new clerks' first job is to become oriented to the daily traffic that flows through the chambers wholly apart from the opinions we must research and write.

There are three kinds of matters that, collectively, I have referred to as the windowsill workload, after the habit of my predecessor, Chief Judge Bailey Aldrich, who collected motions, petitions, and complaints outside of regular cases, storing them on the windowsill behind his desk until he had an opportunity to think about them and discuss them with his colleagues. Such matters constitute a large and important subculture of the justice system that lies outside the usual orbit of comment and analysis. These are not docketed cases and yet are all important to the parties. The decisions disposing of these issues are seldom printed, yet often involve the most painstaking study. I doubt that courts are ever judged on their fairness or efficiency in dealing with such issues, but they should be. These are the unheralded cases, the anonymous litigants, the usually-but-not-always lost causes.

The first group in this subculture consists of "pro se" cases, cases appealed by an individual who does not have, and frequently does not want, a lawyer. This person often is an incarcerated prisoner who, over the years, has acquired a pretty good legal education and is skillfully using the prison library, sending off lengthy petitions, motions, and briefs every few days. Or it may be a citizen with a civil complaint, charging that the entire government of a city has long been conspiring to blacken his good name. Bushels of papers having to do with such cases are received and filed each year. A large number of them prove to be anguished but insubstantial pleadings. The language of many is illiterate, extreme, incomprehensible, or all three. One is tempted to discount the entire classification as "eccentric," but it is one of the unsung glories of our appellate system that such primitive paperwork from these frustrated and sometimes tormented individuals occupies untold hours of serious attention on the part of law clerks and judges. All the papers are read and considered, and, although they are usually found irrelevant, once in a while a crude complaint is seen to have stated a case. A district court will have missed a key fact, or a motion paper will have been simply lost and no action taken for an unconscionable time. I am sure that a narrow cost-benefit analysis would prove the investment of my court and all other appellate courts in understanding and dealing with pro se appeals to be unjustified. But though they are unfortunate and unassisted, these citizens receive high-quality deliberation at the appellate level and count heavily in the calibrations of justice.

A second kind of case coming over a judge's desk apart from regular caseload raises the question as to whether that case has any business being before the appellate court. For example, an objection to appellate jurisdiction may have been raised. The appeal may not be a "final" one; it may not have disposed of the whole case; or it may not have been a timely appeal. Enough here to say that the law has erected a pretty formidable fence around appeals. To enter appellate territory, one has to have the proper key to unlock the gate.

A state prisoner seeks a writ of habeas corpus from a federal district court, is refused, and then seeks to appeal. In this kind of case, unless the district court gives permission to appeal, the court of appeals must first certify that the issues presented are not frivolous. This means that if any one judge thinks the case is substantial, the appeal will be heard. But if three agree that there is nothing of substance, the appeal will be dismissed. Usually the court acts by memoranda circulated among the judges, resulting not in any formal opinion but at most in a short memorandum and order. Sometimes days of clerks' time and many hours of judges' time are involved, with very little on record to show for the effort. Again, I would say that one of the tests of the quality of an appellate court is the thoroughness with which it examines such requests for permission to appeal.

A third and more exposed kind of case claiming the time of judges is the emergency request. Though trial courts face most of the emergency situations in the legal world, appellate courts at times must also act quickly. Cases carrying a sense of urgency include a request for bail pending appeal, a motion for injunction or for stay of an injunction pending appeal, a motion for a summary reversal or for a writ of mandamus accomplishing the same goal, a motion to expedite an appeal, a motion to enjoin transfer of a prisoner to another jurisdiction, and so on. The ingenuity of lawyers is without limit. In the most complicated and serious of these matters a panel of the appellate court must quickly assemble and hold a hearing, deliberate, and issue an opinion, sometimes within a few hours.*

---

* I think that our court must have merited a mention in *Guinness* for expedition in the consideration of a civil case from its inception at the lowest

---

So this windowsill traffic is there, it is important, and it claims time, scholarship, and skill.

THE CYCLE OF WORK

What I have called the most important element in appellate work ways, incremental or graduated decision-making, is the inevitable product of the cyclical patterns that shape the contours of life for appellate judges. While others may think our activity to be very much of a sameness, the cycles of work give judges a frequent and refreshing change of pace and challenge. They enable us to do confining, solitary work, month after month, without becoming desiccated by boredom.

The starting point is the schedule for hearing arguments at court. Each panel of three judges can hear no more than five to seven cases a day, depending on their complexity. A week's total of thirty to thirty-five cases is more than enough to keep three judges and their clerks busy in research and writing for the next three weeks. Some courts hear arguments for more than one week, then recess for six weeks' work in chambers. For me, the cycle is monthly, beginning in September and ending in June, leaving July for catching up on the year's work and, I always hope, most of August for vacation. Some judges may well cut out one or even two stages in a typical cycle, but I have found it natural to think of six. Each gives me a chance to approach a case from a dif-

level until its final disposition by the Supreme Court. On the Monday before Easter in 1978, plaintiff clergymen sought an injunction in the federal district court of New Hampshire against the governor's order to lower the flag in all state institutions on Good Friday. There being no judge then available in New Hampshire, I certified a Massachusetts judge to hear the case. He heard the parties on Tuesday and issued an injunction on Wednesday. One of our circuit judges held an emergency hearing Wednesday, conferred with his colleagues overnight, and set aside the injunction on Thursday. The plaintiffs flew to Washington, where the matter was presented to the full Supreme Court on Friday morning. The Court set aside our order and reinstated the ban against the governor's order to lower the flag. Total elapsed time from bottom to top: four days.

ferent direction. In each phase I am likely to gain some new insight, perhaps at odds with one I had earlier. Each phase involves a different intellectual process:

- I read (or scan) briefs alone, usually at night.
- I talk over each case with my clerks, one of whom has given particular attention to it. I make notes of our colloquy.
- I listen to oral argument in court and ask a few questions.
- I confer with my fellow judges late in the day after the argument.
- I research, discuss, and draft an opinion in chambers or discuss, edit, and redraft the first draft of a clerk.
- I circulate my draft to my colleagues and respond to their suggestions; when they circulate their drafts, I propose changes to which they respond.

These phases, I have come to realize, are not merely sequential, chronological steps. They involve changes of environment, focus, and intensity that call to mind the metallurgical process of tempering a sword blade, alternately heating and cooling or quenching it until it achieves precisely the right condition of strength and ability to retain an edge. This is the kind of process served by the six stages of my decision-making cycle, which regularly alternate between the coolness of solitary reflection and the heat of animated discourse with others. Not only do they alternate, but the variation in the temperature of deliberations increases with each alternation.

Reading briefs is a cool, solitary, relaxed business. Discussing briefs with my clerks is a warmer, more animated, occasionally upsetting exercise. Indeed, clerks and judges may sometimes have vigorous if not heated exchanges. Then oral argument, if it is ordinary, will find the judge mainly listening — really a solitary occupation for the judge, though the courtroom may be crowded. Often, of course, arguments come alive because of the preparation, curiosity, and wit of the judges and the competence and resourcefulness of the lawyers. On such occasions, an oral argument becomes a lively learning venture for the judges and a rigorous testing round for the lawyers.

Whatever kind of argument may have taken place, the postargument conference among the judges raises the temperature, since this is the first time a judge is called on to give his opinion and to indicate if and where he may disagree with his colleagues. The process of collegial consideration has begun, and for this process to be triggered, a certain depth of involvement and warmth of views are necessary. When a judge returns to chambers, however, not only the scene but the atmosphere changes. The judge once again is solitary, cool, reflective, as he begins to dig more deeply into a case. Finally, when the judge and clerks have done their best and have circulated an opinion for comment, the commenting judges know that this is their last chance to affect the opinion of their court. This is the stage at which strongly held and carefully developed opposing views collide. Whether dissents or compromises result, this stage is likely to be attended by the highest temperatures — and sometimes by the precipitous chill of an unexpected quenching of a judge's fondest idea.

If the process works well, the result is what we must refer to as a well-tempered opinion.

Chapter 6

Preparing for Argument

By the middle of the third week of a typical month, the briefs for our next session of court arrive in several heavy cartons. Although my clerks and I are working away on opinions from earlier sessions, we know that we have to make time to prepare, for my way involves a two-step approach to a case before I mount the bench to hear argument: reading briefs and then discussing them with my clerks. This is not the only way; Justice Louis D. Brandeis, for example, preferred not to read briefs before hearing oral argument. He wanted to have a completely open mind, uninfluenced by prior reading or discussion.

Each of my three clerks takes a third of the briefs, and a pile containing copies of all is reserved for me. The clerks' task is to read their briefs with some care and report to the rest of us what the case is about, what the key issues are, where some of the major problems lurk, and what questions might usefully be asked at argument. Again, what I do may not be the best way for others. I suspect that most judges prepare by having their clerks prepare a "bench memorandum." This is a typed memorandum that can be quickly read or reread at the bench; it contains salient facts, issues, contentions, and some thoughtful insights and questions from a clerk. Over the years, I have come to feel that it was better to save the solitary typing time and the equally solitary reading time and invest it in more lively discussion, talking back and forth about the case, taking notes as we go along.

There are from thirty to forty appeals to be heard in a week's sitting. There are at least two and sometimes more parties to each appeal. Each will have a typewritten or printed brief from 15 or 20 to over 100 and even 200 pages long. If one session's briefs were stacked in one pile, it would be from one and a half to two feet high and contain at least 2000 pages, and would not include the still more voluminous records containing transcripts of testimony, exhibits, and pleadings.

What must also be kept in mind is that this reading matter is not pellucid, fast-moving prose. It is from sixty to eighty tales of hard-won, amply justified triumphs of right over wrong (according to the appellees who won below) or of lamentable miscarriages of justice (according to the appellants). The briefs are written usually in plodding, pedestrian sentences, on subjects as different as organized crime and solid state circuitry. Yet they are absolutely critical in American appellate advocacy. They give any advocate, if he is willing to devote the time and the care, the opportunity to say everything he wishes precisely as he wishes. What is written is sure to be read by from three to nine judges and from four or five to a dozen law clerks, several times by some. Honestly, thoroughly, and skillfully done, the brief is the heavy artillery of advocacy on appeal.

As one would expect, there are many monographs, articles, clinical courses, moot court competitions,* and books

* Moot courts are full-dress appellate arguments by law students before a "court" of senior students, professors, lawyers, or even actual judges. As long ago as 1814, Thomas Jefferson replied to a correspondent seeking advice by copying a letter he had written a young person contemplating study of law fifty years earlier: "This is your last and important exercise. no trouble should therefore be spared. if you have any person in your neighborhood engaged in the same study, take each of you different sides of the same cause, and prepare pleadings according to the custom of the bar, where the pl. opens, the def. answers, and the pl. replies. — it would further be of great service to pronounce your orations (having before you only short notes

devised to teach the advocate how to write an effective brief. But, as with most other goods and services, though there is much effort to instruct in their production and distribution, there is very little attention paid to intelligent and discriminating consumption. Thus, the judge largely has to fend for himself.

I am usually so wrapped up in working on my opinions, commenting on those of my colleagues, tending to administrative duties, that I leave most of my brief-reading for my evenings. I am not proud of this. There are better ways to spend one's postprandial hours and better times to undertake such chores. Nevertheless, once every month I read over thirty sets of tedious, lengthy, and technical argumentation. This is the dullest part of our work. If a case is frivolous, I am irritated that it is taking up our time. If it is not, then my reading induces a state of discomfort: I am irritated that I don't know which side is right. I try to take comfort in the thought that after argument, conference, and study, all will at some point come clear, as it always has. But the discomfort remains, lessening only as I begin to make the case a part of me.

The two states, tedium and discomfort, are exacerbated by the sheer quantity of material to be read. If one could spend hours on a set of briefs, with time for reading, comparing, and mulling, one could read creatively and develop a position with some confidence. The more creative the reading, the less tedium; the more clear the right disposition or approach, the less agony of uncertainty. But, like most appellate judges, I simply do not have the luxury of an extra week a month reserved solely for the reading of briefs.

As the three cases that follow illustrate, I do not faithfully read every brief from cover to cover. There are clear signals which make my task manageable in that they tell me when

to assist the memory) in the presence of some person who may be considered as your judge." (Letter of August 30, 1814, in possession of University of Pennsylvania Law School Library.)

it is profitable at this early stage to do close reading and when it is not. If the table of contents, nature of the case, and size of the briefs indicate that the issue is un- complicated and easily understood, I will read rather closely. The appeal may be patently groundless or substan- tial. If the former, my first reading may be my last. If the lat- ter, a full reading takes little time and gives me a good basis for developing an informal "feel." If the case is obviously complex in its facts or law, I will know that, whether it proves to be difficult or not, I shall not be in a position to decide until I have read a great deal. So I will rest content with a general comprehension of the issues.

In some instances, a quick look at briefs will indicate whether the issue is a novel one, where the court is free to make law, and where basic values may determine the out- come. It is this kind of case that sets one musing, thinking ahead, turning over things in one's mind, trying to prepare, not in the sense of doing more research, but in the sense of trying to determine where one really stands on due process, on prisoners' rights, on free speech, on privacy. In this genre of case, a judge senses that an important decision lies ahead. He puts out his antennae. He wants his questions at oral argument to expose concerns that will make his colleagues think. In short, he wants the whole process to be a good one. Even if his initial biases may not prevail, he wants the sys- tem to "work" on the issue at hand, which he senses is one of those which are freighted with significance for society at large.

THE CASES

The Smuggler on the Dock:
A Criminal Case

It is not unusual in a criminal appeal for a wide range of issues — from the substantial to the insignificant — to be presented. That a large proportion of guilty verdicts are appealed and that the issues argued include many insubstantial ones are chiefly the result of the instinct of defense lawyers to protect themselves against later charges of incompetence should their clients try to attack their convictions on the ground of ineffective assistance of counsel. The court-appointed lawyers representing indigent defendants therefore not only prosecute every appeal but raise every possible issue.

The defendant, Albert Hapless, has been convicted of aiding and abetting two other co-defendants, John Derring and Harvey Dew, in their scheme to smuggle marijuana into a coastal state. The co-defendants were aboard the motor yacht *Lucky Lady*, which, near midnight, had rounded the end of a cape jutting into the sea and was heading up a narrow estuary, Rosemary Cove, toward a long lobster wharf when a Coast Guard launch approached. The *Lucky Lady* did a right-about-face, took off like a flash and sped off to sea, but was eventually caught. Several dozen bales of marijuana were seized.

Defendant Hapless, at the time of these events, was observed by Drug Enforcement Administration agents to be sitting on the dock near Fleur L'Heureux, a well-known local prostitute. Ms. L'Heureux, on being apprehended by the agents, seemed nervous. Her clothing appeared excessive for a hot summer night and was oddly bulging. When at last she started to run away, she was arrested and searched. About a dozen plastic envelopes were found taped to her body, some containing marijuana, several empty. Defendant Hapless was then arrested. A search of his background revealed a conviction, over ten years old, when he was eighteen, for possessing with intent to distribute five grams of marijuana.

These facts were established during a short, two-day trial in which the defendant did not testify. Each brief devoted from six to ten pages in presenting its version, adding innuendo in much the same spirit as one tries to put a bit of english into a billiard shot. With my selective reading, or scanning, of each brief began the up-and-down process of considering issues from various points of view.

The briefs discussed no fewer than six issues. The first caught my eye because of its novelty. Defendant, now the appellant, attacked his conviction because he could not have been an aider and abettor in smuggling, since, thanks to the Coast Guard, the *Lucky Lady* never unloaded any contraband on land in the United States. Appellant cited an old Supreme Court case, *Keck* v. *United States*, 172 U.S. 434 (1899),* which looked to old English law and found that "smuggling" meant the "bringing of goods *on land*." In response, the government's brief pointed out how ridiculous a result such a reading would create. Smugglers caught in the act, with every possible proof of their intent to smuggle, being well within the territorial limits of the United States, and on the verge of succeeding when they were arrested, would have to be released. Their release would be based on the meaningless and hypertechnical ground, drawn from the law and custom of another age, that the contraband had not been landed. The government's position seemed incontrovertible to me after a quick reading, but I had to give appellant's counsel credit for a good college try.

Appellant next claimed error in the refusal of the trial court to exclude evidence of his ten-year-old conviction for possession of marijuana. From ancient times, the law has allowed one side to impeach or discredit an opposing witness by introducing evidence of conviction of a felony if it was relevant to prove motive, plan, or absence of mistake. Nevertheless, since such evidence is likely to be taken by the

---

*For the benefit of the non-lawyer reader, this citation means that the opinion is to be found in volume 172 of the printed reports of the Supreme Court, of which there are now over 440. Later on, opinions of federal courts of appeals will be cited as in a given volume of F.2d, this being the abbreviation for the Federal Reporter, Second Series, which, now numbering over 600 volumes, contains all of the opinions of these courts. The supreme court of each state has its own series of reports.

jury as indicating that if defendant committed one crime, he may well have committed another, courts have always been sensitive to the possibility of prejudice. The present, recently rewritten rules of evidence preclude "other crimes" evidence over ten years old unless the court finds the danger of prejudice to be "substantially" outweighed by the probative value. On reading the briefs on this issue, I felt appellant had a good point. Why, after all, did appellant's possession of a small amount of marijuana over ten years ago, when he was a very young man, tend to prove that he was part of a recent plan to smuggle the drug in wholesale quantities? Yet I noted that appellant's brief said nothing about whether trial counsel had objected to the evidence going in. And appellate courts rarely fault trial courts for rulings made in the absence of any objection. The government brief did not help clear up my question; it merely argued that the old conviction *was* relevant to the recent crime, the same substance being involved.

The third issue, raised by defendant's motion for acquittal just before the case was submitted to the jury, was whether there was sufficient evidence of defendant's knowing participation in the scheme to justify a verdict of guilty. The law is that the mere presence of someone at the scene of a crime is usually not enough. Here, the only facts set forth in the briefs that linked defendant to the drug-running operation were his presence at the target dock late at night and his being in company with the prostitute L'Heureux, who was "body-carrying" some drugs and had room to carry more. The merits of an argument based on insufficiency of the evidence cannot usually be determined before all of the testimony is carefully read, so I did not try to dig any deeper or even try to form a tentative opinion. When I read the government's brief, however, I was struck by its failure to cite two recent opinions from our court where the crew members and a passenger of a seventy-foot schooner had been arrested by the Coast Guard shortly after several bales of marijuana had been jettisoned from the ship. We had said that "the intimacy of association on a small vessel" was not enough basis to support a conviction of the crew and that even the close personal relationship between the passenger and the captain was inadequate to support the passenger's conviction.[1] I had not been surprised that appellant's court-appointed counsel had not found these cases, but I was sure that government counsel was well aware of them.

The remaining contentions, which I merely skimmed, were that the judge should have separated Hapless' trial from that of the more deeply involved co-defendants, Derring and Dew; that the prosecutor had prejudiced the jury by promising in his opening that he would prove Hapless was an old friend of Derring and Dew, without offering any evidence by way of fulfilling that promise; and, finally, that the jury had returned inconsistent verdicts, finding defendant guilty of aiding and abetting in a smuggling operation but not guilty of conspiring to smuggle.

I put down the briefs, feeling that appellant had overargued his case on some issues, had been misled into stressing his novel wrinkle on the definition of smuggling, and had paid inadequate attention to the more mundane but promising point of the sufficiency of evidence. I thought appellant would probably lose, but I was annoyed with government counsel. I found his brief a bland boilerplate production. It left me unconvinced that appellant's case, as he irritatingly put it, was "a bundle of hollow reeds," and I was bothered by the brief's ignoring recent pertinent authority within our circuit.

When my clerks and I convened for our seminar on the cases to be argued the following week, the clerk who had drawn this case reported first on the challenge based on the point that the goods never reached shore. She had read the *Keck* case. The justices really had bought, lock, stock, and barrel, old English smuggling law that required a landing. And they did this deliberately, for the dissenting minority of four had vigorously criticized the majority for importing the technicalities of a bygone age. There was no blinking the fact that in the past three quarters of a century Congress had never seen fit to clarify or change its statutory definition of smuggling. So, despite our common-sense reading that smuggling should not depend on hitting the beach, there could be a problem. After all, an inferior court only rarely disavows a Supreme Court opinion, and then only after a number of signposts have been erected by the Court itself and conditions of life and technology have drastically changed. In this case, neither set of events had taken place.

On the issue of the ten-year-old conviction, my clerks fell into a spirited debate. The clerk with responsibility for the case felt that, although it was a close question, the judge was probably within his discretion in allowing the evidence. Another clerk, who had worked in this area in another case, made the point that the new Federal Rules of Evidence were intended to raise the threshold of relevancy, to make it more difficult to admit this kind of inherently prejudicial evidence. He put it this way: "If the prejudice in admitting this conviction doesn't dramatically outweigh any possible relevance, then aren't we saying that all old convictions for minor offenses are admissible?" As the debate waxed, I asked if anyone knew whether defense counsel had objected. We all agreed this was a crucial question to ask counsel. In the meantime, my clerk should have a look at the record.

On the sufficiency of evidence point, the clerk who had worked on a recent similar case chimed in with some energy. In that case an obese man had been convicted of conspiracy to import cocaine on the evidence that he had gone to Colombia in company with a prostitute who, on returning home, was found to be carrying drugs. The prosecution had argued that this pair would not have gone abroad except for illegal business reasons, an argument we rejected in that earlier case as based on "a sort of guilt by unlikely association."[2] We all agreed that this was a serious issue in the case now before us. Yet I could see how naturally one could jump to a conclusion that defendant was probably up to no good in being where he was at such an hour and with such a companion.

This is the kind of situation we often meet in the law: because of some legal principle (here, the criminal law's requirement of proof beyond a reasonable doubt and the allied presumption of innocence), the right legal answer does not correspond with so-called common sense. I resolved to flush out this issue at oral argument, not merely to hear what government counsel would say but to alert my colleagues that I thought that this issue, usually a no-win one, had real substance and should claim their concern.

The remaining issues, my law clerk said, were "a house of cards." She seemed on solid ground. Severance of the trial of one defendant from that of others is a matter of wide discretion for a trial judge; even with three defendants, this trial was neither complicated nor likely to confuse the jury. Similarly, failing to sanction a prosecutor for not backing up his opening with evidence would rarely be reversible error, particularly in the absence of any motion for mistrial or for curative instructions to set the jury straight. The inconsistent verdicts point seemed, as my clerk frankly said, "bogus." A jury is allowed wide latitude. It could rationally find defendant to be an abettor in the act of smuggling while finding him innocent of agreeing or conspiring to formulate the whole scheme.

What at first blush looked like a routine criminal case with an affirmance now seemed to be an open question. Not only was the result up in the air, but we had a wide variety of issues, ranging from the broadly significant one of the interpretation of smuggling, to the application of the new rules of evidence to "other crimes" evidence, down to the most particularistic, fact-laden issue of sufficiency of evidence. As to each issue, laymen might well respond in an instant-opinion poll that it was not at all close: common sense

would have no difficulty in finding enough evidence to convict (after all, where there's smoke, there's fire), or in admitting evidence of the old conviction (as the twig is bent, so
grows the tree), or in paying no attention to the old Supreme
Court case (time makes ancient good uncouth). But if folk
wisdom could justly resolve such cases as this, there would
be no need for a legal profession. So it is that the lawyers
fight and judges deliberate long over what look at first like
easy questions.

The Agency and the Anorectic:
A Civil Case

The subject matter of this case, an appeal from a government agency whose mission is to protect consumers, is intensely technical and scientific. The case record is massive.
The problem for the courts is how to exercise review in such
cases without getting swamped by data that, if not beyond
their competence to judge, may appear to others to be so. As
I lift the briefs out of my briefcase, I am appalled: petitioner's brief, 125 pages; the agency's, 95; petitioner's reply
brief, 50 pages; a hopeful intervenor's brief, 35 pages. I did
not bring home the record of pleadings, testimony, and exhibits (the "appendix") — twelve volumes on my chambers
table standing a foot and a half high. This appeal is in the
form of a petition for review of a decision by the Food and
Drug Administration, sought by a major drug company that
stands to lose tens of millions of dollars invested in a medi-
cament devised to reduce weight in obese persons, that is, an
anorectic (from *anorexia,* meaning "loss of appetite").

The product is seductively named "Thin-King." By increasing one's metabolism, it leads to weight loss and also
allegedly stimulates intellectual productivity. Since over-
stimulation is a danger, the pill contains a counteractive
narcotic. This combination of drugs had been merchandised
for many years but became prominent only after it changed

its name to its present label in the late 1950s. Up to this time there was no question of Thin-King's legality, since the only legal requirement was that such drugs be proven safe for human consumption. In 1962, however, Congress changed the law and required that all drugs meet the test of being proven "effective for their intended purpose."

Accordingly, the legitimacy of some 7000 drugs had to be re-established. The manufacturers had to convince a panel of scientists through "well-controlled investigations," meeting very precise criteria, that they were effective. Thin-King succeeded only to the extent of satisfying a panel that it was "possibly effective," which was not nearly good enough. The FDA refused to approve a new drug application and ordered Thin-King off the market. The manufacturer, Schmarzipan, Incorporated, then brought the petition for review.

As I settled down with the briefs, I had two, and only two, goals in mind: to get some sort of grasp of the facts and to obtain a rough idea of the issues. I also quickly came to the conclusion that each side should be given a full hour for argument rather than the usual twenty or thirty minutes. I soon learned that a consumer group calling itself, enticingly, FIB, an acronym for Fat Is Beautiful, wanted to be allowed to intervene as a party and support the FDA's ruling. Whether FIB was legally entitled to do so was the first question in the case.

A second issue was whether the FDA had overstepped in prescribing in detail what sort of investigations it would credit in the category of well-controlled investigations. A third, and major, issue, occupying some fifty pages of briefs on each side, was whether the agency's detailed criticisms of the quality-control methods used in the tests relied on by Schmarzipan to establish the effectiveness of Thin-King were reasonable or arbitrary. A fourth challenge was directed to the agency's action at the hearing in limiting the time of several of Schmarzipan's witnesses.

Finally, there was a very abstruse, almost metaphysical

issue. The question was whether the FDA's proceeding was "adjudicative" or "legislative." If it fell under a section of the Administrative Procedure Act covering an "adjudication required by statute to be determined on the *record*," then petitioner had the right to complain that a certain panel of experts assigned by the FDA to scrutinize Thin-King's testing methods took into account their own acquaintance with "the literature in the field," which, of course, was not part of the record of this case.

Having broadly absorbed what I have just narrated, I was nothing if not open-minded when I came to my session with my clerks. All of us were somewhat overwhelmed by the mass of technical data that seemed to be important. But we had a few ideas. As for FIB, the consumer group that wanted to intervene, my clerks saw no special interest that would set it apart from people generally. The law of "standing," determining who has enough at stake in a controversy to raise an issue, is a highly structured set of propositions, and I had to agree that the most recent precedents from the Supreme Court would probably preclude FIB's playing much of a role in this appeal. As an afterthought, one clerk asked whether FIB had attempted to participate in proceedings before the FDA; if not, it certainly could not jump into the fray on the appellate level. Oddly enough, this obvious matter had not been addressed by FIB's brief, and I noted the issue so that I might ask the question at oral argument.

The clerk in charge of this case also felt that the attack on the FDA's regulations defining well-controlled investigations was, in his inelegant words, "off the wall." The regulations did not exclude any sensible additional technique; they merely sketched a reasonable minimum of requirements to be met. Moreover, the regulations had been in place for several years; those who waited to challenge them until now had very probably waited too long. We would have to check the time requirements for challenging regulations.

When we came to discuss the laboratory methods used in

gathering the data meant to prove the effectiveness of Thin-King, and the FDA's criticism, we all agreed that the record had to be read closely. The company's reliance, in part, on crude opinion polls submitted to customers concerning the product's effectiveness looked like a weak point in its case, but otherwise we had no wisdom to contribute at the moment. Nor did we have a feel for the FDA's sharply limiting the testimony of Schmarzipan's witnesses. This was probably a necessary agency prerogative.

The last issue, whether the FDA's proceeding was the kind of adjudicative proceeding where nothing that was not in the record could be considered, was agreed to be interesting. None of us had recently worked with the Administrative Procedure Act, and this seemed to be a solid issue.

As we exhausted our limited impressions, I asked my clerk to prepare for me a list of the criticisms made by FDA of the testing procedures used on Thin-King. I was not sure whether or how I would use such a list, but I felt it would at least help me keep my bearings as I listened to argument. I set off to court with absolutely no idea how I would ultimately vote on this case.

The Saga of the Transferred Prisoners:
A Civil Rights Case

Civil rights cases are those in which the plaintiffs claim that their rights as citizens, guaranteed them by the Constitution or by federal laws, have been violated by some government official or agency. One of the distinctive features of civil rights litigation lies in the intellectual tools used in coming to decision. A civil rights case involves more than the fixed and often precise principles of law that govern the conduct of a jury trial in a criminal case or the minute analysis of administrative procedure and scientific facts that so informs the review of a technical agency. It implicates as well the basic values of judges, their sense of the proper balance between the individual and society. Another distinction is focus. "The Smuggler on the Dock" deals with the appellate functions of correcting error and preserving continuity and consistency in the law, and "The Agency and the Anorectic" deals with the traditional agency review function. This case, however, shows a court playing a part (for a time) in influencing the direction of the law in addition to exercising a new kind of monitoring, in which the court is called on to serve as arbiter in matters small as well as great between society and the individual.

There is one final distinction here. Although the other two cases draw on actual legal problems and resemble various parts of a number of real cases, they are fictional. This case is an actual one. I felt I could use it for two reasons. First, so much of the thought is on the record that I shall not be divulging confidences or relying on undisclosed motives.* Second, nothing I might say can possibly affect anyone's view of the law because the decision is no longer law. The Supreme Court reversed our decision and so relegated it to history.

In the fall of 1974, a period of unrest in the Massachusetts Correctional Institute at Norfolk culminated in a series of fires thought to have been set. Plaintiff inmate Fano and his fellow plaintiffs were placed in a segregation unit and subsequently were notified that informants had allegedly linked them to the setting of the fires and the carrying-on of other criminal enterprises. Hearings were held, but the evidence was given the disciplinary board outside the presence of plaintiffs and their counsel. Neither the information given by the informants nor a summary was revealed. Plaintiffs were ordered to be transferred to purportedly more severe maximum-security institutions at Walpole and Bridgewater. The district judge enjoined the transfers, holding that the in-

---

* Where there is a gap in the record, I reserve the right to fill it with some credible but fictional connective tissue, implying no resemblance to what really happened long years ago. When I do so, I shall say so.

mates had been denied procedural due process, guaranteed
by the Fourteenth Amendment. The prison superintendent
and other state officials appealed.

In reading briefs in the other cases, I was exploring a new
factual situation or bafflingly unfamiliar technical territory,
but this case was clearly foreshadowed by others we had had
within the past two years. Federal courts in many parts of
the country found themselves dealing with prisoner litigation in the early 1970s, and because of the paucity of precedent, their decisions made law. We were no exception. Many
of the new decisions recognized that the Constitution did not
stop at the prison gate, but clarity or consensus in analysis
was lacking. In 1970, our court had dipped its toe in these
waters. In *Nolan* v. *Scafati*, 430 F.2d 548, we held that a prisoner's claim that authorities had refused to mail his letter
seeking legal advice from the Massachusetts Civil Liberties
Union should not have been dismissed without a hearing. In
the opinion I wrote for the court, I had said that when substantial interests of prisoners are at stake, "some assurances
of elemental fairness are essential." Hardly a systematic analytical approach.

Not long after, in 1973, we had our full-scale baptism in
Palmigiano v. *Baxter*, 487 F.2d 1280. A life inmate at Rhode
Island's Adult Correctional Institutions, disturbed over the
failure of authorities to give medical assistance to a violently
ill prisoner, advised fellow inmates, as a protest, not to return to their cells. He was charged with "inciting a distur-
bance," a charge for which he could be prosecuted under
state law. At his disciplinary hearing, from which his attorney was barred, he was told that if he did not speak, his
silence would be held against him. He was sentenced to
thirty days of punitive segregation, being locked up full
time, eating his meals in his cell, having no exercise, recrea-
tion, or work.

While we held for the plaintiff as to several limited rights,
Palmigiano's significance for us in this *Fano* v. *Meachum*

case lay in the effort we had made to develop a sensible way
of thinking about prisoners' rights. We had recognized both
the tense and often precarious nature of prison administration and, at the same time, the need for an atmosphere of
fairness if there was to be any hope for present order in
prisons or for prisoners' ultimate adjustment to society
when they were released. Writing for the court, I undertook
a two-step analysis, not being at all original but following
venerable Supreme Court doctrine. The first was to see
whether what the individual had at risk was enough to merit
any due process. This threshold test was simply whether he
might suffer "grievous loss," as the cases put it. Applying
this principle to prisoners, I wrote:

> In a prison setting where liberty is by necessity shrunken to a
> small set of minor amenities, such as work or schooling privi-
> leges, visitations, and some modicum of privacy, it is likely that
> any marked change of status which forecloses such liberties will
> be perceived and felt as a grievous loss.[3]

The second step was to determine *how much* process was
due. What we did was to borrow from the Supreme Court's
approach to the most important rights, such as speech and
religion, where government is required, in taking action that
impinges on such a right, to use the means that interferes
least with that right. But, recognizing that we were not dealing with such a major right in the case of prisoners who
have already lost, in a legal trial, their major liberty, we wa-
tered down the burden on the prison, not requiring it to use
"the least restrictive means" but reasoning as follows:

> While due process safeguards have not as yet been elevated to the
> status of fundamental rights, such as freedom of speech, in rela-
> tion to which the state's interests in administrative efficiency
> must take second place, they are not to be abridged unneces-
> sarily. That is, we think that if the state can accomplish its pur-
> pose just as well by observing some measure of due process as by
> not observing it, it should tread the former path. Where a due
> process safeguard entails little or no administrative burden, it
> should be employed whenever due process is merited.[4]

I should add that I was able to convince only one of my colleagues. The other, a visitor from another circuit, made it crystal clear in a short dissent that he felt that the prisoner had received all the due process he was entitled to.

The analytical framework thus formed, we applied it to a second case, argued the same month as *Palmigiano, Gomes* v. *Travisono*, 490 F.2d 1209. In this case, eleven other Rhode Island inmates, suspected of being troublemakers, were transferred without notice or hearing to out-of-state prisons, where they spent their first two to six weeks in segregation. The district court had ordered a wide range of procedural safeguards for all kinds of transfers. We agreed that a transfer to another state did impose a grievous loss on a prisoner, subjecting him to administrative segregation in the receiving institution, depriving him of rehabilitative, educational, or work programs, visits from family, friends, and attorney, and creating a blot on his record for parole purposes. But we gave narrower remedies than the district court, limiting the burden on the state to providing due process as long as it involved little or no burden. Such, however, would include giving the prisoner notice of reasons for a proposed transfer, a hearing, and a chance to controvert factual assertions. One colleague, in concurring, specifically limited his agreement to transfers out of state. My other colleague, the same visitor who dissented in *Palmigiano*, now dissented at greater length, saying that "the majority has failed to recognize that the consequences of conviction of a crime involve not merely the loss of liberty enjoyable in a free society, but . . . the subsequent impairments which are inevitably associated with membership in a closely supervised prison community."[5]

It was not only our court and others like ours that had grappled with prisoners' rights. The Supreme Court had at last made some significant law in this area in *Wolff* v. *McDonnell*, 418 U.S. 439, in 1974, the year following our two decisions. The Court had held that if a state authorizes "good time" credits for prisoners, which would give them freedom earlier than otherwise, such credits constitute such a liberty interest that they cannot be taken away without minimum due process. The Court had also, by the time *Fano* reached us, decided to review *Palmigiano* and prisoner cases from two other circuits. This, then, was the background and atmosphere. Change was in the air, but in what direction?

Gomes involved an interstate transfer; it was inevitable that we would eventually get an intrastate transfer case like *Fano*. I had mixed feelings. There was a sense of symmetrical completeness in knowing that our court could fill out its doctrine in both contexts. But I also dreaded yet another excursion into a field where I knew feelings were strongly held. One of my colleagues had given me fair notice by his concurrence in *Gomes* that he might well look differently on a transfer within a state.

When my clerks and I had our seminar on this case, there was no need to explain the issues or discuss the law.* We all knew where we had been and that this case would find us a divided court once again. We found ourselves concentrating on details, albeit important ones. The clerk assigned to this case felt that it was important to ask questions that might shed light on whether this kind of transfer was really distinguishable from in-prison punitive segregation. We were not sure, however, that on being transferred to Walpole or Bridgewater, a prisoner would be placed in administrative segregation, as were the prisoners in the *Gomes* case. My clerk also felt it important to nail down whether or not the fact of transfer was entered on an inmate's record. She further pointed to a section of the state's brief that seemed to challenge the district judge's finding that Norfolk was more desirable than Walpole and Bridgewater. I should, we

---

*Although what I say about this case is from what is publicly reported, since any discussion with my clerks is something not revealed by the published opinion, what I present here is my fictional construct of what a discussion could reasonably have been under the circumstances.

agreed, try to see if that finding could stand. We also discussed a clerk's thought that it would be better if the disciplinary board could interview the informant witnesses privately to decide if they were credible and to create at least a minimal record for review by a court.

As I packed these briefs to take to court, I knew we were in for an interesting argument and conference.

REFLECTIONS ON PREPARING FOR ARGUMENT

Although each case is different from all others, and its preparation equally distinctive, I can generalize to a limited extent and list the following major concerns that recur most often as I read briefs and hold preargument discussions with my clerks.

Identifying Threshold Issues of
Jurisdiction and Procedure

The first question for any appellate judge is: Is this case properly before us? Such a question is imposed on courts by the very structure of the law, which both empowers them and limits them. An appellate court is empowered to hear an appeal only if a question is ripe for decision, if a lower court or agency has issued an appealable judgment, and if an issue has not been rendered "moot," that is, deprived of legal significance by superseding events. It is surprising how often a skeptical or inquiring attitude on jurisdiction will uncover a fatal flaw, which the parties have either overlooked or perhaps have hoped the court would overlook.

Occasionally, I will catch some obvious technical defect. My clerks, however, have standing orders to try to be sensitive to hidden questions like the following: Do the parties reside in different states so that there is real diversity of citizenship (and thus a basis for federal court jurisdiction)? Was there a final order below, giving appellate jurisdiction? Is

every party properly before the court? Does the plaintiff
have enough of a special interest in the outcome to have
standing to raise the question? Has the passage of time
made the case moot? Is this a situation in which the federal
court should defer, temporarily or permanently, to a state
court? If this is a suit between citizens of different states, to
what state should we look for the proper law to apply? To
what extent should state law apply and to what extent federal law? What is the proper standard of review? These
questions can be fiendishly recondite and doctrinaire. I expect my clerks, fresh out of good law schools, to spot these
issues.

Understanding Facts, Contentions, Law

After assuring himself that the appeal has hurdled all of the
jurisdictional obstacles, a judge's elemental task is to read
enough in the briefs to understand the argument, to know
what the issue is and what each party contends. This sounds
simple enough, like scanning a table of contents. But at
times it takes literally hours of reading and rereading
merely to comprehend the facts and claims. A patent case
quite often presents a challenge to factual comprehension.
The judge, a complete stranger to the chemical, mechanical,
or electronic enclave of technology in which the patent in
suit is located, has all he can do to pore over the technical
language and study the drawings with the slim hope that
eventually he will grasp what the gadget is and how it
works. He will leave for a later day such questions as: Was
the idea really novel? Was it foreshadowed too much by earlier inventions? Was it infringed by the gadget that defendant has on the market?

Often I find my understanding immensely clarified by
reading what the trial court or agency decided. The briefs of
the parties may have selected those parts of the decision
being reviewed which seemed most vulnerable or most de-

fensible. Sometimes a judge, after reading the briefs of appellant and appellee, feels that they describe two entirely unrelated cases. If he goes back to the decision of the court below, he will regain perspective. If time allows, it is usually worthwhile to read those parts of the record which are at the root of the argument: the actual words of the complaint, the whole instruction given by the judge, what words were used by the attorneys in making their objections, the key testimony of a witness, and the entire statute or regulation being challenged. Obviously, the more one reads, the more one understands. But time must be austerely rationed. The trick involved in the first reading of briefs is to identify those cases where a little extra work at the briefs and parts of the record may uncover a factual or legal question that will help focus the argument on the hard issue in the case.

My principal reliance for understanding, in all but the clearest cases, is on my clerks. The primary purpose served by our conferences is the simple one of helping me assimilate the relevant information I will need to understand the argument, to ask intelligent questions, and to contribute to the conference among the judges. In an uncomplicated case, our discussion will be brief, perhaps only several minutes. It will confirm my preliminary understanding and will enable me to view the key problem with more precision. In short, our discussion will give me more of a "handle" on the case.

In more complex cases, the seminar is more than merely confirmatory. If the briefs total a hundred pages or more, with thirty or forty pages describing in detail a formidable maze of facts leading up to a dozen issues of law, a clerk can spend several hours unraveling, distilling, outlining, selecting, encapsulating, and in a half-hour or so convey to a judge the essential facts, arguments, and the critical issues. Sometimes my clerk will simply construct a chronology of events, giving me a skeleton on which I can hang all the arguments. Sometimes I will receive a chart of the positions of the parties in their various actions against each other. Though I cannot hope to know enough about such a case to form any binding opinion, a good discussion will enable me, with a total investment time of perhaps an hour and a half, to become a reasonably intelligent listener. Were I to attempt to gain the same entrée without any assistance, I would have to spend at least half a day in uninterrupted reading.

One of the by-products of this colloquy between clerks and judge is a perspective, eventually shared by us all, of key legal authorities. My clerks will be familiar with earlier cases decided by our court in somewhat similar situations and will be able to tell me whether, at first sight, this case is closer and harder than the earlier ones or is easier and controlled by them. Their general knowledge of recent decisions by the Supreme Court and other courts of appeals will enable them quite frequently to suggest recent decisions that the parties have missed in their research or have been issued in the weeks since the briefs were filed.

Scenting Weaknesses

I like to think that one of the things a judge develops over time is a judicial nose. Such an organ is exquisitely sensitive, if not allergic, to both strong and faint odors that the briefs exude. The judicial nose, if it is to serve its possessor properly, must distinguish between the scents that are merely unpleasant and those that signify the presence of some endemic disease or weakness. The former are regrettable, reflect no credit on the drafters of the brief, and test the fortitude of the reading judge, but may not indicate malignancy. This kind of benign, if unhelpful, condition is typified by dullness, lengthy sentences, passive verbs, jargon, banal expressions, poor paragraphing, misspelling, lack of organization, obsequious tone, a pretense of righteous anger, snide innuendo, and patronizing pap.

What the judicial nose really tries to scent are signs of rot. Sometimes the way facts are handled reveals the weakness:

there may be the bland omission of a key fact; the facts may be ever so lightly twisted; they may be set forth at exhausting length but with no sense of relevance or importance, in which case the reader suspects that the writer had hoped to tire him before he discovered that the brief was going nowhere. A frequent ploy of counsel is to write the brief as if he could rewrite history: a powerful argument is made by appellant that the judge erred in one of his rulings; the brief is compelling . . . until the appellee points out in his brief that, no objection having been made in the court below, the error has not been preserved for appeal.

The way in which arguments are handled is often illuminating. The most telling discovery a judge can make is that a brief has neglected to deal with an issue. In a complex case of many issues, a quick reading may leave the reader with the impression of the brief's overwhelming strength. A careful rereading may bring to light the missing issue, which may well not have been treated because there was no persuasive way to deal with it. Sometimes such an issue will be recognized but blandly swept aside by the writer with some patronizing comment. Another gambit is the misstating of an opponent's position, which is then demolished. Still another is to be prolix and undiscriminating, including a dozen or more arguments, trivial and serious, in the hope that the court will assume the presence of fire from clouds of billowing smoke.

Finally, the way in which legal authorities are dealt with sometimes gives away the brief's argument. Is a leading case conspicuously absent from the brief? Are there cases prominently relied on in one brief that are not dealt with by the other? Does the brief cite ancient cases only, or those chiefly of lower courts? Does an imposing string of citations of many cases really represent a more or less unanalytical reliance on the earliest? Does a cited case reflect the thoughtful consideration of a court, or is the relevant passage a casual remark in passing, unnecessary to decision?

I have stressed scenting out weaknesses. Of course, if the judicial nose detects nothing to arouse suspicion, the reader soon concludes that a party's case is formidable. When the facts seem fairly set forth, with precise references to the record, when all arguments of one's opponent are recognized and dealt with, when the authorities seem to have been thoroughly canvassed and correctly used, and, above all, when that part of the argument that is or appears to be the weakest is frankly brought front and center and made the focus of the brief — when these tests have been passed with flying colors, the party is on his way to victory. He is not there yet, and may never get there, but he has done all within his power to do so. If he loses, he can justly blame the facts, policy, the law, or the court, but not himself.

My clerks develop their own judicial noses and help frame questions to test a party's law, logic, or common sense. One of the oldest and yet most sophisticated devices is the analogy, applying the principle being urged on the court to some similar situation where the result would be devastating. There is nothing more intriguing to a knowledgeable on-looker than to see a judge pose a colorful and fair analogy to counsel during oral argument and test the rule being argued by applying it to a hypothetical situation — unless it is to see candid and resourceful counsel respond with a compelling reason for the two situations not being really analogous. This sort of give-and-take honors both court and counsel. It is not merely fencing to show off prowess in reasoning by analogy; it is a way, and a good one, of testing whether a rule that may make sense in the case being argued is consistent with rules governing other basically similar situations. Analogy is an instrument of consistency in the law.

Developing a Sense of Policy

An appeal may present only the narrowest of questions: What do the decided cases demand? What does the statute

mean? Was the trial ruling erroneous? Did the evidence support the verdict? In such cases there is no room for an appellate court to be concerned with policy implications. But if
the question presented is a novel one, if legal authority is
divided, if the statute is ambiguous, or — sometimes — if
legal doctrine, though clear, is outrageous, the reviewing
court ought to be concerned with policy in the broadest
sense. I do not mean that the court should try to act like a
legislature, but it should always keep in sight the pole star
question: If we decide this case in this way, what is the underlying principle, and are we prepared to universalize it
and apply it generally? We may have no trouble at all in saying that the seasoned intuition of the police ought to be
enough justification for a search of a rumored Mafia head-
quarters. We balk, however, at allowing tax agents to ran-
sack a business office on mere suspicion. Yet where is there a
meaningful distinction between the two cases?

This is where my discussion of a case with my clerks often
ends. We will have touched laboriously all the bases of jurisdiction, facts, state of the legal authorities. Then we sit back
and ask ourselves, What makes the most sense, most of the
time, for most people, in the long run? Our answer may be
irrelevant in that the law may be settled, whether sensibly
or not. But a surprising part of the time it is a helpful question. I confess that usually it is only after living with a case,
musing over the authorities, putting questions to myself and
trying out answers, drafting and redrafting different approaches, that I arrive at the point where I can say with any
confidence, "This is the sensible solution because . . ." But
at this preargument stage it is useful to begin the search for
policy, even if nothing more comes of it than a question to
put to counsel at argument: "If we decide for you, what
about the next case, with slightly different facts, down the
road?"

Considering Ancillary Decisions To Be Made

Apart from the result to be reached in the appeal under consideration, there are several other types of decision a court must make. A primary question is often whether a case shall be decided on the narrowest possible ground so that the decision will have little precedential value, or whether the court will join in a much more sweeping decision. Then there is a subtle objective: to choose the best approach to the agreed-on result. For example, a ruling excluding evidence could be affirmed because an objection was not properly made, or because, on the merits, the judge ruled correctly. Another objective, probably in the very back of one's mind at this early stage, is whether it may be useful to have the opinion contain some dicta, that is, some statement that is not necessary for decision but may indicate an attitude on the part of the court that could guide judges and lawyers. Some other elements to consider are whether there is a need for prompt decision, whether the decision can rest on the opinion of the district judge, and whether a full-scale opinion or a shorter memorandum is called for. Finally, there is the question of remedy. In both conventional litigation, and especially in the new breed of civil rights litigation seeking institutional reform, the most difficult question may not be liability; it may be what to do about it.

Identifying Tasks for Law Clerks

Though time is short between our preargument seminar and the opening of court, discussion often opens up new areas of quick research. If a case is relied on heavily by a party, it may be advisable for the clerk to check the subsequent history of that case to see if it has been affirmed, followed by others, overruled, criticized, or simply ignored. If certain testimony appears critical, the law clerk may well read it in context and report back to the judge. If the briefs contain

selective quotations from legislative history and if there is
time before this case is reached, the clerk should try to locate and read the whole committee report. If the issue on appeal has been commented on in a respected treatise or law
review article, the clerk could sample the comment and report back. And, finally, as the result of the discussion among
the four of us, the clerk should reduce to writing any pertinent questions to counsel that have been suggested.

*

By the time we have finished discussing thirty or more separate appeals and I have made my notes, it is late Friday afternoon, with court coming in on Monday morning. I begin
to pack for court, reflecting that I am one of very few who
use a briefcase precisely for its nominal purpose. Even leaving out the bulky appendices, I stuff my two cases beyond
their comfortable capacity, winding up with what look more
like saddlebags.

If my description of our preparatory talks conveys the idea
that I leave chambers serenely confident that I have found a
key for each case, it overclaims. I suppose that I could spend
a solid month preparing to hear thirty arguments and still
feel unprepared. As it is, I invest between fifteen to twenty
hours. Certain it is that I never feel anything but inadequate
for most of the complex and difficult cases we hear. I try to
remind myself that I should not despair, that it is too early
to feel mastery, and that at least I have started the process
that will eventually deliver me to the point of conviction
about a decision.

Chapter 7

A Term of Court

AFTER MONTHS, sometimes years, of prelude — including pretrial discovery, trial, the preparation of briefs, and the preargument attention given the case in the chambers of at least three judges — the ritual of oral argument brings persuaders and deciders together in a final confrontation. This is the occasion when bulky briefs and records are put aside while each party's lawyer speaks directly to the judges at the bench. The challenge in planning and making an oral argument differs significantly from that in writing a brief. In constructing an effective brief, the writer may rely on felicity and grace to ease the burden of reading, but his purpose remains to convince the reader through what must largely be an intellectual effort.

The purpose of oral argument, on the other hand, is to appeal to all the springs of motivation, to persuade. Under any circumstances, convincing someone else of the rightness of one's view is a considerable feat. In an appellate argument the task takes on added complications. Not only is time for argument stringently rationed, but an advocate knows that his is only one of a half-dozen cases scheduled for the same day. Moreover, he labors under the uncertainty of not knowing in advance what aspect of the case will be of greatest interest to the court, as well as the certainty that, because of unpredictable questions from the bench, he will be unlikely to control how his precious few minutes will be spent.

The judge will extract from an argument what he himself puts into it. If he has really probed into the briefs and record, homed in on some damning testimony, discovered a crucial case that was not cited, identified some misstatements of law or fact, he can make the oral argument a crucible, burning away the dross and leaving only the pure metal of sound argument. But since thirty or forty cases are to be heard in a session, this kind of performance is rare and depends partly on luck, partly on preparation, and partly on the judge's past experience in a given field.

More often the argument yields modest dividends. Some facts fall into place, and the context is better understood. Some issues drop out of the case, and new ones appear that no one has yet thought about. When this happens, additional briefs may be invited. Counsel occasionally make concessions as to facts, claims, or law, which may profoundly affect the outcome, the approach, or the scope of relief. It may even appear, after colloquy between court and counsel, that the relief desired is quite different from that argued for in the briefs. Sometimes the actual controversy will have disappeared because of changes brought about by the passage of time.

All such products of argument are the result of interaction between court and counsel. Equally important is the opportunity for interaction among the judges. Often when a judge addresses questions to an advocate, he is really communicating with his brethren. As a judge prepares for argument, he and his clerks may discover a serious weakness in a case that at first reading looked invulnerable. In such event, probing questions by one judge may identify for all the hidden weaknesses. By the time the judges confer, the judge who thought the case was an easy affirmance knows that it is close and may even be a reversal. In a sense, therefore, the conference of the judges begins during argument. It is then that the judges first reveal their view of strengths and weaknesses, their biases and values. Their questioning may also

reveal the depth of their interest in the case and the investment of time already made in it, factors that are not lost on
the presiding judge when he makes assignments of cases to
judges for the writing of opinions.

Some time after oral argument comes that step in the
decision process when the judges congregate to exchange
views. That such conferences take place is widely known.
But exactly what goes on and what kind of exchanges take
place remain a mystery. The result, I sense, is the image,
widely shared, of highly articulate and disputative jurists,
bent on hammering home their points in conference until
the fates of the parties are irrevocably decided, leaving only
the grubby ministerial work of writing the opinion to be
done. Some conferences may fit this mold; the great majority, I am sure, do not.

We hold our conferences at the end of each day of argument, having heard from five to seven appeals, from 9:30
A.M. to 3:00 or 3:30 P.M. We three judges gather in chambers
either immediately after recessing court or after a few words
with law clerks to see if any insights they have gained from
oral argument are worth sharing with colleagues. Then we
begin our pondering. One of us — and we observe no set protocol — starts the conversation. It is likely to begin with an
amble around one edge of the case. Only rarely will one of us
so gather his thoughts together that his presentation could
be said to be polished. Indeed, I have often thought that if
we were confronted with an analysis of a case suitable for
the professor's podium, the impression of finality would
make our hackles rise. At this point, if the case has any difficulty, each of us is still probing, talking to test points to
hear how they sound, not to convince others. Sometimes just
saying something out loud is enough to send the thought
packing. The process as we experience it is something like
what I imagine a Quaker meeting to be, speaking as the
spirit moves. This means very little colloquy in some cases;
hours of talk in others.

THE CASES

The Smuggler on the Dock

The judge who had the responsibility of setting the schedule
of arguments had allotted twenty minutes to each side in
this case. After discussing the case with my clerks, I rather
wished a full half-hour had been allowed. But there were six
other cases on the day's list. If counsel were prepared, each
could have made an effective argument in his twenty minutes. Counsel for appellant was a young man, appointed by
the court to represent appellant, who, after paying the legal
fees in connection with his several-day trial, was without
funds. We had seen this lawyer in another case and felt that
he was competent. Sometimes, however, his judgment revealed his inexperience. For example, I noted that in the
back of the courtroom was an intent young man, sitting with
his tense wife and small child — obviously the appellant.
Bringing a client to appellate court for tactical reasons is
seldom a good idea. The thought may be that the sight of the
little family will humanize the court, but it cannot be pleasant for the family and must put pressure on the lawyer. The
assistant United States attorney was a veteran of many
years' service. He had a disquieting manner — perhaps it
was the secret of his survival — of dealing with all challenges to a conviction as if they were patently frivolous,
treating them lightly unless the court was so gullible as to
take some of them seriously. Then he summoned up his resources and, more often than not, prevailed, but without en-
dearing himself to the court in the process.

Appellant's counsel began by going into the facts in minute detail. After a few precious minutes, one of my fellow
judges stopped him and said that all the judges had read the
briefs and were fully aware of the few significant facts. Some
lawyers, after such an interruption, continue to rehearse the
facts as if they had been programmed. This counsel, how-

ever, readily complied and took up the issue he obviously found the most intriguing.

COUNSEL: My position, may it please the court, is simply that my client could not have aided or abetted smuggling, because there was no proof the bales of marijuana were smuggled. As the Supreme Court said in the *Keck* case, the goods must reach land.

JUDGE: But that's an irrational place to draw the line today. Here, the *Lucky Lady* was not only inside the three-mile limit; it was way up the estuary. What if she had made it to the dock, but the goods had not been offloaded when seizure was made?

COUNSEL: Even that wouldn't be smuggling. We have a 1955 case in the 9th circuit, *Wong Bing Nung*, 221 F.2d 917. In that case a seaman had brought goods on a vessel from the Orient. In San Francisco he declared half of them and unloaded them. Half he kept on board, undeclared, and had a friend ask customs if he could offload them. When he learned he could not, he stated his intention of taking them to the Philippines. The officials then seized the merchandise. The court of appeals held this was not yet a completed act of smuggling.

JUDGE: Do you have any other cases?

COUNSEL: No.

JUDGE: Don't you think that's significant? Have you wondered why it is that only you are raising this kind of defense?

COUNSEL: Yes, I have. I guess that other defendants have either been caught after landing the goods or they never knew about the *Keck* case.

JUDGE: But since *Keck*, the law has been changed. No longer must the United States be defrauded of revenue. It is enough that the United States be frustrated in its collecting of documents and information. The importance of the goods passing a point where duties are payable has vanished, hasn't it?

COUNSEL: Yes, Your Honor. That's true. Defendant could

have been convicted under the second paragraph of the statute, 18 U.S. Code, Section 545, for knowingly importing merchandise contrary to law. But that is not what he was charged with. He was charged with smuggling, and *Keck* says that "mere acts of concealment of merchandise on entering the waters of the United States" are only attempts and fall short of the real thing.

At this point the judges were feeling frustrated in not readily being able to reconcile law and common sense, and had no more questions on this issue. Counsel, having very little time left, moved to the next question.

COUNSEL: As a number of circuits have held, "mere association" of a person with others who are linked in a conspiracy is not enough to convict.

To support a verdict of guilty of conspiracy, there must be evidence of knowledge of what is going on and a specific intent to forward the purposes of the enterprise.

JUDGE: But why else would defendant be sitting on the dock late in the evening with a prostitute in a bulging granny dress?

COUNSEL: So far as we know, the two had never met and had never spoken a word to each other. And, as the cases hold, the fact that someone happens to be at a place at the time a crime is committed is not reason enough to convict him of participation in that crime.

JUDGE: Then why was he there?

COUNSEL: That's not my burden. My client is presumed innocent until proven guilty beyond a reasonable doubt.

Counsel's time had expired. He sat down without touching on the issue involving the ten-year-old conviction. He had done pretty well, but not spectacularly. He had held his own on the exotic definition of smuggling but had not exploited the issue relating to sufficiency of the evidence. On this issue

he would not have had to ask us to make new law but
merely could have followed established law. He had failed to
cite the recent cases from our court that would have given
him even more support. He had not chosen to argue the
"aging conviction" issue, which was an exceedingly close
one.

The assistant United States attorney went to the lectern
and began to marshal the facts from the government's point
of view.

JUDGE: What is there that makes this sufficient evidence to
allow a jury to find guilt beyond a reasonable doubt?

PROSECUTOR: This is just too much coincidence to be consistent with innocence.

JUDGE: Is it any more suspicious than the crewmen in
Francomano, where we held that their presence on the boat
wasn't enough to implicate them in any plan to smuggle
marijuana, even though some bales were thrown overboard
under their very eyes?

PROSECUTOR: Yes, Your Honor, this is more suspicious, because there the crew were young men just recruited from
South America and couldn't speak a word of English. Here
defendant is an American, and the jury could infer that he
and the prostitute, another citizen, could speak English.

JUDGE: It's true that the crew in *Francomano* couldn't understand a word of English. But you must remember that
there was a second case involving the same ship, the same
cargo, and another defendant, the friend of the captain who
did speak English. What about the *Mehtala* case?

PROSECUTOR: Yes, I'm familiar with that case. That is more
difficult.

JUDGE: Why didn't you cite it in your brief?

PROSECUTOR: Well, we probably should have.

Here the judges were obviously nettled but were not getting any help from the assistant U.S. attorney. They moved
the argument forward to the smuggling issue.

JUDGE: How *do* you get around *Keck?* After all, the Court did hold that mere concealment was not enough.

PROSECUTOR: But we have a later Supreme Court case, *U.S. v. Ritterman*, 273 U.S. 261 (1927), which held that a defendant carrying undeclared diamonds from Canada into Vermont could be found guilty of smuggling even though he had not passed by a customs house. The Court said that one who wishes to smuggle does not need to wait until he finds a customs house.

JUDGE: What about the *Wong Bing* case that your brother* has talked about?

PROSECUTOR: In that case the intention as to the undeclared goods was to take them to Manila. Here there is no question but that the intent was to land them at Rosemary Cove.

The prosecutor, probably remembering the wisdom that if you don't have the law on your side, you should holler about the facts, now reiterated the factual coincidences. I could see that he was making progress with one of my colleagues, who nodded in sympathy as the argument ended with the rhetorical question "Now what was Hapless doing on the dock? Writing poetry?"

The prosecutor was about to sit down.

JUDGE: You haven't touched on the ten-year conviction issue.

PROSECUTOR: Your Honor, since my brother did not argue it today, I thought I would also rely on my brief as to this issue.

JUDGE: As I understand it, the new rule bars evidence of convictions over ten years old unless the judge makes a finding that the probative value substantially outweighs any prejudice. Did the judge make such a finding?

PROSECUTOR: We think he did. At the close of the govern-

* Reference to a lawyer's adversary as a brother or sister may seem a formal recognition of sibling rivalry, but it is, in fact, a time-honored and valued manner of address from more courtly days. In like spirit do advocates begin their appellate arguments, "May it please the court."

ment's case there had been some discussion as to whether he would let in the record of conviction if the defendant testified. The judge said he was "presently inclined" to let it in, because, as he expressed it, "it shows defendant was no stranger to drugs. I think this is probative enough to meet the requirement of the new rule." Later, defendant took the stand and when I asked about his criminal record, the judge said — and I'm quoting from transcript page 126 — "For the reasons I gave before, I'm going to let this in."

JUDGE: Did defendant object?

PROSECUTOR: No. The judge raised the issue himself and disposed of it. Defense counsel said nothing. We take the position that, there being no objection, defendant would have to argue that letting in the evidence about the old conviction is plain error, something so bad that the conviction must be reversed even though no one objected. We just don't think this error, if it is error, rises to that level.

JUDGE: I can see, whether I agree or not, how the judge could say the old conviction had some probative value. I can even see how he could say that the probative value outweighed prejudice. But how could he possibly say it "substantially" outweighed prejudice?

The prosecutor decided to treat this as rhetorical, not calling for an answer.

JUDGE: You would agree, would you not, that if this is error of which we can take note, we couldn't say it was harmless?

PROSECUTOR: I agree, Your Honor. This was a close case, and if the jury couldn't consider the old conviction, I couldn't say that beyond a reasonable doubt it would still arrive at a guilty verdict without that evidence.

By this time the colloquy had gone several minutes overtime. The prosecutor sat down and defense counsel anxiously sought time for rebuttal. We gave him a minute.

COUNSEL: Thank you, Your Honor. I just wanted to say that

in *Ritterman* the whole context shows that the Court was referring to a boundary on land. If one crossed that boundary,
he need not have passed by a customs house. But the Court
repeated that if goods came by sea, they would have to reach
land. And, second, in the *Wong Bing* case, while it is true
that there was an expression of intent to go on to Manila, it's
also clear that this played no part in the court's decision.

With this, the argument ended and a new set of counsel
approached the counsel table to argue the next case.

*

At the end of the day's cases the court conferred somewhat
as follows:

FIRST JUDGE: This case is a lot closer than I thought, but
I'm not too bothered by that old conviction. The trial judge
has to have wide discretion. And I can't really see much prejudice. Indeed, just because it was so old, I think it wouldn't
count for much. Juries aren't fools. What does bother me,
though, is that antique definition of smuggling that the Supreme Court apparently adopted.

SECOND JUDGE: Well, I admit I'm bothered by that old conviction. This is, as you said at argument, a close case, and
even a little prejudice might tip the scale. The new rule of
evidence is tough. It's a lot for a judge to say that the probative value of this very old charge of possession of retail quantities is so great in this prosecution for aiding a huge wholesale program of distributing that it substantially outweighs
the prejudice. What worries me is that if we say that this is
within the judge's discretion, we'll just about have evis-
cerated the rule. Anything will go if this does. I hate to see
judges start out sloppily with these new rules.

FIRST JUDGE: I see your point. But do you think defense
counsel preserved the point? I gathered from what the prosecutor said that it was the judge who acknowledged that
there was an issue and discussed it. But after he gave his
ruling, counsel didn't say "Boo."

SECOND JUDGE: You may be right. We'll just have to read the record. But I think this would be a dangerous precedent to affirm.

THIRD JUDGE: Isn't either of you bothered by the sufficiency of the evidence? I think that's worrisome.

FIRST JUDGE: It's worrisome that neither counsel, particularly the prosecutor, cited our recent cases.

THIRD JUDGE: Exactly. If there are no other facts than what are reported in the briefs and what they talked about today, I'd be hard put to affirm.

FIRST JUDGE: I wonder if we aren't getting too technical. Here's this fellow on the target dock, with a well-equipped drug-carrying "mule" beside him, when the Coast Guard at the last minute frustrates delivery. How else can you explain why he's there? Isn't there room for common sense?

The subject was exhausted for the time being; there were, after all, other cases waiting their turn. The presiding judge asked each judge how the case should be tentatively noted. Each said he was considering a possible reversal, but for a different reason. It had been a good though brief discussion, with everyone contributing a different insight. Perhaps this sort of discussion took place because the case was of a traditional kind, with familiar issues recalling many past experiences. As of this point, however, the precise thrust and approach of the court's decision could not be predicted.

The Agency and the Anorectic

The setting of this argument differed dramatically from the routine criminal appeal. To begin with, we were playing to a full house. Every seat was occupied by crisp, well-accoutered, professional-looking people — all of them lawyers having something to do with the drug industry. There were several lawyers for Schmarzipan, a local Boston counsel, and some lawyers from New York. The Food and Drug Administration was represented by a woman lawyer in her late

thirties from the consumer affairs branch of the Department
of Justice. She was assisted by a younger man from the Food
and Drug Administration's enforcement policy staff. Each of
the lawyers for the drug companies undoubtedly received a
yearly income probably twice that of both government lawyers. FIB, the hopeful intervenor, was represented by a
rather skeletal young man whose scrawny structure belied
his clients' preference for obesity. We had given him five
minutes to argue that his group should be allowed to intervene as a party.

JUDGE: How does your organization differ from any other
group of Americans?

COUNSEL: Because my people think that the use of drugs to
bring about loss of weight is dangerous. They also feel there
is nothing dangerous about a little obesity.

JUDGE: But your clients presumably feel no more strongly
about this than thin people who don't like drugs or fat people who don't mind drugs but object to efforts to persuade
people to lose weight.

COUNSEL: Perhaps so, but . . .

JUDGE: Before we go further, did FIB seek to participate in
the hearings before the agency?

COUNSEL: Well, we learned about this proceeding late in
the day. I wrote the agency of our interest a week or so
before the hearing . . . but no, Your Honor, we did not ask
to intervene below.

Schmarzipan's lawyer then approached the lectern, with a
few — not more — pieces of paper in his hand. I thought to
myself that he had probably mastered every fact, had in his
mind's eye every page number containing important information. I was right.

He began with a down-to-earth, homespun complaint
about the excesses of well-intentioned regulators. Here was a
product that had been produced for fifteen years, in which
had been invested some $70 million, 150 million doses of
which had been merchandised during this period, with al-

most unanimous acceptance by doctors, an exceptional safety record, and no evidence of adverse interaction of the product's components. His litany of the evils of the deadening hand of bureaucracy was powerful.

JUDGE: Counselor, I understand the point you are making. But I take it that the main issue is whether you have sufficiently proven that Thin-King is not only effective in reducing obesity but also in sharpening the intellect. Don't you have the burden of proving effectiveness for both purposes?

COUNSEL: Well, we don't agree that this is a proper standard.

JUDGE: But we're beyond that point, aren't we? That is, you didn't protest the adoption of that standard when it was published in the Federal Register?

COUNSEL: That is so. But we still think it is unrealistic and an improper delegation of congressional power, as we show in our brief at pages eighteen to twenty-three. Nevertheless, let me go on, assuming that Your Honors uphold the standard. We are fully aware of the reasons advanced for it — that locking fixed dosages of drugs into a combination product is generally not good medical practice. But in our case we have fifteen years and the testimony of the medical profession behind and for us.

JUDGE: Tell us what you submitted as the results of the required "well-controlled investigations."

COUNSEL: In the first place, we submitted the results of experiments with mice, showing that they not only lost weight but increased in intellectual activity. But the FDA's definition of well-controlled investigations didn't include studies of animals. Then we submitted studies done with a group of fifty patients of five doctors, half of whom were a test group and half a control group who were given a placebo. The results showed both appreciable weight loss and increased intellectual activity in the test group. But FDA nitpicked our methods and refused to accept the results. Finally, we canvassed the medical profession scientifically and submitted affidavits of professors and pharmacologists and a poll of some three hundred physicians, all attesting to the efficacy of Thin-King. But the FDA simply stuck up its nose and proclaimed that this was not a well-controlled investigation.

Counsel elaborated on these points for twenty minutes or so. Then, leaving to his brief the issue of curtailment of testimony of Schmarzipan's witnesses, he addressed the question as to whether the proceeding was "adjudicative" or not, and, if so, whether only evidence formally made part of the record could be considered. A proceeding is adjudicative if its aim, like a court's, is to decide rights and duties between the parties; it is contrasted to a legislative hearing, which, like a legislature, lays down a rule to govern many.

COUNSEL: We most earnestly urge, Your Honors, that if the proceeding was the kind of adjudicative hearing required by statute "to be determined on the record," the panel of scientists convened by the FDA should not have relied on "the literature in the field." This was obviously an adjudicative hearing. Important rights were taken away. And even though the statute doesn't specifically require decision to be based on the record, we think the requirement is implicit.

The Justice Department lawyer placed her papers on the lectern. Before she began, one judge asked, "What standard of review do we apply here? How much deference do we give the agency?"

COUNSEL: A narrow standard, Your Honors, and a great deal of deference. Indeed, any expansive view of your reviewing power will result in eleven circuits running off in all directions, entirely frustrating the congressional objective of controlling the composition of drugs. I would say that you could properly set aside an FDA ruling only if you found it utterly arbitrary, without any reasoned basis.

JUDGE: Then you think it's almost a blank check that Congress has given the FDA?

COUNSEL: Almost.

JUDGE: I find that difficult to accept. The more important and technical the kind of control an agency has over people, the less judicial review. George Orwell's 1984 is almost here. Continue.

COUNSEL: If it please the court, I would just say that the intervenor group, FIB, has shown no basis for appearing as a party. I would urge that you not grant their motion to intervene. Unless it had a very particular interest, which we say it did not have, the interests of all such groups, and of citizens in general, must be entrusted to the Department of Justice.

Petitioner challenges the FDA's standard for well-controlled investigations. I need hardly point out that the time for challenging was when notice of the standard was published in the Federal Register. But petitioner was not heard from. As for petitioner's complaint that the regulation excludes studies of animals, this is not true. The definition sets forth the minimum requirements for such investigations. But it does not foreclose studies that go beyond and differ from those minima. In fact, the studies of mice submitted by Schmarzipan were discounted heavily, not because they were studies of rodents, but because the evidence of intellectual productivity was not there. The subjects did lose weight and they did race around frenetically, but racing around frenetically does not necessarily mean intellectual activity or productivity.

JUDGE: Why didn't the study of fifty human patients qualify as a well-controlled investigation?

COUNSEL: Because it wasn't well controlled. There were so many things wrong with it. Our regulations call for explaining procedures, articulating steps taken to minimize experimenter bias, quality-control sheets, particular tests to identify the contribution of each component drug. Here, to give you a case in point, the test group and the control group were never compared in terms of intellectual level or interest or activity. Nor were they screened to exclude the influence of prior use of tranquilizers. And finally, we never could tell what effect was created by any one drug. When you administer a heavy dose of caffeine and follow it by a heavy tranquilizer, you really don't know what you're doing.

JUDGE: This still leaves the study of the three hundred doctors, which you people rejected in a pretty cavalier fashion.

COUNSEL: With all respect, Your Honors, that's because the so-called study was pretty cavalier. Schmarzipan presented these things to the FDA: two articles in a professional magazine that anorectic drugs held great promise, particularly because of their convenience; the affidavit of a professor of medicine that all experiments seeking to test contributions of component drugs are expensive, difficult, and often inconclusive; the affidavit of a pharmacologist that prescription misuse increases in proportion to the number of specific drugs prescribed; and the three hundred responses of doctors to a company questionnaire. These responses were not representative geographically. They harped mainly on the themes of convenience, as distinguished from efficacy, and of the intermeddling of the federal government.

JUDGE: What do you say about the FDA's panel considering the literature in the field?

COUNSEL: There is no statute that requires the adjudication in cases like this to be on the record. Obviously, every administrator has to rely on staff. And for staff to rely on the literature in their field of expertise is merely to confirm that they are experts.

When the judges gathered to discuss this case, they were at an impasse. The data were so voluminous, the issues so technical, that no one could be sure of his final vote. All that the judges could agree on was that this was a difficult case, that it was probably a close case, and that whoever was going to write the opinion had a big piece of work to do.

The Saga of the Transferred Prisoners

The lawyers for both the Commonwealth of Massachusetts and the prisoners were young, yet seasoned and very competent. Both the assistant attorney general and the Prisoners' Rights Project attorneys had participated in a number of ground-breaking cases in prison law. They were well acquainted with all of our First Circuit cases, the Supreme Court cases, and, for that matter, any case on prisoners' rights decided by any court in the country. Each side had a half-hour, and I knew we would have an excellent presentation.*

The commonwealth, having lost in the court below, was first to argue. The assistant attorney general began by economically summarizing the facts.

A.A.G.: We proceed upon two theories, Your Honors. In the first place we contend that *no* process at all was required in this case. There must, as *Wolff* v. *McDonnell* tells us, be a liberty or property interest, some claim of entitlement to that which is taken away. Here there is simply no basis for the district judge taking judicial notice that going to Walpole from Norfolk subjects one to a drastic change in conditions of confinement. This is not the kind of interstate transfer you dealt with in *Gomes*. Here, Norfolk and Walpole are only a mile apart. All we concede is that there are fewer rehabilitation programs at Walpole and that furloughs are more difficult to obtain at Walpole. But most of these plaintiffs had had no furloughs at Norfolk to begin with.

JUDGE: Was this argued to the district court?

A.A.G.: I am not sure that the furlough point was, but we vigorously argued the question as to whether any process at all was called for.

JUDGE: Speaking of *Gomes*, in that case all transferees were kept in administrative segregation in the receiving prison for

---

* What follows is a reconstruction of my notes of the actual argument. It is not verbatim but is substantively faithful.

several weeks. When prisoners are transferred within Massachusetts, does the same process take place?

A.A.G.: No, Your Honor. They have no time in segregation. There is no need to determine their classification, and they go immediately into the general prison population.

JUDGE: Didn't you stipulate on the record that the fact that a prisoner is transferred and the basis for his transfer are made a part of his record that can be considered by the parole board and the furlough board?

A.A.G.: Yes, we did. But of course, this doesn't mean that the notation on the record will in fact delay parole or hold up furloughs.

JUDGE: But it's possible?

A.A.G.: Yes, Your Honor. May I suggest to the court that another case involving a transfer from a medium- to a maximum-security prison, *Preiser* v. *Newkirk*, was argued in the Supreme Court last January.

JUDGE: Do you think we should wait for that decision to come down?

A.A.G.: Yes, Your Honor. I think you would be wise to wait. Now, our second theory is that even if you disagree with us in our claim that no process is ever required in an intrastate prisoner transfer, there must be at least the presence of what objectively looks like a punitive motive. But here there is no loss of "good time" credits, no segregation, no difference in treatment after transfer, no interstate transfer, and no punishment. Indeed, our regulations require the superintendent to refer any possibly criminal actions for outside prosecution.

JUDGE: One thing that bothers me about having the superintendent telling the disciplinary board in confidence what unnamed informants told him is that I can't see how there can be any judicial review. The superintendent could invent a whole series of unfounded inculpating reports.

A.A.G.: Well, we did offer to disclose the confidential reports of the informants to the judge alone in his chambers.

Yes, Your Honor, I see your difficulty. Review is affected. But though the era of complete deference to prison authorities is gone, the pendulum, we think, is starting to swing in the direction of recognizing the extreme burdens under which they labor. For courts to attempt to second-guess every decision to transfer prisoners within a state would just wreak more havoc in what often is already a chaotic situation.

JUDGE: I can sympathize with most of what you say, but why can't the authorities at least summarize generally the informants' data?

A.A.G.: We can't because even a summary, the superintendent feels, would reveal the sources of information to these prisoners. My time is up. I respectfully ask the court to reverse the decision below and remand the case with instructions to dismiss the complaint.

The prisoners' attorney continued the argument.

COUNSEL: The question here, may it please the court, is a much narrower one than the commonwealth's attorney would have you believe. It is simply whether the correctional authorities can ignore a regulation that they themselves have devised to balance the prisoner's right to know what offense he is charged with committing and the institution's problems in maintaining order. At Walpole there is an Institution Order that prescribes that in a disciplinary hearing testimony must be taken in the presence of the accused unless the disciplinary board chairman determines that there is a risk of harm to the informant or to general security and summarizes the information given. In any event, a summary is required. There is no question that the prison regulations recognize transfer as a disciplinary sanction. The fact is that if the district attorney, to whom allegedly criminal matters are referred, decides not to proceed, the basic facts will never be determined. And the prisoner can never effectively appeal the board's decision.

JUDGE: But what governs matters at Walpole doesn't have to be followed at Norfolk?

COUNSEL: It's our contention, Your Honor, that where, as I shall next show, there is a need for some process, and where, at a prison even more difficult to manage, the authorities have adopted procedures with which they can live comfortably, they have struck the balance and should be required to follow their procedures elsewhere. This would not be a case of a court intermeddling. This would be a case of a court accepting the balance adopted by the prison authorities.

Now, Your Honors, as to whether any process is due, the court properly took judicial notice that confinement at Norfolk is traditionally a reward for good behavior. I refer you to the literature cited in our brief. The commonwealth, of course, is not required to have different grades of treatment for prisoners, but once it does, rights in inmates are created. This is analogous to the good time credits in *Wolff*.

JUDGE: What if a prisoner is assigned a different cell, which he doesn't like, or his meal or work or library schedules are changed to his dissatisfaction?

COUNSEL: I think it's clear, Your Honor, that there has to be a grievous loss, a serious loss, to trigger constitutional protection. Here, all the ingredients are present. The basis for the proposed transfer is particular alleged misconduct of the prisoners. The incidents of transfer include higher security controls, fewer rehabilitation opportunities, discontinuity and disruption in prison jobs, and the most important factor: the notation on the record. This follows the prisoner wherever he goes and can affect parole, furlough, work release, and other privileges. So here, where the officials themselves have devised a way of dealing more fairly with data obtained from informants, we contend that the burden shifts to defendants to justify their action, something they cannot do, having adopted the practice at Walpole.

JUDGE: Do you think we should wait for the Court's decision in *Preiser*?

COUNSEL: No. I think *Preiser* is irrelevant. For one thing, there were no standard-setting prison regulations. Moreover, the transfer was not related to the specific alleged misconduct of the prisoner. Let me close, Your Honors, by calling to your attention the obvious opportunity to circumvent the protections recognized in *Wolff* if it is possible to transfer a troublemaker to a tougher kind of confinement by simply invoking proceedings that are called classification rather than disciplinary.

Although virtually every significant fact in the evolution of this case is a matter of public record, the conference among the judges was and must remain off the record and in confidence. We are probably not missing much. Since this appeal was the latest in a series of prisoner cases presenting similar issues, it is likely that each judge had a clear idea not only of his own position but of the probable position of each colleague. The judges also very probably acted on the assumption that no one at this late date was likely to change his position. This was a case in which there was little or no room for compromise. Either prisoners must be afforded more procedural protection before being transferred or they need not be.

REFLECTIONS ON ARGUMENT, CONFERENCE, AND ASSIGNMENTS

On Principles of Effective Argument

I have no desire to contribute to the general literature of advocacy, which stretches back at least to Cicero's "Essay on Argumentation." Rather, I write from a very particular point of view, that of an advocates' consumer. John W. Davis, perhaps the most elegant and respected appellate advocate of his time, once addressed this question to the Association of the Bar of the City of New York: "Supposing fishes had the gift of speech, who would listen to a fisherman's weary discourse on fly-casting . . . if the fish himself could be induced to give his views on the most effective methods of approach?"[1]

I am prompted to give my views by the reflection that, with the passage of time and changing customs and conditions, what may have been effective in one era may miss the mark in another. Not only are the occasions for a lengthy, formal, prepared set speech almost nonexistent in these pressured times, but with increasing frequency a lawyer on appeal will find his opportunity to convince a court limited to fifteen or twenty minutes. This Spartan rationing of time has raised the stakes on counsel's guessing accurately what to say and how to say it in a forum where his control over the agenda varies from none to free rein.

I take as givens the presence of basic qualities such as command of the facts and their location in the record, command of the law both within and outside the briefs, and a manner at once informal and respectful. Additional special qualities contributing most to effective argument when time is sharply limited are the following, in increasing order of importance.

Early Sensing of the Court's Level of Comprehension

There is only one miscalculation as unfortunate as getting into argument wrongly assuming that the court understands the factual context or legal doctrine. It is spinning a long narrative on the wrong assumption that the court does not understand the context or applicable law. Sensing the right level of sophistication in legal discussion is a task for the lawyer's good sense; if instinct does not supply the answer, little else will help. But the advocate will often not be able to guess how deeply the judges have been able to go into the facts. Sometimes they will have mastered a complex factual background, perhaps at the expense of other cases, which may be simple. My suggestion to an advocate who is in

doubt on this point is simply to ask the court whether he
should review the facts in any detail.

Controlled Flexibility

By "controlled flexibility" I mean a relaxed resilience allowing one to respond to a judge's question, coupled with an
internal gyro compass enabling one to return gracefully to a
charted course. Mastery of the pair of talents — yielding to
the sometimes centrifugal force of a judge's query and returning as soon as possible to one's own centripetal force —
is more critical than ever in an era of truncated arguments. I
can give no better sense of an advocate's predicament than
to quote the following exchange between a law student and
me in the course of a lecture I delivered at the University of
California

> STUDENT: Given the short time for argument, would it be better
> if there were just questions from the bench based on close points
> in the case?
> JUDGE COFFIN: Yes, it would be. That's the ideal. The ideal fif-
> teen-minute argument would be in a case where the judges have
> been so thoroughly prepared that they know exactly what they
> want to ask. I wish I could say that I was always in that position,
> but I'm not. So what you have to do is to say to yourself, "The
> court has assigned me fifteen to twenty minutes, or a half hour,
> so if the court just hasn't read these briefs or hasn't absorbed
> them, or if they got up on the wrong side of the bed and don't ask
> any questions, I want to cover what I think would make a good
> argument. On the other hand, if they have done a lot of work and
> if they have a lot of things on their minds, then I'm going to be
> flexible, and I'm going to respond to those questions." With this
> caveat, that the court's questions are not always necessarily the
> questions they should be asking. You will know your case better
> than they will, so you will have to do the delicate thing of an-
> swering their questions, but getting back onto your charted course
> as soon and as politely as you can. It may seem impossible but
> you ought to make the effort. I've seen counsel operate on the
> theory that the court can do no wrong: "So if they are asking
> questions, I'm just going to answer them." But you risk losing
> control of the whole argument, and you wind up without having

gotten to that key issue which ultimately, you will realize, you should have been discussing. You've got quite a job. You have three things to think about: what to do if there are no questions, what to do if there are good questions, and what to do if there are bad questions.[2]

Policy Sense

An advocate is well advised, in preparing for any appellate argument, to ask himself policy questions about his case and his opponent's. As a judge, that is exactly what I am doing as I read briefs and talk with my clerks. There will be many cases where there is no room for considerations based on policy. But, as we noted earlier, there is frequently some ambiguity, some opaqueness in a statute, or a choice to be made between case precedents, that allows, indeed invites, a judge to weigh the policy implications of different routes and results. An advocate, therefore, ought to be able to supply thoughtful answers to such questions as: What are the policy ripples from a holding in your favor? In your opponent's? How would you state the neutral principle of general applicability that can be derived from a holding in your favor? How can we decide for you without being forced also to make an absurd decision in a more extreme case? Where could we draw a rational line that limits this principle?

Disciplined Earnestness

By "disciplined earnestness" I mean a communicated sense of conviction that pushes a case to the limits of its strength but not beyond. One somehow brings together one's words and body language, facial expression and eye contact, to radiate a sense of conviction without making every point a life-and-death issue. This is an ineffable quality. I know it when I see it, but I cannot articulate a formula. Without it, the most eloquent speaker falls a bit flat; with it, attorneys may bumble, stammer, and even read their argument, and yet be effective because they had this ability to say to the court "Look, I mean business. This case is important, not just to my client but to the development of the law. You judges had better do the right thing."

Instinct for the Jugular

In the realm of combative sport, when we speak of an instinct for the jugular, we mean that the athlete somehow knows where his opponent is weakest and concentrates his attack to exploit that weakness. This is part of what we mean when we seek to describe the qualities of appellate advocates, but only a small part. It does not take much wit or courage to strike at the weakest part of an adversary's case. But it takes both qualities to expose the weakest part of one's own case.

It is not pleasant to concentrate on the weakest part of one's case, but when the advocate knows what it is, acknowledges the appearance or actuality of weakness, and then, with as much forcefulness as the issue permits, shows the appearance to be misleading or the weakness to be counterbalanced by other strengths, he becomes known as one who goes for the jugular — the advocate's highest accolade. In this sense it is the advocate's own jugular. It is the weak point that worries the court. When an advocate does the best he can on that issue, he is doing just about all he can do in oral argument. He is being a good advocate whether he speaks eloquently or awkwardly. Implicit in this instinct for the jugular is credibility, the earned respect of the court for the advocate's candor in presenting the whole of his case, defects and all. The first time such an advocate comes to a court's attention, he establishes his credibility; thereafter, his reputation precedes him into the courtroom and constitutes an unspoken but palpable advocacy.

On the Importance of Argument

When judges and, for that matter, lawyers talk about advocacy, they eventually acknowledge a paradox. On the one hand, they sing the praises of the superb advocate; on the other, they concede that a party should not win a lawsuit just because he, she, or it has hired the most capable lawyer. Much of the work of a court, its judges and law clerks, is to see to it that a party does not lose because of the poor work of the lawyer. The question thus arises: If the right side usually wins, why is good argument important?

I begin by observing, as a matter of self-interest, that if a good oral argument can help us fallible judges make a better analysis of a case and contribute more to the sound development of the law with a minimum investment of time and energy, this ought to be justification enough. And it is — for judges, if not for lawyers, whose fees are necessarily based on more than the proposition that a social service has been rendered.

My next answer responsive to this concern is that there are times when the law, facts, and policy considerations are in such balance that a court can reasonably go in either direction. At such times the better advocate can indeed hope to persuade the court to see matters his way. There are times when a brief was poorly or indifferently written, making little impression on the court, but the lawyer presenting the oral argument has thoroughly prepared himself, is inspired, and does a spectacular job, turning the court around in its thinking. I would say that this happens at least once or twice in a court session. Statistically this may be small, but such frequency of cases rescued by oral argument makes court week exciting and the effort of good advocates worthwhile.

There are other, more limited but more frequently encountered uses of effective advocacy. A lawyer who argues well will not lose a good case. This may seem obvious, but just as trial judges can err (the very reason there are appellate courts), so can appellate judges; it is quite possible for them to misunderstand facts and misapply statutes, rules, regulations, and cases. A good argument ensures that a court will not unwittingly go astray.

Another kind of interest served by good argument is that

the approach of the court, although perhaps not the result, will be influenced. Sometimes, for example, it is of critical importance to a regulated industry that a decision be a narrow one, confined to the special facts of the case, rather than one announcing a broad new requirement. Or if a prosecutor has to see a conviction set aside, he hopes that it will make as little precedent for the future as possible. A good advocate, looking to the future, may try to persuade the court to resist expressing dicta, or he may actively seek them, hoping thereby to pave the way for winning some future case.

Finally, the wise advocate will have his eye on the range of remedies that could be chosen by the court. His client may win or lose through circumstances beyond his control, but he can try to help the client win as "big" or lose as "small" as possible.

One footnote to this description of oral argument: it gives us solitary, ivory-towered appellate judges a refreshing chance to hear and talk to other human beings who are neither judges nor law clerks. Oral argument is a dramatic and welcome change in our work cycle.

On the Judges' Conference

Our former chief judge, Bailey Aldrich, refers to a conference as "the semble." I think what he means by this is that what we do is to say how the case *seems* to us at the time. Nothing is solemnized in a binding commitment or irrevocably decided. We know from experience that we may ultimately agree on an opinion quite the opposite of what we had tentatively decided. Just because of this looseness of expectation, we are willing to talk freely.

Our discussion runs the gamut. One of us may be captivated by a technical jurisdictional or procedural point that had not occurred to the others. We may be concerned about the facts revealed by the record; oral argument may have left us up in the air. If one of us can point with authority to a relevant passage in the trial transcript, this moves along our deliberations. One judge may be making considerable progress with an argument until another says, "Yes, but how do you reconcile this with that Fifth Circuit case?" At which the sense of the semble is likely to be "We'll have to see how the writer of the opinion handles this." Sometimes argument has so rubbed away at the words of a statute that we seem to be looking at it for the first time. At such times one thinks back on complicated briefs and convoluted oral arguments and wonders how he ever could have lost sight of the simple and obvious. The opposite is more likely to occur: realizing the complexity of what at first sight had seemed simple.

Occasionally, a judge gives vent to his spleen, making such utterly nonjudicial statements as "We can't hamstring the police. We mustn't overburden the trial judge. If we don't shut the door on this type of lawsuit, we'll be buried. Government is getting too intrusive." Or such ad hominem remarks as "The judge below is a very good one; I'd hate to reverse. This defendant is obviously guilty of a very bad crime; I'd hate to see his conviction set aside." Once such a statement is made, it appears to be what it is, a remark that has no place in the decision process. It has no place because it reflects a value judgment about burdening the police or the courts, about the competence of a judge or the public image of a defendant . . . but nothing about the law or the process of reaching a just decision. Then there are cases that pit philosophy against philosophy or value against value. We can see these coming and resign ourselves to the inevitable conflict.

Often a conference will involve not only discussion of the merits of the key issue but also questions of the breadth of the holding, the impact of the precedent being created, the advisability of limiting language. A decision may be made to take a step in the evolution of the law if, after further analysis, the judges feel that such would be "respectable," by which they do not mean the approbation of society but the making of a close fit between the proposed result and the facts and pre-existing cases, using acceptable legal analysis.

Many conferences involve a debate between the desirability of taking that next step and the difficulty of drawing a sensible line if that next step is taken. The debate is most successful when it is accompanied by clear vision and dispassionate discussion of what case may next present itself if the court moves forward. Matters of timing sometimes prove to be the key: the present case may not be a good one for the announcement of a new rule, or a problem of prosecutorial misconduct may not have reached the stage where a prophylactic rule is justified.

Still another range of ideas discussed in the judges' conference has to do with choosing among the available options as to disposition, form of opinion, and publication. In choosing among dispositions, we will note an "affirm" if we are very clear and sure. Indeed, if we are certain that an appeal should never have been brought, we begin to think about taxing additional costs to the litigious appellant. If we are not sure that the judgment below should be affirmed, if there are days of trial transcript to read or a multitude of legal issues to consider, we will end our conference notes with one or more question marks. Proceeding toward the negative end of the spectrum, we note possible or sure reversals. These dispositions do not exhaust the possibilities. We may affirm on some issues, reverse on others, and on still others remand for further proceedings in accordance with instructions.

As to our options in form, if the decision is very clear and simple, a short order announcing the result and the rule, statute, or case compelling it is sufficient. An appeal that merits some, but not much, reasoning or citation calls for a longer "memorandum and order" or a short per curiam opinion.* Finally, the opinions thought to make some contribution to the understanding, application, or development

---

* A per curiam opinion is usually a brief opinion applying well-known law in a routine way to run-of-the-mill facts. Occasionally, however, the caption may signify that a significant opinion is an extraordinarily collegial production to which all the judges contributed in more or less equal measure.

of the law are "signed opinions" and bear the name of the writer.

Decisions as to whether an opinion merits publication in the printed reports may sometimes be made as early as the conference but usually await the preparation and circulation of the opinion. The issue of publication involves a tension between a reluctance to load the bookshelves of law offices with volumes of opinions that turn on particular, never-repeated sets of facts and the most ordinary application of legal principles, and a recognition that even in the most fact-oriented opinion a perceptive lawyer will learn something about the way in which a court works. We pursue a liberal propublication policy; if any one judge feels that the opinion merits publication, it will be published.

A final avenue open to us is simply to adopt the opinion written by the court below or by the administrative agency. If that opinion not only reaches the result agreed on by the appellate court but reaches it for the reasons deemed sound by that court, it makes little sense to invest the time required to create what in effect would be a duplicate opinion. So on occasion we acknowledge that we cannot improve on what has been written and adopt it in whole or in large part.

Merely to review the kinds of comments and decisions made in conference cannot begin to convey the quality and variety of chemistry that make this step one of the most fascinating in the entire process of appellate decision-making. It is not usually the most crucial or decisive, but, just because it brings together the impressions, biases, and studied views of judges, relevant and irrelevant, in a freewheeling, nonbinding way, it is unpredictable and unfailingly provocative and helpful. The judges themselves bring to a case different strengths and interests, with complementary weaknesses and blind spots. To complicate matters, the same judge can bring different strengths or weaknesses to different cases. The result is that in a day's conference, one judge will be brilliantly analytical in technical matters, and another judge will start with a preferred result and try to work backward toward a supporting analysis. There may be one judge who views some of the cases through a broad philosophical framework; he will be balanced by one who keeps everyone's feet on the ground with his solid common sense. Once in a while a judge will finally illumine a meandering discussion with a pithy statement of the problem in a manner that suggests the right result. And, not least, there will be a judge here and there who has done considerable work on a particular case. To make matters more intriguing, the judges swap these roles, attitudes, and functions from case to case.

The image that comes to mind as we discuss conferences is that of a large stew pot sitting on a low flame, just enough to make it simmer, not boil, while various ingredients are gently added. The judge who is assigned to write the opinion remembers the exchanges, takes them into account, and, consciously or not, adapts his work to the views so exposed. But there are other conferences in which the key issue is best likened to a lightning rod that draws down a powerful electrical discharge and polarizes the thinking of otherwise agreeable, amenable, accommodating judges. For there are some issues where judges, almost against their will, come to a case strongly predisposed. The prisoner versus the warden, the teacher or student against the university, the consumer against the manufacturer, the pregnant woman against the state — such are the dramatis personae of conflicts where the final word of the law has not yet been written, and where, therefore, there is room for the value judgments of judges. When an issue like any of these comes along, a court will frequently have a protagonist for each side and one judge on the fence, who is an obvious candidate to write the opinion.

If the conference has produced any kind of exchange of opinion, it is likely that, before the end, some change of position, some moderating of views, some new indication of openness to new ideas will become evident. Not infrequently a judge, if the case involves a highly charged issue, will come into conference with an equally highly charged credo and deliver it forcefully. After a conference of a half-hour or so of low-keyed, civil talking and listening, this judge is likely to say that he perhaps overstated his point, that he by no means has a closed mind, and that if something sensible could be worked out without changing the law too much, he may very well join the opinion.

Perhaps the most thrilling kind of conference occurs when the judges find themselves in basic agreement, have time to think, and find themselves interacting in creative chemistry whereby one suggests a general idea that leads another to be more specific, building on the general foundation, with another adding still further refinements. This kind of catalytic reaction is most likely to occur in the field of remedy, where the room for improvisation, common sense, and ingenuity is perhaps larger than in the substantive field of rights and obligations where prior case law and statutes may well restrict available options.

In an era when conferences are the commonest of devices, the judges' conference breaks all the rules. It has no protocol, apparatus, staff, minutes, rules, press release. No one stands to gain or lose prestige, position, or power by what he says or does not say. No one is trying to take advantage of another. Each judge on our court, although he may occasionally question the judgment of others, has unlimited trust in the motives of his colleagues. The conference does not, at least as we practice it, aim at, or exert pressure for, a binding decision. For us it is but a step, a significant and helpful step, toward decision. It is part of the graduated process of maturation that is appellate decision-making.

On the Assignment of Cases

There is one last step in the ritual of a monthly term of court — the assigning of each case to a judge for the writing of a suitable opinion, long or short, named or per curiam, published or unpublished. In our court this is the very last act before we separate and return to chambers. In some courts, where the panel of judges changes with each day, the senior presiding judge will divide up the grist of that day. We are a small court, and our panels change only minimally when a fourth judge rotates with the other three. We are able, therefore, to defer assignments until the week's end, when we can form an idea of the workload that must be shared.

Assignment is a little talked-about function, perhaps because those who perform it operate more from intuition, sensitized by experience, than from any conscious set of principles. At its best, wisdom in assigning enables the court to operate at its highest level of sustained productivity. At its worst, thoughtless, unwise, or manipulative assigning could in the short run wreak havoc on a court. The apprehension of such manipulation recommends to many the practice of random assignments or strict rotation.

Our court has always lived, comfortably I think, with the custom of giving the assignment function to the chief judge or the senior judge presiding during a session. Here are the goals I try to achieve with each month's docket: balance the workload in terms of the burden borne; balance it in terms of interest — see that everyone has a chance to deal with frontier issues; exploit expertise in moderation, making sure that each judge eventually gains experience in all fields; respond to displays of interest on the part of individual judges through their questioning at argument; select a writer who is most likely to be able to command a majority.

Then there are lesser considerations. A sampling is illustrative. When we are interpreting our own circuit's precedents or perhaps making new ones, I will ask one of our own judges, rather than a visiting judge, to write such an opinion. Conversely, there may be times when a trial judge or counsel is to receive fairly severe criticism; sometimes an outsider can administer this more effectively and with less embarrassment. Occasionally, the judge's residency in a particular state in the circuit becomes relevant. If a question of state law is involved, a judge who has practiced in that state may be thought able to deal more expeditiously with the case. Sometimes, however, just because a judge has been part of the mainstream of a state's life, he will prefer that an outsider write an opinion that may impose significant changes on a state's conduct. Similarly, though a judge may not feel bound to withdraw from a case involving a company he represented years ago, he may prefer that another be responsible for drafting the opinion.

From time to time, an issue arises that leads the court not merely to decide a case but to announce a significant change of policy affecting trial judges, prosecutors, the bar generally, or state government. Sometimes the controversy is such that it is appropriate that the chief judge or the senior presiding judge speak for the court. As my colleagues and I meet for our final conference of the term, we may, infrequently, indicate cases we think we should not write or cases we would like to write. When we have finished conferring on the last case of the week, I go down the list of assignments. This done, we decamp to our respective chambers.

Chapter 8

The Creation of Opinions

AFTER A TERM of court, the appellate judge's return to chambers signals both a change in location and a change in pace and style of work, the onset of a period of individual, solitary work. The judge brings with him the week's crowded impressions of the arguments of from sixty to seventy-five lawyers and the questions, comments, and views of his colleagues. He settles into chambers.

It is at this point that appellate judges disappear, not merely in a physical sense but in a psychic sense as well. To the non-lawyer the image conjured up by the words "a judge in chambers" is probably that of a Dickensian character, corpulent and bewigged, sipping his tea before a low fire and interrupting his pondering to dip his goose quill into the inkwell and pen a few more profundities — or possibly that of a cadaverous Daumier character, filling his time by chortling over the unhappy fates of the widows and orphans who have appeared before him. In truth, when a judge retires to his chambers to write opinions, he commences a number of processes outwardly unremarkable but inwardly demanding and ultimately rewarding. All are necessary in the creation of opinions — a much more accurate phrase than the narrower and partial one, "the writing of opinions." The processes include thinking, discussing with clerks, doing research of law, becoming intimately acquainted with the record, making notes, writing a first draft, editing and revising.

Even though the published opinions of a judge are perhaps no more than half his total work product, they reflect his unique qualities, values, methods, and approaches. Moreover, the construction of an opinion is the heart and core of appellate judging. This is where the fun and challenge, the agony and frustration are.

On my return to chambers, I confer with my clerks. This conference is a key to what all of us try to do in the next several weeks. After I report anything significant that occurred during argument or conference on cases assigned to me for opinion-writing, I parcel out the cases so that each of us has a set of assignments. We even set tentative dates for completion of rough first drafts. As the weeks pass, I review the schedule to see how we are doing, what cases are proving troublesome, and what a more realistic deadline would be. It is impossible to schedule opinion production as if cases were homogeneous, like so many widgets, but a schedule, even though continually revised, does enable us to avoid falling into the trap of spending an excessive amount of time on cases that may hold infinite intellectual interest but are not difficult to dispose of and are of no significance to anyone other than the parties.

At some point the time comes to begin work on an opinion. I wish I could say that I am clear in my mind as to what I want to achieve in any given assignment and how to go about achieving it. In candor, I confess my feelings of chronic ineptitude and perennial uncertainty. Here is a telling entry from my judge's journal as I started work on one case:

> I am now waist-high in P——, bathed in the unpleasantness of uncertainty. I have been reading "around the case," getting insights from treatises and uncited law review articles. I thought I had hit upon the key, but further reading put me back where I

was. And other work suffers — the production line slows. I am in the dark about other judges, say, Learned Hand. I imagine him to reflect a bit, do a bit of refreshing reading, and then calmly chart and follow his course. But I am like a bounding hunting dog let loose in a field; I race helter-skelter in all directions, ears flapping, until I pick up the scent. It is not an impressive process to watch.

The process of creating a decision is impossible to analyze and articulate in any generally applicable format. As my familiarity with facts and law increases, I gradually develop a feel for strengths and weaknesses that leads me to clues, corroboration, or perhaps dead ends. Before I know it, I am "into" a case, no longer dreading it as an insoluble mystery but feeling that there are keys or handles somewhere and being impatient to find them.

THE CASES

The Smuggler on the Dock

After rereading my argument notes and the briefs in this case, my law clerk and I have an exploratory session. Still reluctant to reverse the conviction, in spite of the serious questions all of us had raised at argument, I decide to review every word of the several-hundred-page transcript to make sure that we have unearthed all the relevant facts and then to see if they are enough to support the finding that defendant Hapless aided and abetted the smuggling operation.

At the same time, I assign my clerk the task of researching the issue involving the definition of "smuggling." We also decide, if nothing more turns up than what is already in the briefs, to try to uphold the district court's common-sense understanding of the term that led it to refuse to dismiss the indictment. So while my clerk is reading the several cases cited in the briefs, going to the digests to see if there are any other or more recent cases that have been overlooked, look-

ing for relevant scholarly articles or notes in law journals, I
begin my journey through the transcript.

I know of no speedy shortcut in reviewing for sufficiency of
evidence, for there may be a significant fact in a most unlikely part of the trial. All that is needed to support a jury's
verdict is just enough evidence to enable a rational jury to
find as it did, even though the court would have taken the
opposite position. I have learned to emulate Theseus when
he entered the Minotaur's maze and to leave a thread behind
me as I go forward. This thread, in the form of a crude index
of major facts and the pages on which they are found, is my
assurance that I can retrace my steps and, when I am in
danger of being overwhelmed by detail, see with some perspective the relation of events.

After several hours I have found nothing other than the
few facts already presented. In my judgment, in the light of
the other cases we had discussed, there was just not enough
evidence to support the inference that Hapless was in on the
plot.

I begin writing, since I now know the record and sense
that this issue of sufficiency of the evidence may well dispose
of the case. I know that whatever my clerk writes on the
wholly legal issue I assigned her will not change what I say
about the evidence. After stating something about the nature
of the case, its procedural history, and the various issues
raised on appeal, I set down the few facts relevant to the motion for acquittal on the ground of insufficient evidence.
Even though I have nothing in my draft opinion that is not
in the briefs, I have gained something from rereading the
transcript of testimony — confidence that what I say is reflected in the record and that the record holds nothing else.
The legal discussion is brief and simple. The several cases in
our circuit are sufficient; there is no need to be encyclopedic.

My law clerk and I then reconvene, and she shows me her
rough draft of the smuggling issue, in which, despite the old
Supreme Court case, we take the position that goods do not
need to be landed on shore for the act of smuggling to have

taken place. It is a solid piece of work. All the facts are persuasively marshaled, but, after reciting all the facts, the draft falters: "Notwithstanding that the Court in *Keck* held that the crime of smuggling was only in the attempt stage until the goods are landed, and that Congress has never clarified the definition, we affirm the action of the district court because . . ." My clerk, finding that the opinion just will not "write," has come to me for guidance.

It had gradually become clear that, like it or not, there is no respectable way to disregard the old Supreme Court case. To put it another way, there was no way to disregard it without implicitly enunciating the principle that we need not follow the law of the top court in the land if we disagreed with it. What has just happened is something that happens quite often in an appellate judge's chambers. The very discipline of writing a reasoned opinion exposes vulnerabilities. We had at least satisfied ourselves that we could not responsibly uphold the government's position on this issue, however sensible it might be.

These two grounds, insufficient evidence and the requirement that goods be landed if they are to be viewed as smuggled, being independent bases for reversal, I see no point in being tentative or opaque concerning admitting the old conviction into evidence. It is high time to nip in the bud any tendency by trial courts to water down the new Rules of Evidence. We gather an impressive amount of case authority and some commentary from treatise-writers. I express our court's incredulity at the thought that a defendant's conviction for possessing a small amount of marijuana so long ago could have any weight, not to mention a substantially greater weight than the prejudice it would create in a contemporary prosecution for his taking part in a wholesale smuggling scheme.

After noting that the other issues do not merit discussion, I have the opinion typed in final form and send it to my colleagues.

The Agency and the Anorectic

This case promised to demand an unusual amount of time. My initial step in dealing with all cases is to try to dispose of smaller matters and clear the decks so that I may have at least several uninterrupted days to immerse myself in the record. Then my task is to become reacquainted with the case sufficiently to have an opinion as to how my clerk and I may best share the labor. I decided that my clerk should address the several issues of the Thin-King case that were almost purely questions of law: whether the hopeful intervenor, FIB, merited being made a party at this stage; whether company witnesses had been improperly limited in their testimony; and the narrow, technical issue of whether the Food and Drug Administration's proceeding was such that no information could be considered unless it was formally made a part of the record. This last matter posed some possible difficulty. Because I wanted to take on a solid case at this time, I undertook to do work of a more factual nature than I usually do. I wanted to see whether the FDA's requirement of well-controlled investigations had improperly excluded some of Schmarzipan's test results and to see if the FDA's criticism of two other sets of experiments was arbitrary or rationally based.

This kind of work would, I suspect, appear to an outsider the most onerous, tedious, and unrewarding of an appellate judge's lot. In fact, I rather relish the chance to leave the ordinary traffic at my desk and lose myself completely in the exhibits and testimony of a complex technical case. At the outset, of course, the language, the subject matter, and the reasoning are alien to me. Gradually, I absorb key points of reference, values, and standards of evaluation. Each time I reread briefs, they reveal more meaning and appear less formidable. As I do when reading a lengthy transcript, I leave behind me a trail of notes.

I first addressed the attack on the FDA's requirement that a drug acceptable for marketing must be demonstrated as effective for its intended uses by adequate and well-controlled investigations. Regulations set forth a number of principles generally recognized by the scientific community as criteria for respectable experiments. Selection of suitable subjects, elimination of experimenter bias, and assurance of comparability in test and control groups as to various factors were among those included. Schmarzipan's objection was that the regulations made no provision for tests run on animals.

After reading several hundred pages of examination and cross-examination of an FDA psychobiologist, I became convinced that the challenge was insubstantial. In the first place, the regulations did not exclude experiments with animals. They simply enumerated minimum requirements; additional proof could be submitted. In the second place, the experiment with mice, while tending to corroborate the dietetic or reducing effectiveness of Thin-King, did not necessarily indicate increased intellectual activity. The mice were astonishingly energetic, even frenzied; whether this reflected useful brain activity was still a matter for speculation.

I then began reading page after page of the laboratory experiment sheets. The fifty-patient study was not very comprehensive. There had been no pre-experiment assessment of those within each group in terms of their intellectual interest, level, or aptitude. As far as anyone knew, the members of the control group could have been at a very low level, and each member of the test group could have had a very high I.Q. I could not fault the FDA for deeming this evidence not probative of effectiveness.

I then went to Schmarzipan's heavy artillery, the poll of some 300 doctors. They were reported, almost unanimously, to have endorsed Thin-King as safe and effective and as something that should continue to be available. The FDA had rejected the poll as insubstantial evidence. To get to the root of the matter, I had to read over a thousand pages of responses to a questionnaire.

The rote affirmative answers, usually stressing convenience to the physician in prescribing and the patient in administering dosages, often conjoined with a diatribe against Washington, with no specific examples demonstrating effectiveness, gave me no basis for confidence in the exercise. On the other hand, the testimony, exhibits, and reports of the FDA experts appeared to me workmanlike and fair. I also had in mind that our task was not to attempt to second-guess the agency in the technical field in which it had expertise, but merely to see what facts and policy concerns were relied on by the agency in making its decision, to see if those facts had some basis in the record, and to decide only if those facts and policy concerns could lead a reasonable person to make the decision the agency had made. I could not say that the FDA had been capricious or unreasonable in discounting this poll. Schmarzipan had had several years and all of its experience and resources to demonstrate in a scientifically acceptable manner the dual effectiveness of Thin-King. If, after all this time, these offerings were the best they could submit, I had no hesitation in recommending that we support the agency's decision. My own conviction was that Thin-King was an effective weight-reducing drug, but that any claim to intellectual stimulation was merely pretense.

I organized my notes and during one intensive ten-hour session in my study at home, I wrote up this part of the opinion, summarizing the experiments, the testing methods, lab sheets, and results. Part of my purpose was to demonstrate to my colleagues, the drug industry, and the agency that, though we had not attempted to be pharmacologists, our review of the record had not been a perfunctory one. In this day of pervasive regulation in matters technical and scientific, there are few more difficult tasks facing appellate courts than finding the path between meaningless rubber-stamping on the one hand and excessively detailed review on the other.

My clerk was now ready with drafts of the other issues. Intervention was easily resolved. FIB, as we had been told at argument, had not tried to intervene below in a timely manner. Nor had it given any excuse for its belated effort. I felt sorry for the group, but I saw no way to allow intervention in this case without serving notice to all that procedural time requirements were not to be taken seriously. The limitation on testimony of the company's witnesses was, our reading of the cases soon revealed, clearly within the discretion of the agency.

The most challenging purely legal issue was whether the FDA's proceeding that had led to the withdrawal of approval of Thin-King was an adjudication "required by statute to be determined on the record." The significance of this requirement lay in the fact that the FDA had relied in part on a panel of experts who gave their opinion, based on their familiarity with the literature in the field, that combining drug components to make a multiple-component drug seldom achieved the effectiveness of tailored dosages of separate drugs. Since a reference to such literature made cross-examination and rebuttal testimony impossible, Schmarzipan's attorneys claimed they had been placed at a disadvantage.

Sometimes, however, the practical need to get on with the business of an agency has persuaded the Congress to allow the decider to take into account his staff's expert opinion. Some permit and license proceedings, for example, are allowed to be decided without all facts or opinion being entered into testimony or made a part of the formal record. We had no trouble in saying that the FDA proceeding was "adjudicatory"; it clearly resulted in taking away Schmarzipan's right to continue to market Thin-King. The difficulty was that, on the one hand, this was obviously an adjudication of great importance to the public and the drug manufacturer, but, on the other hand, there was no specific affirmative statutory requirement that decision be based on the record.

After surveying opinions of other federal courts of appeal,

which were divided on this question, we decided to ally ourselves with a thoughtful analysis which held that, since individual rights and duties were finally determined in adjudicative proceedings, we would presume that decision must be
based on a record unless the Congress had specifically faced
the question and declared a record to be an unnecessary
prerequisite to decision. What we would be saying is that
the policy behind maximizing fairness in adjudicative hearings is so strong that decision on the record will not be discarded without a statute waiving the requirement.

With all the building blocks at hand, I assembled the opinion. I began with the background description I had written
about the proceeding before the agency. As a threshold matter, I first dealt with the issue of FIB's request to intervene.
Then I followed with the technical part of the opinion on
standards and tests, which I had done in one long sitting at
home. Finally, after noting briefly the criticism of the
agency's curtailing of testimony and affirming on these issues, I concluded by proposing a remand of the proceedings
to the FDA to allow it to rethink its position and either forgo
any reliance on the literature or to reopen the record, allowing the particular articles or opinions to be introduced and
subjected to whatever testing or opposing submissions
Schmarzipan might be able to locate. In effect, the FDA won
on all but one point, a fairly minor one but one whose
proper resolution would necessitate holding up the FDA's
final decision for yet some more months. While the defect
was, a layman might say, petty, it is important that agencies
observe the rules of the game.

By the time I had finished canvassing the record, writing
my reflections on the testing methods of Schmarzipan, and
outlining the framework of the opinion, two weeks had
passed. The work my law clerk had done fitted in well. I did
some final editing and, within several weeks from argument,
sent out a fifty-page opinion. I had invested roughly sixty
hours of my time in this case, the equivalent of a full week's

work time. My clerk had spent probably two times this amount. Together, we were able to produce the first draft within a month after oral argument. Had I not been able to have the assistance of a law clerk, the opinion would have taken me away from other work for several additional weeks, and in any event its issuance might well have been delayed by several additional months.

The Saga of the Transferred Prisoners

Since *Fano* v. *Meachum* is an actual case, I summarize the printed opinion. To one who is acquainted with the earlier prison cases, there are no surprises. The facts were few and generally uncontroverted. The applicable law was just one case, the Supreme Court opinion in *Wolff* v. *McDonnell*. The application of this case to the facts in *Fano* was straightforward. There was, therefore, no occasion for extensive research of law, time-consuming reading of the record, or lengthy involvement in the organization and writing of the opinion.

The critical decision lay in how *Wolff* v. *McDonnell* was to be interpreted. *Wolff* dealt with the interest a prisoner has in his earned good time, the credit applicable under state law to his sentence, which he has earned through keeping out of trouble. Such, the Court had said, "has real substance and is sufficiently embraced within Fourteenth Amendment 'liberty' to entitle him to those minimum procedures . . . required by the Due Process Clause."[1] We were, of course, dealing not with taking away a prisoner's good time but with transferring him to a prison with fewer amenities. Our problem was to determine whether in *Wolff* the Supreme Court was placing stress on the effect on the prisoner of taking away his credit or on the fact that the credit had been established under state law. If one looked to the quality of the prisoner's interest, transfer from a more relaxed prison environment to a more severe one would seem to be analogous to a good time credit, which would reduce the length of incarceration. The former had to do with conditions of confinement; the latter, with length of confinement. Each kind seriously affects a prisoner. On the other hand, the Court in *Wolff* also referred to the source of the prisoner's interest, saying, "But the State having created the right to good time and itself recognizing that its deprivation is a sanction authorized for major misconduct, the prisoner's interest has real substance . . ."[2]

It is clear from our opinion that we read *Wolff* as bringing the requirement of due process to the quality, not the source, of the interest at stake. This decision having been made, the opinion logically unfolded in three uncomplicated steps: (1) four paragraphs describing the fires at Norfolk, the kinds of hearings given plaintiffs, the decision to transfer, and the ruling of the district court; (2) five paragraphs referring to our earlier opinions in *Palmigiano* and *Gomes* and most particularly to *Wolff's* holding that the interest in good time credits "has real substance," analyzing the extent of detriment caused by an intrastate transfer from a medium-security institution to a maximum-security one, noting the district court's finding of "substantially more adverse conditions" in the latter, and concluding that a liberty interest existed, warranting the application of the due process clause; and (3) five more paragraphs balancing the loss suffered by an inmate because of a transfer against the burden that procedures would place on prison officials, noting that the balance had been struck at the higher-security unit at Walpole by an order requiring a summary of any information from informants — the relief sought in this case — and concluding that this procedure could not be denied inmates at the lesser-risk institution.

The decision was not a broad proclamation that summaries of informant information must be provided in all cases of intrastate transfer to more severe confinement. It was narrowed to a situation where state corrections officials had already required such summaries at disciplinary hearings in maximum-security institutions. If those who subscribed to this opinion hoped that this fact would be considered significant in subsequent proceedings, they were fated to be disappointed.

REFLECTIONS ON THE
CREATION OF OPINIONS

On Working Up an Opinion

Sometimes, often enough to make me aware of the privilege of being an appellate judge, the process of working up an opinion from the raw materials of the cold record, the contesting briefs, the existing law, history, logic, custom, and such considerations of policy and social justice as the case permits, becomes an intense, all-engulfing, and fulfilling experience. I reproduce here the account of such an experience from my journal.

*

I have just come home early, in the beginning swirls of the season's last blizzard. I have also done something as rare as a blizzard on the eve of spring. I have spent all day in chambers, almost uninterrupted, working on one case, my own from start to finish — or at least till my ruthless editors, my law clerks, begin to work on it.

This is what people must think an appellate judge does all the time when he is not sitting behind a big bench. This is what judges of yesteryear did. It is what I did quite often in my first years at judging. But it is rare enough now to write about.

This adventure crept up on me. It began as a drab piece of goods, so uninteresting that the lawyers on both sides let the case go without oral argument. Each was content to let the briefs speak for themselves. In this case the "speaking" was guttural; the briefs were slim, diffident things, hardly competent. They did cite a few key authorities on both sides, but so ignored the facts and the scholarly debate which has arisen that I was early misled into thinking that this was an easy affirmance.

The case concerned a ruling on jurisdiction, on whether the court had been given the power to hear this particular case. Were the issue one of the court's discretion, a one-line affirmance would be adequate. But the law is a forest of totem poles, and some are bigger than others. And the tallest, most grimacing and heartless is the totem pole of jurisdiction, the idea that judges, whatever their philosophy and values, will honor the boundaries set for cases they can and cannot decide.

Although I began with the assumption that the case was a trivial one, worth perhaps a page or two, I soon came to the realization that if we were to affirm, our opinion would have to be consistent with what other courts, particularly the Supreme Court, have said about the bugaboo Jurisdiction. Then came some dull work — rereading briefs and thumbing through the court papers evidencing almost eight years of futile and dilatory motions, notices, excuses. Far more exciting was to go beyond the briefs, read what the treatise-writers had to say, and realize that the issue in our case had been recognized as a "problem" for at least fifteen years.

The next step, by this time already under way, was my book-collecting phase. My desk is a long and wide work table, usually showing much woodwork between the in- and out-baskets and on either side of my desk blotter. But one case leads to another. Law review articles and treatises suggest others. The books — some from the Supreme Court (with a musty smell if they date from the last century), some from courts of appeal, and some from the district or trial courts — begin to stand in line, first in threes and fours, then in phalanxes of ten or twelve, then in double phalanxes; then scouting parties camp out on a nearby radiator and, in extremis, bivouac on the floor.

Meanwhile, I try to keep track of where I have gone, even though I do not yet know where I am going. So, with a light pencil, I mark the margins near passages of opinions that strike me as useful. These will be trailblazers when later I return, hunting for some half-remembered thought. But this alone is not enough. I also begin to fill pages with brief notes of cases and points made. I wish I could say that this is systematic note-taking, but it isn't. Nevertheless, it is my retrieval system, and this sheaf of papers is my basic working tool.

Exhilaration increases when I have the feeling that I "know the territory." This means being aware of the cases, commentary, and arguments on both sides of the issue. The parties and their briefs are far behind. Now what is in my mind is "the problem," disembodied from the particular facts of my case, and now seen as an institutional contest of some importance between being fair in an individual case and being faithful to the "first principle" of keeping courts within their charted domain. All of this means that at this stage I am in an uncomfortable state of imbalance, sometimes pursuing an approach with enthusiasm until I run into or recall a fact or a legal principle that blocks the road like an overturned trailer truck.

The task of research takes on wings when I find myself gaining fresh insights. I check the cases on which a leading opinion relies, and I find that they do not stand for the proposition for which they are cited. One after another of the supports proves termite-ridden, and the "authority" appears to be stripped down to a court's merely saying so. Or it may be the provocative article of a scholar, placing a new construction on venerable Supreme Court cases. Then I read the cases, as though with a magnifying glass, taking care to see exactly what the facts were, to see whether the justices appeared to focus on a point or simply said something in passing that, taken out of context, may appear to be a solemn pronouncement. And I realize that the scholar in his advocacy was de-emphasizing facts that stood in the way of his theory. I begin to gain the confidence that on this small issue and at this precise time I know more of the subject than any other person. I shall soon forget, pass on to the next case, and begin all over as an amateur. But for this moment I am an expert.

During this phase, logic, precedent, policy, concern for the parties, respect for tradition, excitement over the invitation to boldness and innovation, desire to influence legislation — all were at war with each other. Once in a while, when vexed to despair, I would air a problem before my clerks. This was always helpful. Merely stating the problem somehow helped. Then, even though we ended the discussion without resolution, it helped to put the issues in focus. And sometimes one of the clerks might mention a case, an analogy, or a relevant legal principle that inched me forward in my quest.

A critical step is taken when I take my sheaf of notes, my working tool Number 1, and begin to construct working tool Number 2, an outline of the opinion. Again I would like to be able to say that I quickly marshal the issues and subissues in a crisp symmetrical structure of I's, A's, 1's, and a's. But my outline efforts begin most tentatively. Indeed, at the start, I write in exceedingly small script, as if I were making the most humble offer to the god of Justice. Not only is the script small, but, since I do not yet see clearly the relationship, sequence, or priority of ideas, I list basic topics in different areas on the page, but close together. Then, on another part of the page, after an interval, I'll try another outline, perhaps this time with ideas arranged in some sequence. This may do it, for a starter. Or perhaps a third set of scribbles will appear.

Then I wait a while. Perhaps I have doodled on the outline for an hour or so after breakfast. Then the office beckons and

I plunge into reading the morning mail, making telephone calls to other judges and the clerk of our court, conferring with my law clerks, drafting memoranda on various points in colleagues' opinions, answering mail, and so on. But toward midafternoon, I have a feeling in my viscera that tonight I shall begin to put words on paper. It is a good feeling.

The writing now begins. It begins with my placing a long pad of paper on my desk. Then, without waiting so long that I am intimidated by the pristine blankness, I write "Coffin, Chief Judge," and struggle with my first sentence. The first paragraph is often the hardest. It soon becomes a mess of cross-outs, inserts, and rearrangements. The problem is to give a succinct overall statement of who has sued whom, what kind of a case it is, what the ruling below was, and what the appeal is all about. To compress all this in six to ten lines without doing violence to each item is a challenge for the most austere writer.

Then come such earthy chores as sketching the procedural background, giving the relevant facts, and leading into the issues. This is important and time-consuming work but not exhilarating. If the facts are important and extensive, I will have made an index of the transcript. I will have checked the key facts, and I will laboriously try to tell the story. I know at the time that I will have to edit this down to a leaner frame, but I also know that the only way to write is to put something on paper. I may leave the evening job a disaster, but I have the assurance of experience that, come morning, something, perhaps a great deal, will be salvageable.

As the writing progresses, as the necessary but grubby work of building a foundation is finished, my interest, excitement, and speed increase. As I write on the issues, I try to put as fairly and strongly as I can the contention that I shall rule against. Sometimes, while writing, I will have a new thought. If, after I roll it about in my mind a while, it seems to have no flaws, I'll write it down. Sometimes the next day I will see its unsoundness, or my law clerks will. Sometimes, however, the thought survives. More often than not, the thought will be an effort to say how our decision makes broad and enduring policy sense and how a contrary decision would not do so, if applied generally.

After four or five hours of steady work — with the foundation laid, the issues stated, and innumerable little decisions made as to sequences, what authorities to use and what to leave out, tone and nuances — I find my pen flying over the pages. Speed at this point is a built-in stimulant to succinctness. I am now eager to finish and more easily reject excessive refinement. Or, if a footnote is needed, I shall mark the gap and leave it for the morrow. The result is a shorter draft than I would have made without impatience. Sometimes my clerks, writing during office hours, not sensing the pressure that comes from knowing that sustained writing time is a rare and precious commodity, will present me with long, heavily footnoted drafts that I would never have the time to construct. Then my job is to winnow, shear, simplify. But with my drafts, their job is to see if flesh should be added to the bones.

Next comes the tidying-up of loose ends, going back over my notes in search of little gems and gap-filling footnotes. As I go over my copy before giving it to my secretary, I realize with some apprehension what a collage I expect her to interpret. Not only does my writing degenerate into minute hen tracks, but carets and arrows and inserts affixed with paper clips force me to give a guide's talk on the sequence of each "page," which may consist of a half-dozen pieces of paper.

Miraculously, a legible draft issues from the typewriter, because of the sharp eyes and seasoned intuition of my secretary, who brings to her task over two decades of deciphering my hieroglyphics. I marvel at the clean copy, already the recognizable form of the creature it is to be.

Ahead lie other steps — the humbling experience of seeing

excisions, additions, word substitutions, possibly even quite different approaches, and, once in a great while, the hard-come-by realization that my whole theory and proposed result are wrong. All this from discussions with these acute young people less than half my age. Then come the reactions of my colleagues, ranging from suggestions in phrasing, to rejection of my choicest thoughts, and even at times a profound disagreement with my conclusion. Next comes the slow task of judicial diplomacy, as I try to defend what I deem essential while yielding on points well taken or not worth quibbling about.

Finally, the opinion meets its public — and a deafening silence ensues. Once in a great while I will see the opinion emerge as a subject in a law review article, usually to be dissected and criticized for weaknesses of logic, law, or policy that had never occurred to me, my clerks, or my fellow judges or their clerks.

On Collaborating on an Opinion
with Law Clerks

As is already obvious from the three cases and reflections on my work ways, collaboration with my law clerks takes place at almost every step of the appellate decision process, excluding only the conference among the judges. Even at the opinion-writing stage, collaborating with a law clerk takes many forms. The clerk's participation ranges from a minimum of checking citations and minor editing, to being responsible for parts of an opinion (as we saw in the smuggling prosecution and the review of the FDA proceeding), to crafting short opinions, and to the maximum participation, having initial responsibility for a complex and significant opinion.

In all these situations, the clerk commences his work on a case with the benefit of notes of his own research and discussions with his judge before argument. He has also received his marching orders based on the vote of the judges at their conference following oral argument. Sometimes, as we have seen, the court remains undecided. It will be the task of the writing judge and his clerks to try to find a solution. The judge will frequently indicate on what issues research should be concentrated, and constant discussions between judge and clerk, and with fellow clerks, will take place as options become more sharply identified. As the clerk becomes more familiar with the judge's thought processes, style, and values, these become powerful if subtle sources of direction. The judge's careful review is, of course, the final and definitive control. The duty of exercising this control to the extent that a case warrants it is one of the judge's most demanding obligations. He must so immerse himself in the briefs and record and draft opinion that he is attuned to issues great and small, to both substance and style. He must then work over the draft until he can conscientiously say that it represents him with complete fidelity, not only as to the outcome, but as to approach, order of presentation, emphasis, length, and tone. Sometimes this point will have been reached after only a few word changes; sometimes not until the draft has been wholly rewritten.

A hundred years ago, when the "legal secretary" or law clerk was a new occupation, and perhaps even fifty years ago, the minimum end of the participation spectrum, that of citation-checking and minor editing, would be the characteristic kind of collaboration for most law clerks. It is far from an unimportant task. When I develop the complete first draft of an opinion and am sure of my facts and approach to the law, I will ask a clerk to edit what I have written, but not in depth. Even so, I know the opinion stands to be improved in a dozen different ways: a new case or two uncovered when the clerk checks the subsequent history of the cases I have used; a more accurate way of citing to a case (indicating, for example, that the case is not directly on point, but, rather, is analogically suggestive); loose language cut out, compressed, or sharpened; authority found for some propositions I had deliberately left for my clerk to supply; a fact more precisely stated after the transcript of testimony has been checked. It is because I value the contribution that good editing can make to a judicial opinion that I generally expect each of my clerks to have had heavy editing experience on his school's law journal.

When my clerk and I — or sometimes in major cases all three clerks and I — work in tandem, each taking a distinct part of an opinion, I become the general editor and rewrite person. I must attain the same depth of familiarity with the parts initially written by others as I have with my own portion in order to be able to decide on sequence of discussion, transitions, tone, and emphasis. In a sense, this is not so difficult a task as that of reviewing a draft opinion wholly written by another, for I will have gotten into the record and the cases on one or more significant issues and inevitably will have familiarized myself with the remaining ones.

If my clerk has drafted a short opinion, for example, in a case where the Social Security Administration has denied disability benefits to a claimant, my job is almost totally one of verifying and assessing the facts to determine whether there was "substantial evidence" to justify the finding that the claimant was not permanently disabled from pursuing gainful employment. I read the record assembled by the agency — testimony, medical reports, a vocational expert's opinion of employability, the decision of the administrative law judge who held the hearing.

The most sophisticated challenge for an appellate judge arises when the law clerk has been given his maximum responsibility, that of doing a first draft of a complex opinion. I say this because of both the importance and the difficulty of a judge's knowing when an opinion becomes as nearly as possible what he would have written had he done it all himself. Of course, the judge can avoid this problem by rewriting every single sentence, but in such event the clerk's draft would not have saved him any time.

My own work way is to read the draft quite rapidly to try

to introduce it as soon as possible into my own consciousness to plumb the depth it will. I note or check words that
make me feel uncomfortable, awkward clauses or ponderous
paragraphing, expressions that I think may grate on my colleagues. Then I reread the briefs, giving most attention to
the losing party, noting arguments made that have not been
dealt with in the draft. Perhaps there is a good reason for the
clerk's not dealing with them; perhaps not. If the opinion
depends on the existence and significance of facts, my next
step is most important — going back to the record, reading
all of the relevant testimony, seeing how objections were
made and how the judge's whole charge to the jury reads.
This done, I am now in a position to work with my clerk in
developing his draft into a finished opinion.

In one case I tried to identify how the process works. This
was a criminal case involving eight or ten different issues,
some of which were extremely close, arising out of a several-
week trial of a number of defendants. It was the occasion for
a particularly fruitful collaboration in the creation of an
opinion with one of my law clerks. The lawyers for both the
government and the defendants were unusually able. Such a
combination of factors required two or three solid weeks of
clerk time before the first rough draft appeared. During its
preparation the clerk saw to it that I became involved in
specific issues and was aware of some of the close questions.
Then came my reading, incubation, and more discussion.
After several days of more intensive working together, discussing changes, trying out different language, and redrafting entire sections, both my clerk and I were satisfied that
we had done as well as we could. The collaboration had
proceeded somewhat as follows:

- The opening paragraph my clerk had drafted might have
  qualified as a one-act play, but not as a serious opinion
  where criminal convictions were at stake. (He really did
  not think this would survive but probably had to get it

out of his system before he could settle down and write humble prose.) I substituted my own introduction to set the tone I thought was missing.

- My notes of the oral argument revealed a few significant facts being conceded that were not found in the briefs. We added these.

- My clerk had worked so closely with each issue from the very beginning that he tended to see each one as finely balanced, even though some of the issues no longer appeared at all close. I toned down some of the agonizing introductions to various issues, leaving them out and making them more neutral.

- Surgery was called for on some footnotes. For example, one footnote made a sound response to a very sophisticated argument that might have been, but was not, made. Another distinguished a case that could have been, but was not, cited. Similarly, I found some discussion in the text only marginally pertinent; we dropped this to a footnote.

- There were inevitable numerous, minor editing changes in paragraphing, sentence structure, split infinitives, unnecessary words.

- My major substantive contribution was to eliminate discussion of three issues that both sides had briefed but that were simply not part of the appeal; no objection to the allegedly improper evidence or jury instruction had been called to the trial judge's attention. As we have noted several times in these pages, part of the premise of appellate review is that the lower court has already had a chance to act on an issue. If we did not require points to be raised at trial, lawyers could play games, lulling the trial court by their apparent acquiescence with a ruling, then belatedly claiming error on appeal.

The result of this kind of collaboration is that two to three weeks of clerk time and two to three days or a week of judge time together produced a major opinion. Was it my opinion? In the case we have just reviewed, I had left enough traceable footprints to prove that I was familiar with the record, every nook and cranny of legal argument, and had made the opinion my own in many visible ways. The question would be less convincingly answered if I had made but a few changes in a draft opinion. Here, the challenge to the judge is a subtle one. If the issues are straightforward, if the draft is well organized, diligently researched, economically written, it makes little sense for the judge to make changes just to acquire a spurious feeling of authorship. On the other hand, the judge must somehow know that he has not been seduced into delegating his judgment by the blandishment of a most presentable, polished, and persuasive draft. To arrive at the point where the judge knows that he has done his duty may take, as in the case just summarized, days; it may take hours; sometimes it may take only the fraction of an hour. I suppose that when and how a judge arrives at that point in a given case remains an uncommunicable mystery, the product of accumulated experience, wisdom, intuition, and integrity.

On Principles and Progeny

I have no set formula for the construction of an opinion. The appropriate opinion can be long or short, have a detailed factual background or none, be very precise or very fuzzy, be broad or narrow, have many footnotes or none, cite many cases or few — all depending on the particular case. All that I can safely say is that after I have thoroughly immersed myself in a case, reliving the trial vicariously through the transcript, rereading the briefs and making point-for-point comparisons, getting a feel for the decided cases, statutes, or legislative history, I develop a sense of the way that particular case should be handled. Beyond this inchoate formulation, I confess to resorting more or less regularly to several reliably helpful disciplines in the creation of an opinion.

Immersion in the facts of a case until there develops a feel for the terrain: This may not be called for at all in a case presenting issues of pure law. Or the relevant facts may be few and not in controversy, as in the prisoners' case. But there are many, many appeals in which there are facts overlooked by the parties, under- or overplayed, or taken out of context. A judge treads in such a domain with confidence only if he has made himself privy to all that the record contains. If there is anything that we can instill in our young law clerks, who seldom need instruction in legal analysis, it is a healthy respect for a factual record.

Verification of the procedural framework of the appeal: Appearances, as we have learned, sometimes belie reality. In the case of the Smuggler on the Dock, the objection to admitting the record of the over-ten-year-old conviction had not been clearly preserved. In the FDA case, the question as to whether FIB could be allowed to intervene had not been submitted to the agency. This is not atypical. So my arsenal of disciplines gives a prominent place to checking the procedural posture of each issue.

Exploration beyond the briefs: There is often some law or legislative history imperfectly reflected in the briefs that can be decisive. While not every case invites such excursions, I would say that in any close or significant case a search should be made of treatises in the field, law journal articles, new cases decided since briefs were filed, and the subsequent history of cases cited to see if they have been affirmed or reversed by a higher court. I am rarely satisfied with what the parties report as legislative history. Perhaps this skepticism stems from my own days as a legislator, when I listened to many debates and many remarks "for the record" that had absolutely nothing to do with the outcome. I rarely read a complete legislative debate or committee report without gaining insights not found in the briefs.

I recall one appeal where all of the case authority, some seven or eight cases, was unanimous that the legislative history behind a statute commanded a certain result. The result seemed to be at odds with national policy in this area. A search was indicated and proved productive. It revealed that the eighth case relied on the previous seven, the seventh on the previous six, and so on, back to the first decision, a rather conclusory lower court decision based on a few extracts from the legislative debates. Reading the entire debate placed the matter in quite a different light. Our opinion made so bold as to take on all prior authority. The case went to the Supreme Court, where we were affirmed, the Court obviously being just as impressed as we were by a look at the whole legislative history.

Statement of the opposing contention as fairly and as strongly as possible: This exercise has something of a hair-shirt nature about it. But if I can deal with the other side effectively in its strongest posture, I know our opinion can endure. Sometimes, this forces me to rethink my position; sometimes, to abandon it. On rare occasions I find myself writing two opinions, one for each side. At times I will inflict both opinions on my colleagues and let them share some of my misery.

Articulation of the policy sense behind the position taken in the opinion: A result may be dictated wholly by statute or case law, but I feel a sense of incompleteness if we leave only the impression that "this is so because this is the law." One helpful device is to ask what the implications would be if we decided the opposite way. For example, we may feel that a court or agency has decided something differently from the way we would have decided, and wrongly, too. We are not enthusiastic about affirming, but when we ask about the implications of reversing, we immediately confront the prospect of opening the door to multitudinous appeals and setting ourselves up as the only important deciders, with no deference being given the lower court or agency. As we saw in Chapter 4, one of the pillars of appellate decision-making is a decision from the court below that is not so easily disregarded.

I feel fulfilled when, using one of the above disciplines or in some other way, I make a contribution to the resolution of an appeal that a computer could not make. It is then that I feel I am doing something unique, not fungible. And I take pride in having left my mark in the opinion on a particular case. This may or may not be a case that "makes law." But it is one of my more cherished children.

A judge's professional progeny, his opinions, almost defy accurate appraisal, most of all by him who acknowledges parenthood. In my own case, at the time of the writing of this book, I have been on the appellate bench a full fourteen years and have sired near a thousand formal opinions and half again as many informal memoranda. They have dealt with all the national specialties, such as taxation, patents, commercial law, bankruptcy, admiralty, and antitrust. They have touched on issues concerning the boundaries separating governmental units: federal-state relations, separation of powers, administrative law. The Bill of Rights and statutes implementing it have fed a swelling stream of litigation, in which my court and I have shared, raising questions of criminal procedure, civil liberties, and civil rights. And my opinions have pronounced on a host of statutes, dealing with the environment, consumers, work safety, nuclear power, and abortion.

A great many of these children are long forgotten, for oblivion is the fate of a healthy majority of decided cases. A very small number of others have also vanished, but their disappearance was more memorable; these are the decisions that were reversed by the Supreme Court either directly or by the force of some decision on point in another case. Some that I had always thought promising and others that have surprised me by their influence are the cases that have endured for at least a few years as authorities in their field or niche. But a final group, which may not be nearly so respected, and indeed may include the forgotten and the reversed, is my favorite. It contains all the cases where I was privileged to feel creative in the process of constructing an opinion. Whether they had lasting significance or not, they provided the occasion, often enough to give permanent color to my working existence, for the steady satisfaction, continuing challenge, and frequent joy of creating judicial opinions.

Chapter 9

The Workings of Collegiality

IN DESCRIBING part of the essence of an appellate court as "collegial," I refer to the ancient meaning of "college," not a highly departmentalized institution but "an association of individuals having certain powers, rights, and duties, and engaged in some common pursuit." In applying the term collegial to an appellate court, we are using it with maximum precision, for the judges on such a court are a small and intimate band of brothers and sisters. They are all peers, having no real superior, their chief judge (in the federal system) being selected by seniority to bear certain administrative responsibilities. Their association with each other is long-lasting, often for the duration of their professional lives. They are independent, owing allegiance to no person or group. They have differing biases, values, and philosophies, but they share the common discipline of the law and a single fidelity — to their court and their joint product, the law it makes.

When I contemplate this mixture of qualities, I can think of no other contemporary institutional grouping that reaches this level of intimate, equal, permanent, independent, and single-minded collegiality. The editors of a large newspaper bring to their conference table their individual, sharply honed specialties. The members of a legislative committee cannot forget their allegiance to their constituents and parties. A firm of lawyers or a doctors' group practice relies on the diverse specialties of members. Coworkers in an executive branch agency or department function within a well-recognized hierarchy. Perhaps the faculty of a small college or a farmers' cooperative is a close analogue.

Because I believe this special kind of collegiality has much to do with the flavor, quality, and — at their best — the wisdom of appellate opinions, and because I have found little in judicial literature on this intensely personal relationship, I want to describe its workings in our court. I have another reason. I am by no means certain that the working relationships we have enjoyed on our court for at least the last decade and a half are typical of courts with three to five times as many judges. And change is inevitable for us. From our origin in 1891 until 1980, after most of this book was written, we remained at the smallest possible size for an appellate court, three judges. Although, like all federal courts of appeals, we continue to sit in panels of three to hear each case, Congress has authorized a fourth judge, and I suspect that a few years hence we shall be a court of seven or more. So what I describe may well be not only a special case of collegiality but an endangered species. That the qualities associated with smallness may endure even though smallness itself may not is my fervent hope.

Collegiality has several faces. One is intimacy. But it is intimacy beyond affection. It begins with a deep if selective knowledge of one another; no one knows our societal values, biases, and thought ways better than a colleague, even though he may never master the names of our children. It is fed from the spring of our common enterprise. It manifests itself in an abiding concern for each other and the court, with the ardent hope that there need never be a choice between the two. If there were, however, the latter would prevail, not despite intimacy but because of it. There is no instinct for competition; at argument there is no desire to appear to outperform colleagues. There is no envy, but rather satisfaction if a colleague shines brightly. Of course, we would be less than human if we did not feel twinges of "I wish I'd said that." But on the whole, on a court composed of able judges who do not feel the sting of a sense of inferiority or insecurity, there is as little pettiness and enmity as one can expect among people working together.

These feelings coalesce to produce customary conduct that is characterized by openness and forgiveness. By openness I mean an absence of dissimulation, maneuvering, or exploitation. We say what we mean, and, though much of our energy is spent in trying to convince each other, we rely on the words that clothe the thought. There is no additional sales pitch. Two judges may well exchange views to perfect an approach differing from that of their third colleague, but they do not "gang up" on that colleague. There are no secret two-way deals. As for forgiveness, we all need this dispensation, for we may have misled our colleagues by misciting a case, by forgetting to pass on critical information, by omitting to carry out some assigned duty, by misstating some fact in an opinion. There is no hiding such an error or its source. But I have never heard any bitter recriminations; each knows that the erring colleague needs no criticism from anyone else, any more than the pass receiver who drops the ball in the end zone.

One might think that such closeness of association and feelings of fraternity would set the stage for a continuing drama of brotherly self-sacrifice. In fact, despite closeness and good will, one thing that is never asked or given in the context of judicial duties is a favor. No matter how hard and long judges have slaved over an opinion and how much they may want the votes of colleagues, I have never known one to ask support for any other reason than that his opinion has been found convincing. Not only are the bonds of intimate association not exploited, as they might be in the business or political world by way of some reciprocal back-scratching,

but the dominant atmosphere is that of constant and institutionalized criticism. The whole reason for there being more
than one judge on an appellate court is that the different
perceptions, premises, logic, and values of three or more
judges ensure a better judgment. In these differences and in
the process of criticism, response, and resolution lies the virtue of the appellate process. The heart of collegiality is unremitting criticism.

Lest this overview of the strengths of collegiality appear a
bit too cloying, I hasten to add that there is a cost side to the
calculus. There are days when the best of colleagues rub
each other the wrong way, when the comments of another
seem like thinly veiled barbs aimed at oneself, when one is
misunderstood by the world and appreciated by no one.
Judges can occasionally wallow in self-pity as well as the
next person. They can snap out a cutting remark if tired,
frustrated, or pressed in discussing an important and emo-
tion-laden issue. But usually the sharpshooter, all too conscious of loss of control, soon finds a way to make amends.

In addition to such rare and minor lapses of civility, there
is always the need to subordinate one's preferences to some
extent. Unlike a solitary trial judge, a judge in a collegial
setting must compromise on many matters of substance. In
doing so, he not only suffers a temporary feeling of chafing
under consensus but often wonders whether he has sacri-
ficed any principle of value in accommodating to his colleagues. Another kind of self-suppression is restraint on style.
Merely to feel a responsibility for trying to achieve a consensus, if reasonably possible, tends to make me rub off the corners in what I write, dull the shiny surfaces, even play down
any aspiration to literary elegance, and homogenize language, for fear a colleague will deem it overrefined and be
uncomfortable with it. Even though the result is usually a
better judicial product, I occasionally yearn for opportunities to say exactly what I wish — without trimming, hedg-
ing, softening, or dropping thoughts.

Having made this confession, I reaffirm my conviction that such chafing is a small price to pay, or a small investment to make, in return for candid, open, and caring collegiality.

THE CASES

The Smuggler on the Dock

This case is the most collegial of our trilogy, which should come as no surprise when we recall the fairly active questioning by all the judges at oral argument and the points of view expressed in the judges' conference. Each judge had been most disturbed by a different issue.

After I finished my draft opinion, I had a few thoughts about the concerns my colleagues had expressed. Since none of us is enthusiastic about reversing a judgment because of insufficient evidence to support a jury verdict of guilty, I assured both colleagues that I had thoroughly canvassed the trial testimony and found no significant fact that had been omitted from the briefs. I also noted the critical pages in the transcript for them to read. I thought it well also, because of one judge's obvious skepticism about accepting the ancient definition of "smuggling," to say that I had unsuccessfully tried to draft language affirming the lower court on this point. I enclosed a copy of my effort so that they could see for themselves how it looked.

In several days' time both judges responded. While each concurred in the result, reversing and setting aside the judgment of conviction, each had different suggestions. Both judges accepted the section of the opinion concerning the insufficiency of evidence. Our experience with two recent cases presenting comparable situations made further persuasion unnecessary once we saw the facts clearly.

But the judge who I knew was not enthusiastic about the traditional definition of smuggling, though not saying that I

was wrong in following the definition in the *Keck* case, saw
no need for us to rule on the issue. After all, since the case
was to be reversed for a good reason, why must we decide
any other issue? He disliked our being the first court in recent times to adopt the old ruling and perhaps contribute to
upsetting a number of other convictions. Moreover, perhaps
before another case arose, Congress might clarify the law.

I could not dispute the fact that there was no need to
decide this issue in order to decide the case. What I did
suggest was that, after noting that we need not face this
issue, we evidence our concern about the old definition,
suggest that *Keck* is not easily disregarded, and express our
hope for remedial legislation. Communications of this nature between courts and Congress, in which a court calls attention to some weak spot in a statute needing repair, is seldom effective, yet there is always a chance that some
committee staff member will note the suggestion and prepare corrective legislation. Then, too, the suggestion may
elicit law journal commentary. And most pertinent, prosecutors in the circuit are forewarned that, before choosing a
particular statute to serve as the foundation of an indictment, they should make sure that some outdated meaning
has not been given it by the Supreme Court. There usually
is, as in this case, another statute that will fairly apply to the
facts. My colleague was completely happy with this approach. We had substituted a dictum for a holding. This
would perhaps be considered bad form in the law schools,
but it was, I felt, a sensible approach under the circumstances.

My other colleague's problem was with my treatment of
the admission of evidence of the ten-year-old conviction for
possession of a small amount of marijuana. He agreed with
me that the evidence should have been excluded under the
new rules of evidence. But he was most reluctant for us to
find that admitting this evidence was so egregiously in error
that the trial judge must be found, even without any objec-

tion having been made at trial, to have so abused his discretion — to have committed "plain error" — that reversal was
in order. He also pointed out that defendant's counsel had
not chosen to argue this issue orally, evidently not considering it very important. Although such an omission should
have no weight in legal analysis, it inevitably, in a close
case, has some influence.

My colleague did not rest after expressing his view, but
graciously took the trouble of drafting a substitute passage
that described the procedural posture on this issue, the absence of any objection at the time the judge finally ruled on
admissibility, and then stated that we could not quite hold
this to be plain error, although it went "dangerously to the
verge" of being such. I should have preferred to come right
out and call this plain error, but I did not think this was an
occasion for provoking a partial dissent. The proposed substitution served notice on trial judges and lawyers that this
kind of evidence is to be analyzed with utmost care and its
admission not encouraged. In due time we may have enough
experience with the new rule to sense whether there is a
need for further guidance.

The opinion, now reflecting our common ground for decision and also the gradations of our views on the two other issues, was ready to go. While it bears my name as writing
judge, this was a truly collegial opinion.

The Agency and the Anorectic

In this case my colleagues understandably took a longer
time to reply. They and their clerks reread briefs and
checked parts of the record I had found most important. To
the extent that I interpreted what certain cited cases meant,
they quickly developed their sense of whether I was correct.
But this kind of case is overwhelmingly factual, the facts and
various expert opinions being extraordinarily technical and
the record appendix being several thousand pages long.

It is simply not feasible for the nonwriting judges to spend as much time on such a case as the writing judge. This poses something of a dilemma. Judicial review must be by the whole court, not by just one of its judges. But the judges on the court cannot all be equally involved. The dilemma is practically if not logically resolved if the writing judge reports enough of the factual basis for the decision being reviewed, the principles followed in arriving at the decision, the specific attacks on the decision, and detailed assessment of both the principles supporting and the alleged defects in the decision for the other judges to do some spot-checking themselves and develop some feel, based on what they see in the record, for the rationality or irrationality of the agency's action.

I was gratified when my colleagues concurred in this case. Each judge sent me a list of a dozen or so minor corrections or suggestions. One small but important change in my draft required a footnote making clear that we expected the additional proceedings to be conducted with expedition. We left to the discretion of the FDA whether, if its final decision was to withdraw Thin-King from the market, it should make the order effective immediately on reaching its decision or await the termination of all future appellate proceedings, which might well provide the manufacturer with an extra year or so of marketing this long-litigated drug. This done, the opinion went to the printer.

The Saga of the Transferred Prisoners

Fano v. *Meachum* was a case where, because the members of the court had had ample opportunity to stake out their positions in earlier cases, there was no room for collegiality in the sense of exploring possible accommodations of opposing views. It is not surprising that, without extensive delay, the court agreed to disagree.

One colleague concurred in my draft opinion; my other

colleague submitted a succinct and thoughtful dissent. He began by recognizing that transfers, even within a state, could have a major impact on a prisoner's life. But Massachusetts had not created any statutory right for inmates to be at one correctional institution rather than another. The question was not only whether an individual suffered a grievous loss but also whether an individual had any right to protection against that loss. Looking at the problems inherent in maintaining secure and safe prisons, and considering that inmates are involuntary inhabitants and sometimes dangerous and unpredictable, our dissenting brother concluded that authorities must be able to act at times on "educated guesses based on suspicion" and that minimal due process, while perhaps wise, is not required by the Constitution. The dissent did, however, take the position that a prisoner's record, insofar as it receives consideration for parole purposes, should not contain any references to transfers if the charges on which the transfer was based were not established in accordance with due process. This seemed to me a nice piece of fine-tuning.

Our majority opinion and the dissent were issued on June 25, 1975. We stayed, or held up, carrying out our order transferring the inmates back to their original institution pending possible Supreme Court review. The prisoners urged us to vacate that stay on the ground that every circuit court which had considered intrastate transfers had held that due process should be observed. We denied their motion.

Exactly one year to the day after we issued our opinion, the Supreme Court acted, reversing our decision in an opinion written by Justice Byron White. Since the prison superintendent, Meachum, had filed the petition for review, the case took on its new title, *Meachum* v. *Fano*, 427 U.S. 215. The Court rejected at the outset the proposition that *"any* grievous loss visited upon a person by the State is sufficient to invoke the procedural protections of the Due Process

Clause."[1] The "determining factor," the opinion continued, "is the nature of the interest rather than its weight."[2] It went on to observe that an inmate is by definition someone who has already lost his liberty by constitutional means and that the Constitution does not require different grades of prison or an "audit" of a decision to assign a convict to one institution rather than another. The key to the Court's decision in *Wolff* v. *McDonnell*, we were told, was the fact that a liberty interest based on a state-created right was at stake. Here there was no state-imposed limitation on the power of officials to transfer prisoners. The conclusion: whatever expectation the prisoner may have in remaining at a particular prison so long as he behaves himself, it is too ephemeral and insubstantial to trigger procedural due process protections "as long as prison officials have discretion to transfer him for whatever reason or for no reason at all."[3]

Three justices dissented. Justice John Paul Stevens wrote for them, expressing concern not merely with the result but with the approach taken, which recognized that a liberty interest could have only two sources — the Constitution or a state law.

> If man were a creature of the State, the analysis would be correct. But neither the Bill of Rights nor the laws of sovereign States create the liberty which the Due Process Clause protects. The relevant constitutional provisions are limitations on the power of the sovereign to infringe on the liberty of the citizen. The relevant state laws either create property rights, or they curtail the freedom of the citizen who must live in an ordered society. Of course, law is essential to the exercise and enjoyment of individual liberty in a complex society. But it is not the source of liberty, and surely not the exclusive source.[4]

This observation on the source of liberty did not end his analysis, for these inmates, all serving sentences under unimpeached convictions, had been deprived of at least a considerable amount of their liberty after what must be assumed to have been fair trials. But Justice Stevens interpreted prior Supreme Court precedent as recognizing that even though one is in legal custody after conviction, there remains some liberty protectible by due process. If not, "if the inmates' protected liberty interests are no greater than the State chooses to allow, he is really little more than the slave described in the 19th century cases."[5] The justice concluded by confessing his inability "to identify a principled basis for differentiating between a transfer from the general prison population to solitary confinement and a transfer involving equally disparate conditions between one physical facility and another."[6]

A strong dissent and propositions that I think are sound, but for the moment at least they are not the law. And neither is our court's opinion in *Fano* v. *Meachum*.

REFLECTIONS ON KINDS OF COLLEGIALITY

On Anticipatory Collegiality

Of the several kinds of work situations in which collegiality can play important but different roles, what I call "anticipatory collegiality" is by all odds the most effective kind and, for the most part, is practiced only by judges who know each other very well. It is the instinctive and unself-conscious sensitivity to one's colleagues' sensibilities exhibited by a judge as he talks with or writes to his fellow judges. In writing an opinion he has a sixth sense of the way his colleagues are likely to react to each position and nuance. He recalls not only the questions asked by his fellows during argument and their comments during conferences on cases, but their biases, predispositions, values, and philosophies as years of service together have revealed them to him.

If I am taking a position that differs from what I think one of my colleagues would prefer, I will either state his position as fairly and strongly in the opinion as I can and proceed to deal with it, or, if for some reason there is no place in the opinion for such a discussion, I will cover the same ground in my covering letter forwarded with the opinion. In either event, my colleague will know that I have not casually rejected what I believe would be his preferred route. In our first case, that of the Smuggler on the Dock, my sending along to the other judges the discarded draft that attempted to reject the old (but sanctified) definition of smuggling was a variant of this kind of anticipatory collegiality.

The sensitive use of words is another manifestation of such collegiality. Sometimes a law clerk will submit to me a draft of some part of an opinion or of a memorandum to another judge, and I will find myself changing words and phrases almost without hesitation or thought. When I am asked why I made the changes, I hesitate. Then I answer somewhat like this: "We are using some words here that look perfectly neutral to you and to me, but to Judge ——— they are loaded with secondary and tertiary meanings. They are bound to emit bad vibrations." This is probably not too different from the attempt of a musician to explain how he knows when he is in tune with his fellow orchestra members.

Sometimes anticipatory collegiality requires no particular knowledge about one's colleagues. For example, whether I am sitting with old colleagues or with visiting judges, if my draft opinion addresses a close question or ploughs new ground, I will note in my covering letter what I have done that might go beyond anything we had talked about at our conference. I want my colleagues to know where to focus their attention. I may also try to indicate why I took the path I did, although I realize that if the opinion itself does not fly, no apologia will make it acceptable. Nevertheless, if I discuss the problems I encountered in trying to write the opinion as we had tentatively agreed, or point to some facts we had overlooked or to a persuasive opinion we had not focused on, I am assured of a fair hearing.

This kind of advance notice and anticipation of predictable response does not, of course, avoid the deeply grounded struggles. But it does help avoid unnecessary disputations, and it is useful in narrowing the scope of dispute and in advancing the dialogue. In so doing, it spares both time and tempers.

On Responsive Collegiality

A more common kind of collegiality is that encountered when nonwriting judges respond to draft opinions of the writing judge. There are varied gradations of response, some subtle, some not. Here are some typical responses and rough translations of their meaning:

- "A prodigious piece of work. I am more than happy to concur." This is saved for a job superbly well done or an equal occasion for superlatives — a tedious case from which one is happy to be spared.
- "I concur and have no suggestions." Probably both a dull and a simple case, which will not be printed in the permanent reports. The opinion might be perfected by detailed criticism, but it reached the correct result quite respectably and is not worth the time or trouble to change.
- "I gladly concur and have only the following nitpicks." A minor opinion but one worth publishing and therefore worth polishing.
- "I willingly concur but have a few suggestions of substance." The opinion is important enough to justify the reader's suggesting that some language be dropped, some be added, some footnotes deleted, and so forth. None of these suggestions is worth fighting about, but the opinion-writer would do well to consider them carefully.
- "I would like to concur but am troubled about one problem. Would you think about this and see if I have a point?" Chances are the point is a good one and the

opinion-writer will come back with a paragraph or footnote dealing with it.

- "I regret to say that I am troubled by your conclusion
  that . . . I enclose suggested new pages 8A to 13A to
  replace your pages 8 to 15." Only a close and trusted colleague would venture to respond thus. But this is an actual quotation from one of my case files. After shudder-
  ing slightly, I read the substitution, found much of it an
  improvement, and, later, came back with my redraft of
  his redraft.

- "I am sorry to say, particularly in light of the work you
  have obviously done, that I am in basic disagreement
  with your approach. I enclose a brief dissent." Or the
  memorandum may say, "While I can go along with the
  result, I thoroughly disagree with your reasoning. I enclose a separate concurring opinion." Sometimes, but
  not always, this kind of message heralds the inevitable:
  the differences are so deep that any further effort to resolve them is ill advised.

When I receive such memoranda from my fellow judges, I
cannot help feeling an instinctive emotional reaction that is
irrelevant and best immediately forgotten. If my colleague
applauds my work, I feel a thrill of triumph. If it is obvious
that he has "problems," grave reservations, or profound disagreement, I am filled with anguish. Any substantial criticism of one's best efforts cannot fail to assault one's pride.
Fortunately, a bit of time sees the anguish pass and I am
able to think constructively about the criticism, avoiding a
posture of either haughty rejection or servile acceptance.
What is likely to emerge could be selective acceptance of
some thoughts, with others questioned or rejected; critical
comment on the criticism, thus continuing the dialogue; a
devising of some new language that avoids the issue; perhaps the disposing of the case on an entirely different issue;
or sometimes the realization that my colleague's idea is far

better than mine and that I can build on it, with a substantial redraft of part or all of the opinion. In all these instances the criticism of a colleague becomes a resource of added strength, resulting in an improved product for the court.

In a large appellate court, where judges may not know each other very well or sit with each other very often, it may well be the better part of valor for a judge to be content with an opinion so long as it does not do violence to his views. But in our small and intimate court, we consider it our mission in life to work as hard as we can to make our colleague's signed opinion as sound and readable as possible. We therefore do not hesitate to proffer suggestions concerning wording, organization, footnotes, the use of authorities, and so on, sometimes to a degree others find mystifying. There is one rule we impose on ourselves that makes this tolerable: if we don't like something in a colleague's opinion, we feel bound in most cases to submit substitute wording.

It is surprising what this simple requirement does for us. In the first place, we frequently find, when we put pen to paper and try to improve on our colleague's draft, that we are unable to come up with anything really better. In the second place, if we are able to show how a supposed defect can be remedied, a thoughtful memorandum containing suggested language is far more effective in changing another's position than loosely phrased talk.

When the response is nothing less than complete disagreement, one might think it would automatically signal a dissent. Not necessarily. Sometimes a disagreeing response provokes a reply from the opinion-writer that succeeds in convincing the skeptic. At other times the writer is moved to alter his opinion and the critic is content to see the opinion narrowed, the rhetoric changed, a footnote put into the text or some text made a footnote or the emphasis shifted. And there are occasions when the response so moves the writer that he is willing to change his position as much as 180 degrees.

There are times, however, when a dissent should be encouraged. I am not referring only to cases where a judge has a strong and deep conviction that the majority is wrong; here, of course, the judge should proclaim his differences. But there are other cases in which the issue is both important and evenly balanced and, while the court may be divided, both the majority and the minority can see the reason in the other's position. Such was obviously the case of the transferred prisoners. Often, in such a situation, all the judges will welcome a dissent in order to reflect the closeness of the issue, to advance reasoned analysis, and perhaps even to stimulate the Supreme Court to accept the case for review. On such occasions, it happens that even judges on the majority side do not hesitate to make suggestions that help strengthen the dissent.

On Simultaneous Collegiality

There is, finally, the total and immediate experience I call "simultaneous collegiality." I have found it mainly in two kinds of cases. The first is the emergency hearing on a request for bail, for an injunction, or for a stay of a lower court's order pending an appeal. Sometimes these matters can be handled by a single judge. Others require either a minimum of two judges or a full panel of three. With uncanny regularity, they are likely to materialize on a Friday afternoon, in mid-August, or on a holiday eve. When this happens, we drop everything else. Our pulses quicken. Cases are hurriedly gathered in each set of chambers. Phone calls to colleagues are frequent and long. We decide within a few hours or overnight. The process, compared to our usual pace, is dramatically telescoped, but within the few hours the case has received the intense focus of at least two judges and their clerks. At such times I can fully appreciate the loneliness of the district judge as he makes his solitary decisions. I give profound thanks that I have two colleagues whose wisdom, instinct, and experience are poured into the crucible of decision.

The second kind of decision-making warranting the caption of simultaneous collegiality is found in cases of great moment and urgency and of high public interest. Issues arising from litigation involving school desegregation, the closing or upgrading of jails and other public institutions, disputes involving key public officials and governmental bodies are examples. In such cases there will be detailed contributions from each judge.

One case of recent memory will illustrate how the process works. We heard full oral argument on an appeal from the district court's denial of an injunction. Because of his denial, one of the parties was to take an important, irreversible action in ten days unless we ruled within that period and reversed the district court. When we ended our judges' conference, we sensed in varying degrees that we would wind up affirming, but all of us were deeply concerned, because the issue was of large significance. Each of us agreed to go over a different issue during the next several days and let the others know if there was a real likelihood of reversible error based on that issue.

I had undertaken the responsibility to write the opinion as a whole, and spent the following week reading the thick record, discussing issues with my clerk, writing up the issue I had agreed to look at first, and talking with my colleagues. Drawing on our own research and my sense of the other judges' reactions at our conference and in our telephone conversations, my clerk and I drafted in one day the rest of the opinion and sent it out by express mail so that the other judges could review the text over the weekend. They carefully went over what we had written and on Monday phoned in their suggestions, including a very good section that gave valuable guidance to the district court in future proceedings. Although total time from oral argument to the issuance of the opinion was only ten days, my feeling was that the case received maximum consideration from all three judicial chambers — but in a much shorter period of time than was usual. In other words, we had invested as much thought and as many hours within a span of five to eight actual working days as we do on other cases that may take months.

On Collegial Governance

Thus far, we have been seeing how collegiality works in the deciding of cases — the mission of the judiciary. Like other collegial bodies, however, the judiciaries of both the states and the federal government have, to a very large degree, the responsibility of self-governance. This includes making rules to govern judges (legislative), administering properties, finances, and personnel (executive), and monitoring the conduct of judicial officials and employees (judicial). The first two functions have been highly developed and institutionalized; the third function has been performed more informally. The traditional nature of collegial bodies, such as guilds and universities, is such that governance is not the province of specialists but is rather one more function to be shared by all peers in the community. So it is with the judiciary.

The federal system of judicial governance consists of both a regional and a national level. The regions are the eleven judicial circuits. Within each circuit, both the district courts and the court of appeals, some of them having hundreds of judicial officers and other employees, have their own sometimes formidable management and housekeeping duties. But the critical institution that has oversight responsibility for both sets of courts is the judicial council of the circuit, created by Congress in response to a plea by the federal judiciary that it be allowed to manage its own affairs. It consists of all the active circuit judges within a circuit and has as its charter a simple statute that empowers it to make such orders as are necessary in the interests of "the active and expeditious administration of the business of the courts within its circuit.''[7] Until recent years the thrust of a council's oversight was casual and informal. It would initiate requests for filling vacancies or appointing additional personnel, review and approve new rules for district courts, and occasionally deal with problems posed by the conduct of a judge, the last often being the inevitable lessening of his powers because of aging. In such cases the chief judge, through quiet talks and gentle suasion, would eventually, without the necessity of formal complaint and hearing, obtain the retirement of the judge.

Recently, particularly in the large circuits, councils have become more formal institutions, with agenda, standing committees of judges, regularly scheduled meetings, and a secretariat under the supervision of a new court official, the circuit executive. Many have adopted for the first time rather elaborate procedures for considering, hearing, and adjudicating complaints against judges. These procedures were set up in the anticipation that councils could impose minor sanctions, like censure, but that the more serious cases would result in recommendations by a council to the Judicial Conference of the United States, the federal judiciary's top policy-making body. The most serious cases would result in recommendations by the conference to the Congress that the latter body consider impeachment proceedings. In such a case, the Congress would have laid before it a fully developed, investigated, and considered set of charges, evidence, and preliminary findings, all this presumably simplifying any subsequent impeachment proceedings.

Congress itself has been considering various approaches toward strengthening and making more formal the governance of the federal judiciary. One proposal would provide for membership of district judges on the judicial councils, thus providing some expertise from the district court level in the consideration of management problems, as well as the guarantee of knowledgeable and sensitive persons in any disciplinary proceedings involving district judges. Another proposal would make more clear the statutory charter of circuit

councils and enact in statutory form such disciplinary procedures as those voluntarily adopted by many of the circuits.
Other proposals would go further and create a specialized
disciplinary staff and court.

The apex of the federal judicial community and its governance at the national level is the Judicial Conference of the
United States, its professional staff resources, the Administrative Office of the U.S. Courts, and the Federal Judicial
Center, with its network of committees. By law, the conference, meeting twice a year, consists of the chief justice of the
United States, the chief judges of the eleven circuits, one district judge from each circuit, and the chief judges of the
Court of Claims and the Court of Customs and Patent Appeals. The staff support for the federal judiciary is lodged in
two agencies, the Administrative Office of the United States
Courts and the Federal Judicial Center. The Administrative
Office, although not free from the thrust of endemic growth,
is still small — just under 500 people. Its mission is to help
the federal judiciary manage with efficiency its personnel,
budgetary, statistical, supply, and space needs. More often
than not, it is of help. The key officials of the Administrative
Office serve as the Secretariat of the Judicial Conference,
rapporteurs of committees, and a source of technical expertise on all administrative matters.

A newer entity, the Federal Judicial Center, is the research
and educational arm of the federal judiciary. For over a decade it has mounted research programs designed to improve
the management of cases, the use of computers in both administration and legal research, the processing of appeals,
and the gathering, testing, and analyzing of data bearing on
all phases of the judicial process, from the selection of juries
to the publication of opinions. In carrying out its mission of
continuing education, it organizes seminars for district and
circuit judges, newly appointed and veterans alike, clerks of
court, circuit executives, probation officers, magistrates, and
bankruptcy judges.

The third linchpin of the governance apparatus of the Judicial Conference is its committee system. Over the past four decades of governance in the federal judiciary, standing committees have been created to deal with such major functions as rules, court administration, and budget. Then there are committees having more specialized concerns, reflecting the entire spectrum of the judicial department — juries, the criminal law, probation, magistrates, bankruptcy — and committees monitoring the financial reporting of judges and giving ethical advice to them. Finally, there are special-purpose committees set up to deal with a specific project or problem. At my last count there were twenty-six committees and subcommittees involving the participation of roughly 180 judges, approximating one third of the federal judiciary. In short, one out of three judges has something to do with governing his colleagues. This involvement, moreover, is the result merely of committee work at the national level. We should also recognize that every district and circuit court having more than three or four judges relies on committees of judges to perform important functions, and that nearly all the judicial councils of the circuits similarly operate by judicial committees.

Herein lies a subtle threat to the federal judiciary, and perhaps to that of many states — the increasing diversion of judicial minds to the performance of tasks bearing only a remote relationship to the judging process. The process is now all too familiar. A legal scholar, a senator or congressional representative, the attorney general, the American Bar Association or one of its specialized sections, or some other institution or individual, will come forward with an idea calculated to develop or improve standards governing judicial personnel and proceedings, expedite the litigation process, modernize communications, and facilitate the gathering, reporting, and analyzing of data. The idea will be referred to a committee of the Judicial Conference.

Once a committee is asked (or specially organized) to look into something, the die is cast. The committee predictably finds that the problem is more serious and widespread than has been supposed; there are various alternative remedies that require study; the committee should remain in existence; it should be authorized to contract with an institution for an expert survey; all judges should respond to the questionnaire, and circuit councils and conferences should discuss the committee's proposals; and judges should communicate their views by a date certain or remain silent at their peril. Eventually a final report is filed, recommending some new procedures, criteria, standards, guidelines, periodic meetings, or the systematic collection, analysis, and submission of data.

To argue against such proposals is, I know, to fight progress. But the drawback is that each new requirement levies on judicial time and further bureaucratizes and centralizes the judiciary, the genius of which has been its independence, its deliberateness, and the quality of its thought. Years ago there may have been enough slack in the judicial workload to absorb this extra demand on judges for other objectives than to decide cases as best they can. But as we have seen, the judiciary has risen to the challenge of increasing litigation by trebling its output of decisions. It is now at the point where every new administrative or non-case-related chore or function carries with it a cost in judges' diminished capacity to decide cases.

My instinct for survival, admittedly far easier to apply in the smallest of the circuits, is to think small, to be skeptical of proposals that require added staff, meetings, or reports, to resist forming permanent committees, to suspend judgment on much of the sophisticated technology designed to spare us from our labors. I do not say that my mind is closed; only that I am increasingly concerned that the devices of technology and the systems of modern management which are invoked to solve the problems of quantity and expedition may divert our energies from the goal of the highest quality of justice.

III
THOUGHT WAYS

Chapter 10

Craft Skills
and Social Values

WE SHALL CONSIDER the thought ways of a judge from several
viewpoints, ranging from "What underlies judges' thinking?" and "What is the public view of the way in which
judges think?" to "What do scholars think ought to influence
judges' thinking?" and "How right are the scholars?" and
"What, if any, frontiers of thought remain to be explored by
judges?"

I have been careful not to attempt to answer the question
"How do judges think?" or even "How do I think?" Not only
do I lack any ambition to prescribe for my profession, but
unless a judge were an extraordinary introvert and a psychi-
atrically trained one at that, he could not begin to describe
with candor and completeness what goes on in a judicial
mind in the deciding of a case. Nevertheless, there are steps
that can be taken to dispel mythology, illumine an underlying common framework of precepts shared by all judges,
highlight kinds of widely shared preconceptions, trace the
flow of the mainstream of scholarly thought about how
judges should approach their work, and test whether there is
room for any new thinking and, if so, the direction in which
this might lie.

THE JUDGE AS JOBBIST

Our point of beginning is to recognize that, though judging is a profession, with such implications of higher learning as may inhere in the word, it is also a craft, with certain principles, rules, and devices that are applied by all members, from the traffic court judge to the chief justice of the United States. To use a favorite word of Learned Hand, we are "jobbists." We know that most of our decisions that contribute to the law of today are destined for oblivion tomorrow. While we take pride in whatever contribution we may be favored to make, we take equal pride in the way in which the contribution is crafted. As Judge Hand put it, "In all chosen jobs the craftsman must be at work, and the craftsman . . . gets his hire as he goes."[1]

To the extent that we do our job well, using the disciplines of our guild well, we move from mere jobbist to craftsman and occasionally to master craftsman when we write an opinion that marshals facts and precedents, logic and analogy, and the broad policy implications of the decision in contemporary society so that the result is seen as fair, expectable, and perhaps even inevitable.

The first set of thought ways of a judge is, therefore, the framework of precepts and ways of using them that judges share by reason of their craft and court. Certainly judges derive fulfillment from practicing their trade with competence and sometimes with excellence, but their performance is judged according to the extent to which they succeed or fail in doing so. At present, judgment on these largely technical grounds is the province of a judge's peers, lawyers, academic scholars, and editors of the law journals. But I have the conviction that lay people can develop an understanding of the reasonable expectations of, and restraints on, the judicial craft; they can achieve a capacity for making fair assessments.

The tools, doctrines, and techniques in this craft-dominated part of a judge's thought ways were discussed in Chapter 4 in the section entitled "The Conventions Affecting Decision." They also played by far the major role in reaching decision in the three cases we followed in Part II. In this respect, the cases mirror the general judicial experience of an appellate judge. For although, as we shall see, moral values, ideas of social utility, and philosophical insights occasionally play a significant role, most issues in most cases are resolved by the precepts common to judges and the courts on which they sit.

Cases during trial and appellate argument are hotly contested, and the pros and cons seem, even as late as the judges' conference after argument, to weigh evenly, but the processes of hearing argument, studying the briefs and record, researching the law, and consulting with law clerks and colleagues will lead a court in the large majority of cases to a consensus on both the outcome and the approach to be taken, whatever may be the background or philosophical bent of the individual judges. Craft-related factors, such as a case on point or clearly analogous, analysis of the evidence or a ruling by the trial court, a procedural or jurisdictional requirement, a compelling public policy, a close reading of legislative history, and considerations of institutional appropriateness, will in the end decide most cases.

Not only do judges share this body of craft skills and learning, but judges on the same kind and level of court develop thought patterns peculiar to that court. Some are precepts, some represent favored techniques, but others are attitudes embracing moral judgments, views of sound social policy, and sometimes even philosophical convictions. Some are good, some bad — depending on the values of the observer-critic, but all are especially relevant to one kind of court.

The court of first resort, the most accessible to all the people, is the municipal or local court. For the parties appearing in that court, the important considerations are the judge's attitudes toward speeding, first offenders, repeaters, drug cases, white-collar crime, probation, bail, alternative service in lieu of fine or imprisonment, restitution of property stolen, mothers versus fathers in child custody cases, and the like. Even more important are the judge's underlying reservoir of compassion, knowledge of human nature, and common sense. I would say that the special kind of thought way characteristic of what I call "the people's court" of first resort has to do with making and effectively communicating judgments about people, on a one-to-one basis.

The next level is that of a court of general trial jurisdiction, the superior court of a state or a federal district court. The attitudes and habits of mind that count in the eyes of all whose fate is to be settled in that court are to some extent those we have just discussed. But they also include the judge's attitude toward discovery, pretrial conferences, stimulating settlements, letting in or keeping out evidence, interjecting much or little during the trial; his attitudes at sentencing toward the defendant, the crime, and the goals of sentencing; and his approaches to devising appropriate remedies in civil cases. Strangely, the trial judge, though often straitjacketed by the law, has more freedom in all these areas than judges on higher courts. In addition, the trial judge in a court of general jurisdiction must administer a complicated institution, deal with all kinds of court personnel, jurors, witnesses, litigants, lawyers, press, and public, and somehow manage to keep moving a steadily increasing stream of cases. The special thought ways of such a judge, largely unshared by judges on higher or lower courts, draw on the prudential lore and mutually supporting attitudes of the administrator, manager, diplomat, psychiatrist, and public relations expert. Finally, the trial judge must have the courage and resourcefulness to make difficult decisions alone and under heavy pressures of time and public emotion.

The appellate courts, the top courts of a state or federal circuit, have their own special concerns: maintaining fidelity to their own precedents or, conversely, deciding whether, when, and how to modify or overrule them; keeping watch over, and seeking to improve, the appellate process; exercising oversight and supervisory power over the entire court family, from judges to prosecutors, jurors, and the bar; and developing folkways, thought patterns, subtle signals, and modulated responses that make up their own brand of collegiality.

THE JUDGE AS INTERPRETER OF VALUES

Although the skills of the craft determine the outcome of most cases, the public and the press sense that in some of the most important cases there is more at work than professional judgment alone. Otherwise judges of high quality would always reach the same result. Moreover, the public expects judicial decisions to be in harmony with its moral values and to contribute to the health and progress of society. Sometimes, as when, in a time of crisis, it looks with disfavor on conscientious objectors or aliens, it invokes a cool utilitarian arithmetic — greatest good for the greatest number, and the devil take the hindmost. Perhaps the most remembered example of the results of discordance between public expectations and judicial performance was the 1857 decision of the Supreme Court in *Dred Scott* v. *Sandford*, 19 Howard 393, which held that when a slaveholder took his slave into free territory and then back into a slave state, the slave status of the human property continued. This, wrote one distinguished scholar, "was one of the most dramatic episodes which aroused public opinion in the North and touched off the war four years later."[2]

This instinct for the "something else" in judicial decision-making, whether it be social utility or harmony with society's moral values or both, has led to an effort by citizens to analyze and label judges. The result has not been successful. The public's perception of the judiciary is at best spotty. Knowledge about the thought ways of judges, as distinguished from their work ways and folkways, seems to have originated in myth and to be perpetuated by convention. According to that convention, judges can be neatly pigeonholed as enforcing "law and order" or as being "soft on criminals," as using "strict" or "loose" construction, as favoring "judicial restraint" or "judicial activism," and, finally, as being "conservative" or "liberal." Indeed, judges are filed under one or more of these pairings as if craft constraints played no part at all.

The fact that these four dichotomies exhaust the philosophic vocabulary of most editorial writers, political interest groups, and ordinary citizens is proof of the low state of the art of judge-watching. If these familiar labels ever etched a consistent profile, that day is past. Justice Hugo Black, for example, found ample scope for a "loose" interpretation of the Fourteenth Amendment's admonition that no state shall "deprive any person of life, liberty, or property without due process of law." Indeed, he was the principal architect of the view that the entire Bill of Rights was binding on the states by reason of its "incorporation" into the Fourteenth Amendment. But he was as literal or as "strict" as he could be whenever the First Amendment came into play. To take a more current example, if the justices of the Supreme Court named by President Richard Nixon were supposed to be exemplars of strict construction, restraint, and conservatism, what do we make of the fact that among their ranks were the author and some of the major supporters of *Roe* v. *Wade*, 410 U.S. 113 (1973), which declared the hitherto unrecognized right of a woman to an abortion in the first three months of her pregnancy? This decision was among the most innovative, value-laden, and controversial examples of constitutional extrapolation that have issued from the Court in recent years.

All that I think can be justly said about the utility of applying overworked labels to judges is that they are appropriate to some judges on some issues some of the time. But to use them as generic descriptions characterizing judges on supposedly major points of difference exaggerates the extent to which they may fairly apply. They also carry such emotional freight that they more often terminate than advance thought. Yet the public instinct is well if not accurately grounded, for a judge does inevitably have moral values and personal views about the causes and cures of our society's ills.

The values of one type, common to judges and lay persons alike, are instant responses to certain inflammatory stimuli. We carry as part of this baggage such reactions as repugnance to or liking for a political party, a homosexual, a social revolutionary, a community leader; an attitude toward counsel preconditioned by reputation; intense aversion to the events giving rise to the litigation, such as the murder of a police officer or the vending of child pornography; a preexisting view of the strengths and frailties of an official or agency whose acts are at issue, including, on the part of appellate judges, such a view of the trial judge. These factors are value judgments that have the potential of influencing decision. Since judges are human beings, such reactions cannot be prevented from entering their minds, but they can and should be identified, exposed to self-conscious analysis, and ruthlessly excised as far as humanly possible before decisions are made. Sometimes a postargument conference among judges will perform its greatest service when one of these reactions is brought to the surface by conversation. Like various forms of mold, they cannot withstand sunlight. This process suggests what often happens when a jury has been exposed to pretrial publicity about a defendant: after a conscientious and skillful trial judge has discussed the irrelevance of such information in the trial of the case before them and put the jurors on their honor not to assign any

weight to it, the jury will usually prove to have merited the
confidence placed in it. Another disinfectant is the very process of writing down reasons for a decision. If the real reason
is one that cannot stand the light of day, the hesitation of the
pen signals to the morally aware judge that he has just been
saved from his prejudices.

A second set of values often derives from the social, economic, and political background of the judge. Sometimes
these values spring very specifically from the nature of the
law practice in which the judge had engaged. In negligence
and products-liability cases, for example, resorting to the in-
stinctual thought patterns one had as a plaintiff's or defendant's lawyer is a hard habit to overcome. So is yielding to
the analysis natural to a judge's former role as a prosecutor
or defense lawyer. There is nothing like a very close, hard-
fought labor-management case to test a judicial panel's ability to rise above its prejudices. For the judge who developed
a regulatory program as a government official or who challenged one on behalf of a company, a case pitting an enforcement agency against a regulated industry may summon
battle-hardened instincts. If a judge's prior law practice does
not bear on a particular case, his schooling or religion or
other personal experience may.

Still relatively new on the scene are the social reform–
oriented, class-action suits against government institutions
and private employers, which thrust students and teachers
against school boards and universities, tenants against land-
lords and housing authorities, welfare recipients against
state welfare departments, prisoners against wardens,
women, nonwhites, the elderly, and homosexuals against
their employers, abortion-seeking women against state legislators, environmentalists against industrialists and utility
companies. Judges may vary widely in their predispositions,
being proestablishment in some categories, proplaintiff in
others, depending on their background. The difference between the good judge and the poor one is not that the former

has been sterilized of all taint of his own experience but that he knows his enemy, himself, and is on guard.

A third group of values is neither good nor bad. Insofar as these values defy rational justification for their automatic application in any one case, they exert an influence quite apart from the merits of the case. They are essentially a mystery. Determining why a judge should embrace one set of attitudes rather than another is probably a task for the most sophisticated jurisprudence — or tea leaves. The fact is that judges often differ in the weights they assign to certain values in the judicial process. For some reason it also seems to be true that these values tend to be divided into two contesting groups.

The two respected generals in the field of judicial decision are Process and Substance. The former commands such battalions as reliance on the adversary process, deference to the trial judge or expert agency, the finality of decision, the administrative difficulty or workability of implementing a judicially imposed rule or standard, and the need to prevent the courts from being deluged with cases. Serving under the escutcheon of Substance are the battalions devoted to achieving a correct and fair result, a sound administrative policy, faithfulness to precedent, justice done despite unequal abilities of counsel, and standing to right a wrong by anyone to whom a wrong has been done.

Ideally, and frequently, Process and Substance fight toward the same end. But sometimes faithfulness to Process results in the exclusion of a party or an issue from the litigation, in the countenancing of certain errors committed by the trial court, in tolerating agency decisions that, while wrong from a court's point of view, are not quite irrational. By the same token, faithfulness to Substance may mean that a fair, wise, and legally sound decision is rendered at the expense of deference to other courts, agencies, or governmental units, or to established procedures.

Each of these warring concepts is worthy. Each reflects a

value with a positive weight. One can easily understand how
a judge could defer to an intelligent and painstaking decision by a trial judge after a hard-fought trial and conclude
that there is virtue in finality, without further prolonging litigation. But one can also sympathize with the appellate
judge who feels that that decision would jeopardize the future sensible development of the law or would frustrate
legislative policy or, simply, would be unfair. Similarly, a
judge may be deeply concerned with the danger of overbur-
dening the courts and may take a restrictive view on allowing access to them — or he may be just as deeply concerned
about the denial of such access by what to him appear as
overtechnical rulings.

A judge can look at a claim of deprivation of constitutional
rights from the point of view of a harassed official or under-
funded institution and conclude that to expect adherence to
high standards of conduct is just not workable. But his colleague can look at the individual's sense of loss and the frustration of his expectation of fairness and come to an opposite
conclusion.

So it is clear that judges do bring to their work certain
moral values and views of social policy arising from their
own nature, social and economic background, and prior
practice, and perhaps from their reflections about the proper
role of courts. These values and views are for the most part
unacknowledged and unreasoned, but their existence
teaches us that it makes no more sense to deny that judges
have values than it does to pretend that their work should be
judged solely by craft standards or that the common simplistic labels assigned to judges provide any adequate or
helpful basis for judgment.

These attitudes are the stuff of philosophy; they represent
legitimate but conflicting values. They themselves are not
philosophies. They may be splinters, implying that somewhere there is a larger plank. But they lack any guide or key
that enables the judge to derive a decision from a broader

system of principles in a logical and internally consistent way, satisfying both his intellect and his universe of moral values.

No wonder. For we judges are not jurisprudents. We arrive at our decisions most of the time without trying to tap the wellsprings of jurisprudential or moral philosophy. The insights and thinking of the scholars of the law come to us in articles and books, or in essays about the ideas in the articles and books, or talks with people who have read the essays or articles or books. Sometimes a ruling is determined by a Supreme Court case or doctrine we are bound to follow. Yet there is often some area left open by the cases for the play of larger insights and values. There is no institutionalized way of digesting and using these resources, but they exist in abundance. We shall inquire how jurisprudence has contributed and may still contribute to the thought ways of a judge.

Chapter 11

Loss of Innocence
and the
Quest for Legitimacy

THE JUDICIAL GARDEN OF EDEN

In the beginning there was no need for judges or lay people to concern themselves with the question of what factors, other than craft skills, might legitimately or properly be considered by judges. There was no question of the legitimacy of judicial decisions, because judges were not viewed as making or changing law. The notion through the eighteenth and nineteenth centuries, when the common law reigned in this country, with very few statutes challenging its hegemony, was that "law" existed wholly apart from men and that the task of judges was simply to find and declare it. Since, by assumption, judges were not imposing their own values or making any other human contribution than their service as a conduit, their decisions announcing the true law were legitimate beyond question. The only appropriate basis for criticism might be that the judge was not sufficiently perceptive.

This concept has been referred to as the oracular theory of judging, the essence of which is that "judging was not regarded in the nineteenth century as an exercise in making law. Rather, law was conceived of as a mystical body of permanent truths, and the judge was seen as one who declared what these truths were and made them intelligible — as an oracle who 'found' and interpreted the law."[1] While this terminology suggests a religious concept of law, the judiciary being its priesthood, the oracular tradition is equally consistent with the view of law as science. Indeed, the establishment of law as a science properly included in the curriculum of a university was the mission of Christopher Columbus Langdell, dean of the Harvard Law School from 1870 to 1895. The tenets of his credo were that "law is a science" and that "all the available materials of that science are contained in printed books," the books being the reports of judicial opinions that a student had to study, compare, and classify, as would a student of chemistry or biology.[2]

Although the concept of law as pure science was more sophisticated and less arbitrary than that of law as religion or mystical reality, it still presupposed that there was only one correct answer to every legal problem. That answer would give itself up to the judge who applied himself with disciplined intelligence to the problem; there was no need or room for a judge's values or sense of the evolution of society. In this view of the law, a judge could be criticized for his shortcomings as a scientist, but the legitimacy of his approach was unquestioned.

Holmes and the Tree of Knowledge

Then, in 1880, Oliver Wendell Holmes, Jr., published "The Common Law," in which he effectively exposed the subjectivity implicit in the oracular theory. Judges, Holmes pointed out, were called on to choose between public policies, that is, to be legislators:

> Whenever a doubtful case arises, with certain analogies on one side and other analogies on the other . . . what really is before us is a conflict between two social desires, each of which seeks to ex-

tend its dominion over the case, and which cannot both have their way . . . When there is doubt the simple tool of logic does not suffice, and even if it is disguised and unconscious, the judges are called on to exercise the sovereign prerogative of choice.[3]

Holmes left no doubt as to the nature and source of judgment when this sovereign prerogative was exercised:

> In substance the growth of the law is legislative. And this in a deeper sense than that what the courts declare to have always been the law is in fact new. It is legislative in its grounds. The very considerations which judges most rarely mention, and always with an apology, are the secret root from which the law draws all the juices of life. I mean, of course, considerations of what is expedient for the community concerned.[4]

This was the moment of truth. But there is a price to be paid for eating the fruit of the tree of knowledge. If judges do not speak as oracles, drawing either on a body of mystical knowledge or on science, but reflect personal values in exercising the "sovereign prerogative of choice," then suitable principles for controlling and limiting the scope of such choices must be found. If not, this country would find itself in the anomalous position of having granted open-ended power to its least democratic element.

Shortly after "The Common Law" was published, Professor J. B. Thayer of Harvard Law School published an article that was to have a long-enduring influence. He wrote:

> The judicial function is merely that of fixing the outside border of reasonable legislative action, the boundary beyond which the taxing power, the power of eminent domain, police power, and legislative power in general, cannot go without violating the prohibitions of the Constitution or crossing the line of its grants.[5]

A court, Thayer concluded, could set aside a legislative act only if it had made such an egregious mistake that the statute was irrational. In short, "whatever choice is rational is constitutional."[6]

This was Thayer's effort to identify principles that could serve as unwritten law, keeping judges from exercising power in an arbitrary or unprincipled way. The quest for legitimacy had begun.

A HALF-CENTURY OF FERMENT: THREE SCHOOLS

While Thayer's teaching was a purely negative command to judges to defer to legislatures, other ideas embodying more positive demands on judges were fermenting in the minds of academics and some jurists during the first half of this century. All took as their premise that the law was not a pre-existing reality hovering in the atmosphere, ready to be found by perceptive judges. All agreed that judges were not possessed of a roving commission. And all struggled for meaningful guidance.

The first set of ideas, embraced in various ways by Dean Roscoe Pound, Justice Brandeis, the then Professor Frankfurter, and others, called on judges to pay greater attention to the social context of cases, nonlegal facts, and empirical observations of changing conditions. These ideas came to march under the banner Pound had given them, Sociological Jurisprudence.

Drawing on Sociological Jurisprudence, but leaving it far behind, came the lusty Legal Realists, led by Judge Jerome Frank. Coming full circle from nineteenth-century oracular approaches, the Legal Realists debunked rules, principles, and the aspiration for certainty as mere myths cloaking the willfulness inherent in judicial decisions. Nothing positive was attempted as guidance, except perhaps a greater use of experts and recourse to mature psychological insights into one's own biases, the assumption being that once the myths were exposed, judges would have no trouble in promulgating rational decisions that would shape a just society.

This excessive reliance on psychological maturity led to harder analysis and the Legal Process school, which advocated building into the judging process a cultivated awareness of the different competences of the various branches of government and a sense of what was appropriate for legislatures, agencies, other judicial systems, and private parties to decide, as distinguished from the courts. For example, legislatures are so much better equipped to gather and analyze complex facts, weigh competing social interests, and develop broad policy that courts should only rarely attempt to substitute their judgment for that of legislatures. Thus did Legal Process advocates emphasize institutional constraints.

The legal historian G. Edward White gives us this capsule summary of a half-century of ferment:

> No longer, then, was the twentieth-century appellate judge an oracle; he was, depending on the theory advanced, primarily a social engineer, or a "hunch player" who understood and trusted his instincts, or a craftsman in the "reasoned elaboration" of justifications for his power.[7]

As the first half-century came to a close, the Legal Process school, already the acknowledged leader, took on added prestige. In the first place, Justice Frankfurter, his contributions to Sociological Jurisprudence long past, had come to be looked to as an apostle of restraint on the part of the courts. In a 1955 essay entitled "John Marshall and the Judicial Function,"[8] he endeavored to give a "distillation of sixteen years of reflection." He began with a recognition of the vast changes in the scope of law since the time of Chief Justice John Marshall. "Law," he wrote, "has been an essential accompaniment of the shift from 'watchdog government' . . . to the service state . . . Profound social changes continue to be in the making, due to movements of industrialization, urbanization, and permeating egalitarian ideas."

Noting the response of lawyers and courts to these changes in seeking "in the Fourteenth Amendment resources for curbing legislative responses to new pressures," the justice proceeded to reveal his uneasiness with "the slippery

slope of due process," referring to the due process and equal
protection clauses as "vague and admonitory," "ambulant,"
of "dubious . . . appropriateness for judicial enforcement."
He accepted the fact that judges were called on to make
judgments on these issues, "demanding . . . a breadth of
outlook and an invincible disinterestedness rooted in temperament and confirmed by discipline." Yet his essay, full of
"undertones of a judge's perplexities," concluded with his
wish that courts set the standards of what is fair and just in
"appropriate" cases but that these standards be largely applied by others throughout government.

In 1958, Circuit Judge Learned Hand, then eighty-seven,
delivered the Holmes Lectures at the Harvard Law School.
Always a prestigious forum, the series took on added incan-
descence from the rare combination of excellence and lon-
gevity embodied by the lecturer. The wisdom was that of
one who had seen almost, though not quite, enough of government and law, aspiration and frustration. Perhaps more
than Frankfurter, Hand took a n.ost restrictive view of judicial review of legislation, seeing its sole justification as being
the only means "to prevent the defeat of the venture at
hand,"[9] that is, to prevent impasse or totally unchecked departmental supremacy. He said in words reminiscent of
Thayer that he would "confine the power to the need that
evoked it: that is, it was and always has been necessary to
distinguish between the frontiers of another Department's
authority and the propriety of its choices within those frontiers."[10] When Hand came to analyze under what circumstances courts should intervene to protect individual rights
against governmental actions within their proper boundaries, he ended on a note of despondency, saying, "I do not
know what the doctrine is as to the scope of [the due process
clauses of the Fifth and Fourteenth Amendments] . . . I have
never been able to understand on what basis it [court intervention in such cases] does or can rest except as a *coup de
main.*"[11]

Not only had these two titans of the law lent their im-

mense prestige to the teachings of limitation and restraint of
the Legal Process school, but younger scholars contributed
enlightening glosses. Only one year after Judge Hand's
Holmes Lectures, Professor Herbert Wechsler, of Columbia
Law School, mounted the same rostrum. He ventured one
step further than had Hand and Frankfurter in attempting to
provide some positive guidance for deciding cases under the
spacious clauses of the Constitution in a disciplined and respectable manner. He developed the thesis that although
courts, in reviewing actions of the other branches on constitutional issues, inevitably must make value choices, they
must not function as "a naked power organ." If their decisions are to have legal quality they must be "entirely principled." He defined a principled decision as "one that rests
on reasons with respect to all the issues in the case, reasons
that in their generality and their neutrality transcend any
immediate result that is involved."[12] So the "theory of neutral principles" became part of our lexicon. It goes beyond a
call to mere internal coherence, since Wechsler's neutral
principles are value judgments, but they are judgments that
have been tested to see if they could be applied in all similar
cases.

The most recent leading contributor to the lengthening
tradition of the Legal Process school was the late Alexander
M. Bickel, of Yale Law School. He stressed what he called
the "passive virtues," devices that leave the Supreme Court
(with which he was chiefly concerned) leeway to decide
whether, when, and how much to adjudicate. He encouraged
the Court to permit experimentation, seasoning and evolving dialogue in the legitimating process applied to emerging
values. He urged that the Court engage in "a continuing
colloquy with the political institutions and with society at
large."[13] Such an approach can and sometimes does achieve,
he felt, a singular and valued accommodation "between authoritarian judicialism and the practice of democracy."[14]

Bickel, however, recognized that not all cases will yield to the gradual approach of colloquy. He acknowledged that "the function of the Justices . . . is to immerse themselves in the tradition of our society . . . in history and . . . in the thought and the vision of the philosophers and the poets. The Justices will then be fit to extract 'fundamental presuppositions' from their deepest selves, but in fact from the evolving morality of our tradition."[15] But this function is not to be performed lightly. The validity of any "fundamental presuppositions" is to be "convincingly demonstrated, and their application to particular facts carried to the last decimal."[16]

Bickel's most precise attempt to formulate the role of a judge's values in the decision process builds on a statement of Justice Frankfurter in *Sweezy* v. *New Hampshire*, 354 U.S. 234 (1957). In the course of an opinion holding for the Court that government may not force teachers to disclose political associations in such a way as to inhibit their freedom to teach and to learn, the justice recognized that two rights were in conflict, the individual's right to political privacy and the state's right of self-protection, and that striking the balance implies the exercise of judgment, a task committed to the Court. In words considerably bolder than those he had used two years earlier in his essay on John Marshall, when he looked on the due process and equal protection clauses as dubiously appropriate for enforcement, the justice wrote:

> This [exercising judgment] is the inescapable judicial task in giving substantive content, legally enforced, to the Due Process Clause, and it is a task ultimately committed to this Court. It must not be an exercise of whim or will. It must be an overriding judgment founded on something much deeper and more justifiable than personal preference. As far as it lies within human limitations, it must be an impersonal judgment. It must rest on fundamental presuppositions rooted in history to which widespread acceptance may fairly be attributed.[17]

Bickel commented that the qualifying clause, "to which widespread acceptance may fairly be attributed," is critical.

But he did not mean that the Court "is restricted to declaring an existing national consensus," for other institutions are more fitted to express an existing consensus. Bickel concluded: "What is meant, rather, is that the Court should declare as law only such principles as will — in time, but in a rather immediate foreseeable future — gain general assent . . . . The Court is a leader of opinion, not a mere register of it, but it must lead opinion, not merely impose its own; and — the short of it is — it labors under the obligation to succeed."[18]

Here, then, now over thirty years after midcentury, is the dominant school of American jurisprudence. Its ethical wellspring is Bentham's utilitarianism — the greatest good for the greatest number. Yet there is acceptance of the fact that the "vague and admonitory" due process and equal protection clauses exist to protect individual rights. The school has long specialized in giving practical guidance for judges in its precepts respecting institutional competence. Although Bickel recognized an area of some amplitude for the application of moral values and views of society's future movement — perhaps more than is generally thought — the chief teachings of the school are fidelity to process and neutral principles, humility in invoking the power of the judiciary, restraint, and deference to other branches, sovereignties, and court systems.*

---

*Two younger scholars of the school have recently added their gloss. In *Democracy and Distrust: A Theory of Judicial Review* (Cambridge: Harvard University Press, 1980), John Hart Ely would have the courts restrict themselves to assuring that deprived or "insular" minorities have open channels to, and fair procedural treatment by, the processes of government. In *Judicial Review and the National Political Process* (Chicago: University of Chicago Press, 1980), Jesse H. Choper would limit judicial review to issues involving the rights of individuals vis-à-vis government and legislative attempts to expand or contract judicial authority, leaving to political processes issues dealing with the boundaries of power between the states and the federal government and between the Congress and the executive branch.

Chapter 12

A Time for
Reappraisal

IT IS FAIR to say that all of the basic principles, precepts, and cautions of the Legal Process school of thought were developed and articulated by the end of the 1950s. On the assumption that ways of thinking about the proper role of judges in constitutional adjudication are not likely to be eternal truths, worthy of being graven in stone for all time, I have thought it relevant that we review the decades since midcentury and even look toward the end of the century to see if anything has happened, is happening, or is likely to happen, both inside and outside the law, that invites new thoughts about the judging process.

THE PROBLEM OF LEGITIMACY —
A CLOSER LOOK

First of all, it is prudent to keep the problem not only in mind but in perspective. The "problem" giving rise to the search for some all-inclusive philosophy or set of principles that can effectively constrain judges in their review of legislative acts or in their monitoring of social institutions is that the federal judiciary, unlike the legislature or the executive, is not elected, is not, therefore, "democratic." Since we now know that a judge does not merely find the law but makes it, we crave some guaranty of legitimacy, some assurance that we shall not be at the mercy of the personal predilections of an autocrat.

It is my thesis that the common view of the problem is distorted, and, because it is, the search for principles to harness judges is conducted in too strident a manner and with simplistic and absolutist expectations that are unrealistic. In the first place, the frequent reference to the judiciary as "the least democratic branch" conveys the suggestion that somehow something has crept into our scheme of things which is out of tune, a discordant note in the democratic harmony. Every time we hear it, it is a reminder that each generation, in a sense, is a new Constitutional Convention, and must decide for itself whether it accepts those seminal principles thrashed out in that hot Philadelphia summer long ago. Those principles resulted in something unique in the annals of the creation of states and fitted no pre-existing mold.

The Founding Fathers were a mixture of idealists and practical men of affairs, and what they created was a mixture, bottomed on a deep distrust of any person, any group, any institution having absolute power. They knew that government would seldom — and then not for long — be in the hands of people as wise and disinterested as Plato's guardian class. The form of government they created was not a democracy in the old Athenian or town-meeting sense. It was not even a representative democracy in the English and continental sense, in which Parliament can do no wrong. It defies a generic label and claims no simple pedigree. We have to settle on the word "mixed." For there is no word or ringing phrase that connotes a theory of government attributing most of the power of society most of the time to three different kinds of officials but so devised that no one official or group can easily be placed in the position of having the last word; making all officialdom subject to the rights and privileges of individuals; and assigning as interpreter of the charter and monitor of official conduct the branch least dependent on and most secure from the citizenry and its elected representatives.

Each branch is subject to our well-known but unprecedented system of checks and balances, which by no means tracks democratic factors. The less democratic Senate can block the more democratic House; the President's veto has a weight equal to that of two-thirds minus one of each house; small states have the same say in the Senate as large states; courts may invalidate legislation, but the Congress may reenact laws, appropriate funds, specify the rules of court procedures, and establish the number, level, and jurisdiction of inferior courts.

Perhaps not so well known is the extent to which each branch is, or is not, otherwise accountable. "Accountability" in government is a talisman of fairly recent origin. Its origin is the world of business, where every branch and unit of an enterprise can, under increasingly sophisticated cost-accounting techniques, be held accountable for its contribution to the overall profit. Since profit is the single and final criterion, measurement of performance in specific terms is feasible. But the accountability of people, of officials, is a more elusive goal.

We think of elections as the supreme machinery of accountability. But even in regard to the President, who perhaps is our most accountable official, election or defeat is a very rough sort of accounting, its precise meaning having been debated by experts for years. As for the unremitting publicity to which the President is exposed, this instrument for determining accountability is to some extent offset by his ability to use both the resources of government and the media to his advantage. The accountability of legislators is even more problematical. Here again, the accounting is a rough one, defying both prediction and retrospective analysis. The incumbent's "image" is ever more important, and judging him on his record is ever more difficult.

The process by which a bill becomes law entails so many

votes at so many stages that a legislator can portray his
position on a major issue as either support or opposition by
selecting the stage at which he reports: a vote in subcommit-
tee, in full committee, an unrecorded aye or nay, an unrecorded (standing) division vote, a teller vote, or a recorded
aye or nay vote. This could be on an amendment, on a motion to recommit (kill) the bill, on final passage, on a motion
to reconsider, or on the conference report. Even the most determined citizen, after obtaining his senator's or representative's "voting record," faces a formidable task in making
an accurate performance audit to see how well his legislator
has lived up to campaign promises. Even if this assessment
can be fairly made, it does not inform the voter whether the
person he elected to Congress has been really effective, responsible, and wise.

There is probably less room for accountability in the vast
reaches of the bureaucracy. The bright lights and creative
spirits in the civil service are generally identified and re-
warded, but the career-security system makes it extremely
difficult for a superior, not to mention a citizen, to deal
appropriately with substandard performance. The least
imaginative, efficient, and productive either climb in the
service, perhaps at a slow rate, or remain locked into a
grade until retirement.

As for judges, we have taken note in earlier chapters of the
measures for enhancing accountability: a review as of right
of any trial court decision; the need to convince a majority
of any appellate court; the discipline of putting facts, reasoning, and conclusions in writing; the existence of well-recognized rules of the judging craft; the possibility of review by
the Supreme Court; and criticism by the bar, law school
faculties, and the academic journals. In the realm of judicial
conduct, we have observed that judges are subjected to the
most demanding ethical code in government. Finally, we
have alluded to the expanded role being accorded the judicial councils of the circuits in acting on complaints against
judges.

The quest for further standards of judicial accountability in the form of principles of decision that can supply some assurance of legitimacy will always go on. But the quest should be pursued in the knowledge that judges are today subject to a relatively high degree of accountability, not notably less effective than that to which officials in the other branches are realistically subject.

CHINKS IN THE ARMOR

If, in retrospect, the problem of an "undemocratic" judiciary was overstated by the reigning Legal Process school, so also was the adequacy of that school's solutions to the problem. However salutary the insistence on neutral principles and the caution to practice self-restraint, chinks in the armor began to be visible.

On further reflection, it was no longer self-evident that general principles could supplant Holmes's "sovereign prerogative of choice." When one attractive neutral principle was placed in contest with another equally appealing, equally neutral principle, how was a hard case to be resolved?

One logically available approach, consistent with the spirit of the Legal Process school, was not to attempt to resolve such a case. But with a rising tide of cases in the 1960s and 1970s pitting individuals asserting their rights against public institutions trying to carry out important social missions, any suggestion that courts abandon the field was greeted as an abdication by the judiciary of its historic role as protector of individual liberties.

Then, too, there was increased awareness that the caution of judicial restraint was not entirely self-explanatory or free from value judgments. When a court, at the behest of a government agency, enjoins on national security grounds publication of a book by a former government employee containing only unclassified material, because the author violated his contractual promise to submit any writing for prepublication review, and, despite the lack of any statute or contract authorizing the remedy, it summarily imposes a constructive trust on all profits,* has the court practiced self-restraint? It has if one begins with the notion that society's interests are presumptively superior to the individual's and are to be limited only for serious cause. But if one instead presumes the priority of individual rights, the court has joined with the other branches as an activist proponent of society's interests against individual rights.

A fundamentally similar problem with the principle of restraint is posed in the converse situation, when a court dismisses a suit brought by an individual against a state. If a court holds, as did the Supreme Court majority in the case of the transferred prisoners, that a prisoner does not have a sufficient liberty interest in his present surroundings to warrant due process before he is transferred to a harsher prison, has the court been restrained? Again, it depends on one's starting point. If society's rights as reflected in state legislative and executive decisions are presumptively superior, the Court was restrained in declining to interfere with those decisions. But if one begins with the assumption of the presumptive priority of individual rights, a decision burdening the individual without any strong showing of government need could legitimately be said to be activist.†

My point is not that the Court was necessarily wrong in *Meachum* v. *Fano*, but that the counsel of restraint, like the counsel of adherence to neutral principles, either may not give clear direction or, when it does give direction, is not a value-free approach to deciding cases. These limitations of the principal tenets of the Legal Process school became increasingly more apparent as more and more of the explosive

---

*These were the facts and holdings in *Snepp* v. *United States*, 100 Supreme Court Reporter 763, decided on February 19, 1980, by the United States Supreme Court.

†This, indeed, is how the majority looked to the dissenting justices. See Mr. Justice Stevens's dissent, quoted on pages 180 and 181.

issues of the last two decades found their way into the courtroom.

THREE DECADES OF SOCIAL CHANGE

Perhaps the most illuminating exercise that can be undertaken in connection with any reappraisal of conventional
thinking about judging is to look back over the three decades
since midcentury and see where society has changed and
how the emphases in public law have changed. We may also
be close enough to the end of the century to begin to see the
shape of times to come — a shape that bears on any evolving
thought ways of judges.

The country, of course, has grown. When I was a law student, in the 1940s, we were 130 million people. We are now
over half again as many. More significant is the change in
the conditions under which life is lived. We are now intensely urban, interdependent, and dependent on services.
As Justice Frankfurter observed, we have passed from the
watchdog state to the service state. We rely more heavily on
institutions. A professor must not only teach well but must
be a cooperating part of a faculty. A lawyer is subject to
rules enforced by a bar association. A worker must abide by
policies and decisions of a union. A doctor must work as part
of, or in close cooperation with, a hospital staff. A man or
woman in business must follow the regulations and orders of
a panoply of agencies, local, state, and national. From child-
hood on, we become creatures of institutions — public
schools, universities, unions, professional associations, regulatory commissions, laws governing our occupations and our
recreations. If we become ill, old, handicapped, or convicted,
we live our lives in institutions.

As we increase in numbers, as institutions play a larger
part in our lives, and as more and more of us satisfy our material needs, our priorities undergo a subtle but distinct
change. We prize what are becoming scarce commodi-

ties — our personal liberty and our privacy. Although our options may be limited, we demand fairness. Just because people have no choice but to buy from big corporations, they insist they not be misled. Just because urban dwellers no longer have several acres around their dwellings, they care deeply that the urban renewal project planned for their neighborhood involve a thorough environmental-impact study. One may be a teacher or a student in a large school or university, oppressed by the numbers of surrounding humanity; he cherishes all the more the freedom to communicate his views to a few kindred spirits. A tenant in a huge, low-income housing project, without a visible landlord, wants some way to complain about lack of heat, plumbing catastrophes, poor security. When a person on welfare finds his monthly check reduced by a few crucial dollars, he wants to know why. A prisoner is called before a disciplinary hearing; his privileges are reduced. He wants a chance to show he did not do what he is charged with doing.

In short, since World War II, America has become an urban, crowded, affluent, yet threatened society, ever more dependent on the workings of institutions and increasingly aware of its vulnerability and the importance of individuals' receiving fair treatment by these institutions, over which we have so little control. During these years we have also developed a highly sensitized justice nerve, possessed enough of the time by enough of the people on the most fundamental matters that we are entitled to be called a justice-oriented society.

SEA CHANGES IN LITIGATION

Some reflection of these external and internal conditions of our living together is found in an impressive series of sea changes in the public law of the land since the 1950s. The roles of the courts in private law have been and remain those of settling disputes, maintaining consistency in the law, and guiding its evolution. In the field of public law, the courts' major role can be viewed as that of monitoring the institutions of government in their dealings with individuals. Monitoring in its most traditional form is confined to the justice establishment — overseeing the conduct of law enforcement officials, prosecutors, trial judges, juries, and the conduct of trials. A wider-ranging kind of monitoring that has seen dramatic development since 1950 concerns society's extrajudicial institutions — not only confining governmental branches, departments, and agencies within their constitutional and statutory boundaries, but ensuring that governmental institutions and even some private bodies observe equal treatment and fair play in administering their affairs.

I detect several major thrusts of expansion in the monitoring role of the courts. The first is what I term Phase I of the civil rights revolution, the pioneering desegregation cases that proliferated in the wake of the Supreme Court's 1954 decision in *Brown* v. *Board of Education of Topeka*. The ramifications of Phase I are still being felt, now most notably in sections of the country other than the South, as the courts face allegations of more complex or subtle forms of discrimination by school boards.

A second is the enlargement of the civil liberties of criminal defendants wrought by the Supreme Court under the chief justiceship of Earl Warren in the 1950s and 1960s, a movement that may have slowed with respect to some procedural rights but has not entirely halted.

Third, also in the 1960s, Phase II of the civil rights revolution emerged, ranging beyond school desegregation and invoking the long-unused weapon of the Reconstruction era. This is Section 1983, Title 42 of the United States Code, the statutory authority of most contemporary "civil rights suits" to vindicate hitherto unasserted rights.

Fourth, in the late 1960s and 1970s there developed a new dimension to the courts' monitoring activities, added not by

activist judicial decisions but by the Congress. Within not
much more than a decade, the enactment of fifty or more
major, people-oriented federal statutes — dealing with environmental protection, health, and occupational safety; ban-
ning discrimination on the basis of race, sex, and age; and
providing a right of access to information held by the government — has added up to an impressive statutory bill of
rights, the enforcement of which Congress has entrusted to
the courts. Similar developments have occurred in a number
of the states.

Finally, prefigured by school desegregation cases in the
South but spreading in earnest in the 1970s and now only
beginning to be understood, Phase III of the civil rights revolution appeared — class action civil rights litigation concentrating on broad-scale remedies.

The speed, scope, and depth of change in the quality and
quantity of traffic through the federal appellate courts of
this nation have been such that even I, who have not served
an extraordinarily long time on our bench, have experienced
a major part of that change. When I became a judge, in the
mid-1960s, most of our work was of the conventional kind of
judicial review — criminal appeals, habeas corpus, agency
review, cases involving citizens of different states in which
we passed on questions of state law, and a steady quota of
tax, patent, admiralty, and other cases involving federal
statutes. Within the next two or three years, the profile of
federal litigation changed dramatically.

To a judge who left the country in, say, 1965 and returned
in 1970, the new kinds of cases would have seemed exotic,
extreme, imaginative, and when he sat down to deal with
them, challenging. Servicemen and -women challenged the
military for everything from discharge procedures and the
forbidding of short hair wigs to the denial of pregnancy
leave. Students and teachers fought dress codes, discharge
or nonrenewal of contracts, and punishment for assigning
controversial reading material. Recipients of welfare con-

tested reduction of benefits without hearing. Tenants of public or subsidized housing projects challenged residency requirements, rent increases without hearing, evictions for
reporting building-code violations, inadequate security measures. Civil servants challenged qualifying examinations, age
ceilings, disqualification of ex-convicts, rules forbidding
them to run for office. Prisoners fought rules hindering their
communication with counsel, censorship of their mail, limitations on books they wished to read, disciplinary hearings
without notice or opportunity to defend, summary transfers
to other prisons.

As Phase II of the civil rights revolution moved into Phase
III, the individual plaintiff has yielded to a broad class; the
defendant is likely to be not merely one individual or institution but another class; the relief sought is not so likely to be
an order preventing certain conduct as one commanding
certain conduct; and the impact on society of a successful
suit is apt to be much more significant. This kind of litigation goes beyond invoking the courts as monitors; it is no
less than an engine of structural change.[1]

Although this new wave of litigation has broken on our
shore only recently, it comes as a distinct surprise, in analyzing each facet of this kind of lawsuit, to realize how different it is from the kinds of cases courts have dealt with
traditionally. In a law journal article entitled "The Frontier
of Remedies: A Call for Exploration,"[2] I catalogued the differences in this manner:

	Conventional Adjudication	New Model
The Issue	Likely to be of private rights and duties. If public body involved, issue likely to be procedural.	Likely to involve substantive rights and means of compelling a public body to effectuate those rights.

	Conventional Adjudication	*New Model*
Parties	Likely to be one "person" suing another.	Likely to be a class of individuals suing a class of officials, public institutions, political entities.
Critical Facts	Historical (what has happened) and adjudicative (relevant to rights and liabilities of the two parties).	Predictive (situation as it is likely to exist during life of decree) and legislative (relevant to continuing decree).
Governing Principle	Legal precedents.	Strategy, tactics, and potential outcomes not informed by legal precedent.
Taking of Evidence	Adversary hearing and rules of evidence.	Wide participation, relaxed standards, more expert opinions.
Relief Sought	Declaration of rights, negative injunction, damages; normally narrow, closely tied to legal injury.	Affirmative injunction, affecting many beyond parties; potentially broad.
Framing of Decree	Imposed by court after hearing evidence.	Large amount of negotiation.
Impact	Confined to parties.	Affects a large segment of society.

	Conventional Adjudication	New Model
Duration of Court Involvement	One-time judgment.	Continuing decree; subject to reopening and amendment.
Role of Judge	Passive: adjudicative in resolving dispute between two parties in a one-time, normally self-executing judgment.	Active: legislative in framing criteria; executive in implementing decree.
Review	Abuse of discretion and error of law; sufficiency of evidence and legal precedents important.	Contribution of appellate court to policy, strategy, and tactics more important than monitoring fact findings or legal principles.

These differences add up to a unique and separate genre of litigation, which, because of the wide representation of plaintiffs and the nature and scope of relief sought, has an impact out of proportion to the number of suits. The impact is felt at every level of government, local, county, state, and federal, as well as in many important nongovernmental institutions. It is not surprising, therefore, that much of the sophisticated current debate concerning the legitimacy of judicial social ordering is stimulated by this kind of institutional-reform litigation, in which the court's controversial role lies in devising and implementing remedies.

THE PRESSURES OF SCARCITY

All this seems quite enough of a harvest for the decades since the 1950s. But to all the pressures that have led to the civil

rights revolution in all its phases, to the elaborate structure
of recently enacted people-oriented statutes, and to the perennial interest in civil liberties, there must be added the
pressures of limits to resources, energy, space, privilege,
opportunity, wealth, travel, education, and many other necessities and amenities to which we are only now being introduced, after two centuries of faith in infinite growth, resources, and opportunities.

It takes no great gifts as a "futurologist" to make several
predictions about some of the basic conditions that promise
to color at least the remainder of this century.

- The future is likely to see population (even our fairly
  stable population) pressing inexorably against limited
  material resources, energy, and space. To the extent that
  there can be international controls limiting excesses in
  national exploitation of the resources of the planet, those
  limitations will be felt as additional pressures. As Robert Heilbroner prophesies, we must be prepared to accept redefinitions of "the legitimate boundaries of power
  and the permissible sanctuaries of freedom, for a future
  in which the exercise of power must inevitably increase
  and many present areas of freedom, especially in economic life, be curtailed.[3]
- These pressures will be intensified by the continuing ex-
  pansiveness of individual demands, aspirations, and expectations.
- People will increasingly aspire to "justice-determined"
  distribution of goods and services in short supply. This
  means that they will expect access to the forums of decision, equality and consideration, and fairness of procedures. And they will have an abundance of lawyers to
  help them.*

* At this writing, the lawyer population of the country is approaching
500,000; by the year 2000 there will be an estimated one million, or about
one lawyer for every 250 persons. (Robert B. McKay, "The Lawyer in the
Year 2000: Three Views, A New Species," *Alabama Law Review*, vol. 25, no.
1, p. 6.)

- The conflict caused by finite resources, open-ended aspirations, and an ever more acute justice nerve will lead agencies, institutions, statutes, and regulations to govern in ever greater detail a democratic society striving to balance competing claims.
- The litigation of the future will be increasingly class-, structure-, and institution-oriented. It will have an affinity to single-issue politics, for it is a short step from an organization with a mailing list to a class action seeking from a court the relief that is denied by the electoral process.

With the end — for at least a time — of the Augustan Age of plenty, access to government, including the courts, fairness in institutional proceedings, equality of consideration and treatment, and residual privacy in a crowded world will be increasingly cherished individual objectives. Their recognition will not be without institutional inconvenience, expense, and frustration, but protection of the smaller liberties in a shrinking world may be the price of a stable and cohesive society. In sum, the new conditions of societal life promise to be such as to elevate in new kinds of ways and to greater intensity and higher degrees of refinement the age-old issue of the proper balance between the rights of the individual and the rights of the state.

Thomas S. Kuhn has written a seminal tract entitled *The Structure of Scientific Revolutions*.[4] In it, he traces the complete upheavals in thought systems wrought by Galileo, Darwin, and others. He defines scientific revolutions as "noncumulative developmental episodes in which an older paradigm is replaced in whole or in part by an incompatible new one."[5] A conventional thesis meets, with increasing frequency, anomalies, resistances, and inconsistencies. Pressure builds up. Then, perhaps quite accidentally, a new theory is proposed that is quickly seen to resolve the problems dammed up during the time the old theory held sway.

While I am aware of no credible descriptions of the judg-

ing process that would involve concepts as mutually exclusive as those of Ptolemy and Copernicus, indications of
change are in the air. The limitations in the tenets of the
Legal Process school; the three decades of turbulent social
change since midcentury; the equally dramatic changes that
have occurred in socially significant litigation; the implications of the latest generation of structural reform litigation;
and, most of all, the impending pressures of scarcity of
space, material resources, energy, and privacy and those of
growing regulation — all these suggest at the very least that
thought about what judges do and how they, in turn, should
be judged is not a closed book.

Chapter 13

A Judge Seeks
His Bearings

EVEN THIS BRIEF TOUR of the headlands of American jurisprudence suggests that a search for doctrine legitimating judicial lawmaking changes direction as the perceived problems
change. A century ago the focus was on the inquiry: What is
the nature of law? The idea that law was something to be
derived from some oracular source yielded to the concept
that law could and should be scientifically derived from the
principles implicit in decided cases. Then came recognition
of the fact that as judges applied general principles to concrete cases they were, to a greater or lesser degree, making and not merely discovering law.

This realization led to the question: If law is not a pre-existing body of doctrine, but is to some extent created by
judicial decision, to what sources should judges look? The
schools of Sociological Jurisprudence and Legal Realism addressed this question. Their answers seemed so open-ended
that concerned scholars found it natural to seek the proper
boundaries for judges. The Legal Process school found them
in self-denying ordinances of restraint and deference to other
decision-making bodies, both private and public. There
were, in short, some kinds of problems not nearly so well
adapted to judicial resolution as to executive or legislative
action, or to private negotiation and accommodation.

Now the developments in law, the new patterns of litigation, and the changing conditions of society dating from the
1950s, together with a likely future of less material abundance for the individual and more intrusive regulation, increasingly rivet attention on the nature, source, and weight
of individual rights vis-à-vis those of society. The looming
question is how to deal with these contesting interests. How
judges respond, to use Justice Holmes's phrase, to these "felt
necessities" of our times will be the basis for the judgment
of the people on how well judges have contributed to a just
society. Such a judgment may or may not be suspended
until the nature and extent of the contribution of judges can
be discerned. In the meantime, the practicing judge must
consider his options, seek his bearings, choose, and act.

CURRENT JURISPRUDENCE:
RIGHTS IN CLUSTERS

One option is to accept as immutable the present configura-
tion of individual rights against the state. A stranger to our
planet, however, might have difficulty in fitting a thumbnail
summary into any logical scheme. The one characteristic of
our jurisprudence as we practice it would clearly appear to
him to be a compulsion to deal with rights in clusters, with
wide disparity in the treatment of differing clusters. And by
no means do we always have a consistent rationale for constituting our clusters.

For example, in the important sphere of the First Amendment,* we distinguish between "pure speech" and conduct
that, though not speech, may yet carry a message. The latter
is much more easily regulated by the state than the former,
although courts frequently face most difficult questions in
determining what is speech and what is action. Similarly,

---

*"Congress shall make no law respecting an establishment of religion, or
prohibiting the free exercise thereof; or abridging the freedom of speech, or
of the press; or the right of the people peaceably to assemble, and to petition the Government for a redress of grievances."

picketing and leafleting on public property are almost sacrosanct, but the same activities have little chance on private property, even though the public may widely and freely use that property.

An even less tidy situation exists in classifying rights in accordance with the quality of their protection under the equal protection clause of the Fourteenth Amendment.* Here, until recently, there were only two kinds: if an interest was "fundamental" or if people were grouped by statutes in "suspect" classifications, a law affecting such interest or making such a classification would be subjected to the most rigorous scrutiny. The courts require that the government must be able to demonstrate a compelling interest in the aim sought to be achieved and that there is no less burdensome alternative that would achieve the same end. Very few laws can withstand such scrutiny. But if the interests at stake are not fundamental, and if the classification is not suspect, then government action cannot be successfully challenged if a "rational" state interest can be imagined. Almost any law can withstand such a relaxed scrutiny.

Just what the criteria are that determine whether a right is fundamental is inexplicable. The most obvious interests are freedom of speech and of religion, for there is a constitutional amendment ensuring their protection. But the right to travel, equally protected as "fundamental," has no such pedigree. So also with "suspect" classifications. Classification by race is easily understood as triggering maximum scrutiny and protection. Yet there are other classifications of the underprivileged whose pedigree goes back only to a footnote in the Supreme Court case of *United States* v. *Carolene Products*, 304 U.S. 144, 152 n 4 (1938).†

* "No State shall . . . deny to any person within its jurisdiction the equal protection of the laws."

† Nor need we enquire . . . whether prejudice against discrete and insular minorities may be a special condition, which tends seriously to curtail the operation of those political processes ordinarily to be relied upon to protect minorities, and which may call for a correspondingly more searching judicial inquiry . . ."

To complicate matters further, I should add that between the mountain of maximum protection and the marsh of minimum scrutiny, there is a meadowland reserved for cases involving classification by sex: the law will stand if it bears a "substantial" relation to some legitimate governmental need. This test lies somewhere on the scale between compelling need and rational state interest.

If all this looks somewhat chaotic, we face a neater dichotomy of rights when we survey the due process clause of the Fourteenth Amendment.* It can be fairly summarized as follows. Not only economic rights but liberty interests of an individual must have a source in specific clauses of the Constitution, a federal statute, or a state law. If there is no such pedigree, the threatened loss to an individual of some right, interest, or privilege, even if felt rather deeply, does not pose an occasion for protection of the individual against society. The point is well made in the cases we discussed under the heading of "The Saga of the Transferred Prisoners." In the final disposition of that litigation, the Supreme Court announced that since there was no state-created limitation on the power of officials to transfer an inmate from one prison to another, the federal courts had no business invoking due process in the name of the Constitution. It was only the dissent that advanced the philosophy that ours was a government in which rights existed in individuals unless they were taken away by positive law, rather than that they did not exist unless they were specifically granted by positive law.

At present, therefore, only if an interest specifically cognizable by federal or state law is at stake will government action against that interest be subjected to a due process scrutiny. If, however, such an interest exists, the scrutiny is likely to be rigorous and the state called on to give advance

---

*"No State shall . . . deprive any person of life, liberty, or property, without due process of law."

notice, hold a hearing in which there will be opportunity for a person to develop his own case and expose weaknesses in the state's case, to have an impartial adjudicator, some kind of record, reasons for decision, and opportunity for review. In short, in the field of procedural due process, if an interest rises to the magic threshold of being protectible, the arsenal of protective devices available is formidable. If, however, one state does not recognize as protectible the same interest that another recognizes, the federal Constitution will not be invoked in the former, but will be completely applicable in the latter. The gap is a wide one — a full panoply of protection for a "recognized" interest; none for a lesser interest.

In sum, we have today, in dealing with individual rights against the state, a jurisprudence of clusters and discontinuity. In some cases, not necessarily the most serious for the individual, courts will hold institutions to very high standards of rationality and procedural nicety. In all others, practically any justification in the nature of a prudential administrative or a utilitarian reason will support the state's encroaching on the interest of an individual. We seem, therefore, to be operating on the basis of a sharply etched dichotomy of rights — an aristocracy and a peasant class.

Abandonment of the Field

Another option for the judge is that of withdrawal. Such a response on the part of the courts would release, according to the mythology, legislatures and executive branch officials from their subservience to judicial fiat. According to Thayer's doctrine, preached also by Hand and Frankfurter, "holding democracy in judicial tutelage is not the most promising way to foster disciplined responsibility in a people."[1] To put it another way, if courts would restrain themselves from requiring new duties and obligations of people, groups, institutions, and government, legislatures would reawaken to their responsibility and fulfill their coequal role as faithful interpreters of the Constitution. This thesis proceeds on the assumption that to the extent that courts decide constitutional issues, legislatures are shielded from the need to come to grips with them. If only courts would restrain themselves, there would remain room for the gentler processes of colloquy, reflection, and constructive response by one branch to the subtle promptings of another.

One response to this way of thinking is that the structure and the workings of the Congress and other legislatures just do not lend themselves to predictably adequate constitutional analysis. The judiciary committees, of course, do have staffs competent in this field. But other committees, dealing with health, housing, welfare, pollution, consumers, taxes, the armed services and the draft, and myriad other fields, cannot all support constitutional experts. Yet each committee forges the laws under its jurisdiction. When a bill reaches the floor, there is no constitutionally oriented devil's advocate to probe either equality of treatment or procedural fairness. Even if there were such a constitutional ombudsman, many problems encountered in applying a law to 220 million people could not possibly be foreseen. Moreover, our system is based on the proposition that all branches share the constitutional responsibility. Each office-holder, whether in the executive branch, the legislature, or judiciary, takes an oath to support the Constitution. To discourage any branch from exerting its effort at any stage would seem to be both unnecessary and unrealistic. Particularly in a shrinking world, where individual rights are viewed as increasingly important, it does not seem sensible to reduce the access of people to any part of government, especially to the courts.

In short, Congress has more than it can do without engaging in farseeing constitutional analysis. (And this applies to state legislatures, as well.) I doubt that Congress spends much time worrying over whether courts will strike down some of its acts. While undoubtedly any legislature does not like to see its work undone, it is not powerless to work its will; more often than not it has the power of the last word. Were courts to sit back and wait for a resurgence of constitutional sensitivity, I suspect that the wait would be long and probably fruitless. The key to a more realistic relationship lies, I think, in courts doing what they think they have to do, respecting all real evidence of legislative intent, and legislatures doing what they think they have to do.

This is not a formula of repose. Nor is it a formula of simplicity, as it would be if, like some continental countries, we were willing to make the legislature supreme in everything. It is a formula calculated to create tension. This is why, in thinking about our Constitution, I do not see justice as accurately represented by such a static, inert symbol as a set of scales. I think the appropriate image may be a coiled spring whose tension yields to and limits the pressures of a majoritarian government on one side and the demands on behalf of individual rights on the other.

THE WELL OF MORAL PHILOSOPHY

In addition to the options of confining judicial vision to the conventional wisdom of the present, and of pulling back the scope of judicial activity, there is the third option, where there is any freedom of decision, of drawing on contemporary moral philosophy. In contrast to the simple dualism of the approach taken by the Supreme Court in cases involving individual rights, latter-day philosophers attempt much more ambitious statements of the source and significance of individual rights.

One leading contemporary philosopher, John Rawls, asks us, as a way of testing the validity of our thinking, to assume that our principles of justice flow from an original agreement among people who are rational, who do not yet know their own place in society in terms of wealth, talents, luck, or achievement, and who are not altruistic. Such persons, not associated with any particular age, society, or govern-

ment, in defining their fundamental ground rules of association would, according to Rawls, reject utilitarianism; that is,
"since each desires to protect his interests . . . no one has a
reason to acquiesce in an enduring loss for himself in order
to bring about a greater net balance of satisfaction."[2]
Rawls's First Principle, accordingly, is "Each person is to
have an equal right to the most extensive basic liberty compatible with a similar liberty for others."[3] Rawls would,
under what he calls his First Priority Rule, allow a liberty to
be restricted only for the sake of liberty, as, for example,
when the price of giving a perfect trial to a litigant would involve so much time, personnel, and funds that the system
could not be made available to all without bringing government to a halt.

Another noted philosopher, Ronald Dworkin, directs his
attention more explicitly to the importance of courts to individual rights. He makes the argument that the Constitution
reflects moral concepts that courts are obligated to utilize in
protecting the rights of individuals against the state. He
frames the target area:

> The bulk of the law — that part which defines and implements
> social, economic, and foreign policy — cannot be neutral. It must
> state, in its greatest part, the majority's view of common good.
> The institution of rights is therefore crucial, because it represents
> the majority's promise to the minorities that their dignity and
> equality will be respected. When the divisions among the groups
> are most violent, then this gesture, if law is to work, must be
> most sincere . . . If the Government does not take rights
> seriously, then it does not take law seriously either.[4]

Dworkin spells out the implications of his basic view that
our system posits that individuals have rights rooted in
moral concepts that may be enforced against the state by
courts that must be prepared to interpret those concepts. He
addresses the "vague" clauses of the Constitution, the due
process and equal protection clauses, and rejects the conclusion that rights under these clauses are limited "to those

recognized by a limited group of people at a fixed date of history."⁵ To make his point clear, he draws a distinction between "concepts," which are commodious ideas or values requiring fresh thinking to be applied in specific situations, and "conceptions," which are already fixed and specific embodiments of a more general concept. He calls this "a distinction that philosophers have made but lawyers have not yet appreciated," adding:

> Suppose I tell my children simply that I expect them not to treat others unfairly. I no doubt have in mind examples of the conduct I mean to discourage, but I would not accept that my "meaning" was limited to these examples, for two reasons. First I would expect my children to apply my instruction to situations I had not and could not have thought about. Second, I stand ready to admit that some particular act I had thought was fair when I spoke was in fact unfair, or vice versa, if one of my children is able to convince me of that later; in that case I should want to say that my instructions covered the case he cited, not that I had changed my instructions. I might say that I meant the family to be guided by the concept of fairness, not by any specific *conception* of fairness I might have had in mind.⁶

Dworkin therefore concludes that it is a mistake to call the broad due process and equal protection clauses vague. "The clauses are vague only if we take them to be botched or incomplete or schematic attempts to lay down particular conceptions. If we take them as appeals to moral concepts they could not be made more precise by being more detailed."⁷ He also rejects the argument that legislatures are better equipped or have special title to make constitutional decisions in cases involving individuals who assert rights against the state, pointing out that the United States long ago adopted the political theory that the majority must be restrained! "To make the majority judge in its own cause seems inconsistent and unjust."⁸

Where individual rights and government interests confront each other, Dworkin refuses to invoke the familiar metaphor of "balancing interests." In the first place, one who

takes rights seriously must, he urges, either accept the Kant-
ian idea that human dignity inherent in one's being a
member of the human community is inconsistent with certain treatment, or believe that, as he and Rawls do, that "the
weaker members of a political community are entitled to the
same concern and respect of their government as the more
powerful members have secured for themselves."[9]

The teachings of such philosophers add up to a quite different blend from that of the Legal Process school of
thought. The emphasis on fairness, the entitlement of each
person to equal respect, the view of the great clauses in the
Bill of Rights as concepts, susceptible of adjustment in each
era rather than as fixed, specific conceptions, the recognition
that the authoritative construction of these clauses is not the
province of the majority, and the caution that the proper
approach to individual rights is not simply a "balancing" of
the rights of individuals against those of society, but rather a
tilt toward the individual — all these spell a different, in-
dividual-oriented jurisprudence. Rawls and Dworkin are
only two of the contemporary jurisprudential thinkers.
There are many others, colleagues, followers, and critics. Indeed, there seems to be a renaissance in thinking about law
and moral philosophy, rights, and judges.[10] This does not
mean that such thinking has as yet become part of the judicial landscape. The task of translating abstract principles
into rules applicable to concrete cases is formidable, and the
areas where judges are free to apply new principles are few
and far between.

Nevertheless, the seeds have been sown, and Dworkin has
issued the call to lawyers and legal thinkers to engage in the
development of moral theory in regard to individual rights
as they did in the development of legal sociology and legal
economics. He writes, "Constitutional law can make no gen-
uine advance until it isolates the problem of rights against
the state and makes that problem part of its own agenda.
That argues for a fusion of constitutional law and moral

theory, a connection that, incredibly, has yet to take place."[11]

PRACTICAL REASONING

Although we have discussed the reigning theory of the identification and protection of rights, the alternative of withdrawal from controversial decisions about rights, and the newer jurisprudence as options open to the practicing judge, the choices in real life are not so absolute or mutually exclusive. One observer has accurately portrayed the predicament of the judge as he contemplates the conflicting claims of the philosophers:

> Legal doctrine cannot afford the luxury of becoming a professional's intellectual pastime. The relevance of moral philosophy to the development of norms for governing a society of ordinary people lies in a few broad generalizations: Utilitarianism, for example, emphasizes that we are part of a social whole; Kantianism reminds us, on the other hand, that we are not mere appendages of the social body. And the task of judges, to maintain the balance between these poles while the philosophers are still out, requires practical reasoning that does not yield easily to unified field theories. To look for more is to ignore the injunction of one of the first philosophers [Aristotle] to seek "precision in each class of things just as far as the nature of the subject admits."[12]

This precisely describes my own pluralism. I find merit in one school for a certain range of problems and merit in another for another range. Where the ranges seem to overlap in my mind, I have to choose between sets of principles or systems, well knowing that my very eclecticism clashes with the fundamental tenets of most of the competing systems. As I look ahead, I confess that I see a need for a principled approach to a finer-tuning, a nicer calibration linking private interests and their protection than allowed by the prevailing dualism. I see such a development in the law as a creative and sensitive response to emerging end-of-century conditions and expectations. But this state of affairs does not come cheaply. If American society is to make room for its acutely sensitized justice nerve, if it aspires to join Rawls in believing that "justice is the first virtue of social institutions, as truth is of systems of thought,"[13] it must pay a price.

If courts are not to be intolerably crowded, litigation crushingly expensive, and decisions oppressively delayed, there must be measurable movement of dispute resolution out of the courts. What is needed is as much constructive thinking about the dejudicialization of some kinds of contests over rights and duties as there has been about the perfection of formal court procedures. To prevent the overheating of the justice system, there must be confidence in, and easy access to, less formal justice subsystems.

By a justice subsystem I mean an extrajudicial system within an institution like a prison, university, school system, welfare or housing agency that identifies and protects rights and privileges, allocates responsibilities, and imposes sanctions fairly and consistently under reasonable standards. The citizen would have access to courts only if the subsystem's resolution was seen as substantially failing to provide justice.* The 1970s saw the burgeoning of what came to be called a dispute resolution movement, leading, by 1979, to experimental neighborhood justice centers in a hundred U.S. cities, employing techniques ranging from conciliation and mediation to binding arbitration. By 1980 a sufficient consensus had formed to make possible passage of the Dispute Resolution Act, establishing a Dispute Resolution Center in the United States Department of Justice, supplied with seed money to encourage additional experimentation.[14]

---

* A promising example of such a subsystem is the establishment of inmate grievance procedures in federal prisons. Federal inmates have widely resorted to these procedures (one third of all inmates in 1976), achieving some changes in correctional policy. The availability of this in-house system has, so observers think, contributed to the decline in federal prisoner cases in federal courts during a period when state prisoner petitions more than trebled. ("Recommended Procedures for Handling Prisoner Civil Rights Cases in the Federal Courts" [Washington, D.C.: The Federal Judicial Center, 1980], p. 2.)

If such subsystems, devices, and procedures short of full-fledged judges and courts are to play a significant part in bringing justice to the people, that same people must succeed in rising to the challenge of self-discipline where other societies have failed. We need only recall that the Greeks, at the end of their classical era, were ever more avid in seizing additional rights and privileges while resisting any suggestion that they assume increased responsibilities.

Another recent phenomenon that enhances the possibility of a more sensitive identification of individual rights and delineation of protections without simply adding to the burdens of federal courts is the increasing willingness of state courts to go beyond the boundaries of rights staked out by the Supreme Court. A kind of "inverse federalism" is taking place; state courts are now frequently setting the pace and direction. State constitutional texts, histories, and traditions have created a special framework, and recent constitutional revisions and amendments have given more precise, current, and authoritative sanction for what have been called "new states' rights." State courts have, in some circumstances, accorded greater freedom of expression to individuals and the press. They have developed more exacting standards governing the admission in evidence of confessions and the fruits of searches and seizures. They have resisted efforts to reduce the size and to discard the requirement of unanimity of juries. They have afforded a wide array of procedural rights in prison disciplinary proceedings and have issued a large number of "privacy" rulings protective of such interests as the wearing of long hair and the engaging by consenting adults in sexual activity.[15]

In addition to the depressurizing contributions of justice subsystems and rights-sensitive state courts, there are opportunities for judges themselves to make room in their work for both a kind of utilitarianism and a heightened sensitivity to individual rights. I refer to the need for judges in their role as shapers and implementers of remedies to consider the optimum limits of performance of institutions and

officials. I have called this the workability factor and have
defined it as "the extent to which a rule protecting a right,
enforcing a duty, or setting a standard of conduct — which
is consistent with and in the interests of social justice — can
be pronounced with reasonable expectation of effective ob-
servance without impairing the essential functioning of those
to whom the rule applies."[16]

In this era of broad-based, open-ended, class action litigation seeking basic structural reform in institutions, the role
of the judge is radically different from what it was a century
ago. The question of what is the law often proves much less
difficult, given the finding of liability (of a municipality,
school system, prison, or welfare administration), than the
question of what should be done. The judge is at this point
no longer concerned with finding or making law; his concern
is to try to see to it that practical steps are taken to bring the
institution into compliance with constitutional requirements. Here a different kind of restraint is needed from what
we have considered in connection with identifying and
weighing rights.

The restraint is one of timing, of giving opportunity to institutional defendants, after a finding of liability, to harness
their own familiarity and expertise for devising a workable
remedy. But if this fails, then courts, trial and appellate, are
called on not only to use their traditional craft skills but to
draw on the innovative genius of the common law and equity jurisprudence to deal with these new problems in newer
and more effective ways.[17]

In short, just as there is a coiled-spring tension between
the commands of the majority and the rights of the individual under the Constitution, there is a tension between absolutist theories concerning individual rights and utilitarian
theory concerning the interest and convenience of society as
a whole. But the newer area inviting creative thought, that
of remedies, though utilitarian in the sense that the objective is to arrive at useful courses of action, is philosophically

neutral. That is, much of the challenge to judicial thinking about remedies is simply a call to acute analysis, farsighted planning, and effective administration.

THE JUDGE AT THE CENTER

As we come to the end of our survey of judicial thought ways, do we find any general propositions of universal application? Perhaps. But they will fall far short of giving people precise measuring sticks to enable us to assess the performance of judges in their time, for it is now clear that judges are inescapably part of the social process and that their work can be fully measured on important questions only by the impact of their work over time.

Judging is most certainly not a matter of mystical revelation. Neither is it all logic or all science. Nor is it all a matter of institutional competence or a search for neutral principles. Finally, it is not the systematic application of a comprehensive theory of social utility or moral values.

Judging is a mixture of all of these, the formula for the wisest and most just mixture remaining as yet unrevealed. We know that the good judge diligently applies himself to the disciplines and skills of the craft. We know also, to use Judge Learned Hand's words, that "he must discover some composition with the dominant trends of his time."[18] That discovery may be illumined by insights drawn from moral philosophy. We realize, too, that the judge, laboring in the vineyard of specific disputes, finds himself working out practical solutions and crafting tailored remedies that are calculated to recognize rights and at the same time respect the need for responsible governance and direction.

In so doing, the judge strives, in cases that allow him that freedom, to come to terms with the crossing currents of society and, consistent with his craft and the limitations of his institution, to contribute to a just future. He knows, if he is wise, that "the Constitution contain[s] ambiguities, not ab-

solute truths, and that the process of judging [is] one of temporarily choosing among competing principles more than
one of declaring the law for all time."[19] And he knows also
that the only judgment that counts, the judgment of history,
as to whether he has truly served the best interest of a just
society, must await another day.

FINAL REFLECTIONS ON ACCOUNTABILITY

The entire purpose of this book has been to shed as much
light as possible on the subject of judging to help non-judges
of all ranks and ages to understand judges. We have approached the subject from different directions. We have
recognized that, at various times, the questions and the standards of judgment may change. We have seen that both the
skills of the profession and broader social values enter into
the process, as well as the separate order of perceptions and
executive ability inherent in the planning and execution of
remedies. We have attempted to demonstrate that the gap
between the accountability of the executive and legislative
branches and that of the judiciary is not so wide as many assume. We have spelled out the demanding systems of judicial review and collegial governance, which aim to correct
errors of law and abnormalities of conduct. Having said this
much, I must acknowledge its inadequacy and make a final
point about this evanescent concept of accountability.

We have always found it easier to build procedures to
prevent or correct gross error or misconduct than to stimulate better quality. The very word *accountability* has a negative tinge to it — being answerable. One is not called on to
answer why one did an outstanding job, or even why one did
not do such a job, only why the job was as poor as it was. It
seems to me that while there may be other and better ways
of guarding against breach of the public trust, these at best
will not ensure excellence. Even if we could establish some
prestigious performance-rating bureau that could give the

most penetrating evaluation of legislators, bureaucrats, and judges, we would have created, in effect, a fourth branch of government with incalculable power over the other three. We would have finally opted for Plato's guardian oligarchy.

On the whole, with some glaring exceptions, we have the quality of public servants we deserve. What we deserve depends on the depth of our understanding and expectations. I tend to think that the quality of individual members of the Congress, in terms of breadth of outlook, sophistication, and devotion to the public good, has improved in the past quarter-century. I think also that the civil service today is better than ever, with its constant influx of brighter and better-educated young people. As for judges, I cannot help thinking that the judiciary, both state and federal, has, in the past dozen years, dramatically expanded its quantitative output per judge in an era when the law was becoming ever more complex — a collective job performance that I suspect is unrivaled in the history of the judicial profession.

But the deeper participation of the public through increased understanding and a voice informed by that understanding is critical. For this is at the heart of the kind of accountability that has a positive thrust. Not only must mountebanks and incompetents be seen and declared as such, but competence and excellence ought to be recognized. Censure is only a negative weapon. Part of our problem lies in our habitual demeaning of all public servants. To the extent that our stereotypes cast senators and representatives as cynical and vapid windbags, bureaucrats as self- and time-serving manipulators of red tape, and judges as pompous pettifoggers, we discourage a wider pursuit of excellence.

Just as in a business, a military unit, or a university, the atmosphere of expectation as to standards has something to do with performance. History offers, at different periods, in different countries, for different kinds of public service, a gallery of rare but inspiring exemplars. To go back over a thousand years to the great days of the T'ang dynasty, there was the corps of Chinese officials who had been educated in the humanities and selected in democratic competition by public examination. In more recent times, we think of the elite cadre of French officials, the *inspecteurs;* the British Civil Service and the Foreign Office; the Indian Civil Service, particularly in the days before India's independence; the Austrian Civil Service; the British judiciary; both the British Parliament and the United States Congress in their splendid moments; and, high on any list, the remarkable group gathered at Philadelphia in 1787 to draft a Constitution. My own conviction is that much of the excellence observed in all these groups arose from the participants' consciousness that much was expected of them by the people.

To be a significant force, the expectations must be discriminating. Citizens, individually and in groups, politicians, columnists, editorial writers, commentators, feature editors, investigative reporters, must know what they can realistically expect from their public servants. When justifiable expectations are fulfilled, respect and credit should be given freely. When they are not realized, criticism and censure should issue just as freely. Respect and censure, selectively meted out, based on appraisal of the performances of officials in the light of knowledge of the roles, powers, freedoms, restraints, and values governing them, are the lubricants of affirmative accountability. Applied in many ways and on many levels, they can strengthen the relatively few and clumsy mechanisms that our Constitution and laws have given us.

*

Judges in the United States are a unique species. They share some of the functions of judges from time immemorial, but have been given their distinctively American mixture of power and responsibility by a century and a half of colonial experience and by nearly two centuries of life under the Constitution. Drawn from the busy thoroughfares of the practice or teaching of law, or service in politics and in local, state, or national government, judges become strangers in our midst. Theirs is a separate way of life and work.

I have attempted to portray the work of appellate judges and the ways in which one of their number carries on this work. One underlying premise has been that a more perceptive view of the nature of appellate decision-making on the part of lay persons cannot fail to improve the quality of citizenship. Another premise, or perhaps an article of faith, has been that to the extent that the public and the press know what should be deemed good or excellent in the work of their appellate judges, and what must be seen as shoddy, sloppy, or meretricious, such knowledge becomes a subtle yet powerful force for improving the quality of judges and their work.

A final purpose applies to all judges, state and federal, trial and appellate. Their most elusive mission is that of safeguarding individual rights in a majoritarian society with due regard to the legitimate interests of that society. The search for the approach most likely to accomplish this mission seems to be never-ending. I confess that if we ever did unearth what was universally conceded as "the right approach" for all judges, I should feel that judging would have lost much of its zest and challenge. In the meantime, the continuing quest itself, if shared broadly and sensitively by citizens in addition to judges, goes far toward making tolerable the coiled-spring tension under which we have been chartered to live.

NOTES/INDEX

Notes

Chapter 1. On Judging Judges

1. Benjamin Cardozo, *The Nature of the Judicial Process* (New Haven: Yale University Press, 1921).
2. Jerome Frank, *Law and the Modern Mind* (New York: Coward McCann, 1930).
3. With the advent of sustained investigative reporting on a single event, institution, or issue, such a book as *The Brethren*, by Robert Woodward and Scott Armstrong (New York: Simon and Schuster, 1979), presents to the lay public a great quantity of data, as well as some controversial interpretations, concerning the workings of the Supreme Court.
4. Learned Hand, *The Spirit of Liberty* (New York: Alfred A. Knopf, 1952), p. 81.

Chapter 2. The Appellate Idea in History

1. For much of the overview of history in this chapter, I am indebted to John H. Wigmore's *A Panorama of the World's Legal Systems* (Washington, D.C.: Washington Law Book Company, 1936). Where no specific reference is indicated, the source is Wigmore. Although *Panorama* is an aging work by a renowned scholar of the law of evidence, who was writing for fun rather than prestige or profit, I have not found its like for interest and stimulation.
2. Will Durant, *Our Oriental Heritage* (New York: Simon and Schuster, 1954), p. 127.
3. Ibid., p. 232.
4. Exodus 18:13–22.
5. This description of the ancient Hebrew judicial system, in addition to relying on Wigmore, is largely drawn from Roland de Vaux, "Ancient Israel," *Social Institutions* (New York: McGraw-Hill, 1965), vol. 1, pp. 152–153.

254   *Notes*

6. "Rabbinical Courts: Modern-Day Solomons," *Columbia Journal of Law and Social Problems*, vol. 6, no. 1, p. 52, reprinted in *Studies in Jewish Jurisprudence*, edited by Edward M. Gershfield (New York: Hermon Press, 1971), vol. 2.
7. René David and John E. C. Brierley, *Major Legal Systems in the World Today*, second edition (New York: The Free Press, 1978), p. 480.
8. Durant, *Our Oriental Heritage*, p. 444.
9. Plutarch, *The Lives of the Noble Grecians and Romans*, translated by John Dryden (New York: Random House, Modern Library), p. 107.
10. Ibid., p. 108.
11. Will Durant, *The Life of Greece* (New York: Simon and Schuster, 1939), pp. 116, 247, 257, and 260.
12. Wigmore, *Panorama*, pp. 313–314, citing W. S. Ferguson, *The Fall of the Athenian Empire: Law and Politics in Athens* (Cambridge Ancient History, 1927), vol. 5, p. 349.
13. Acts 23:28–30.
14. David and Brierley, *Major Legal Systems*, pp. 35–36.
15. Montesquieu, *The Spirit of Laws* (Chicago: Encyclopedia Britannica, Inc., 1952), p. 239.
16. Ibid., p. 245.
17. Ibid., p. 247.
18. Ibid., pp. 247–251.
19. Ibid., pp. 249–251.
20. David and Brierley, *Major Legal Systems*, p. 37.
21. Montesquieu, *The Spirit of Laws*, p. 259.
22. Ibid., p. 257.
23. David and Brierley, *Major Legal Systems*, pp. 37–40.
24. Will Durant, *The Age of Faith* (New York: Simon and Schuster, 1950), pp. 691–693.
25. William Holdsworth, *A History of English Law*, seventh edition (London: Methuen, 1956), vol. 1, pp. 3–4.
26. Ibid., p. 63.
27. S. B. Chrimes, introductory essay to Holdsworth, *History of English Law*, p. 34.
28. Holdsworth, *History of English Law*, p. 214.
29. Ibid., p. 584.
30. David and Brierley, *Major Legal Systems*, p. 313.
31. Holdsworth, *History of English Law*, pp. 1–2.
32. David and Brierley, *Major Legal Systems*, p. 335.
33. Ibid., pp. 124 and 131.
34. John Henry Merryman and David S. Clark, *Comparative Law: Western European and Latin American Legal Systems* (Indianapolis: Bobbs-Merrill, 1978), pp. 184–185, quoting John P. Dawson, *The Oracles of the Law* (Ann Arbor: University of Michigan Press, 1968), pp. 369–371.

35. Merryman and Clark, *Comparative Law*, p. 189, quoting Merryman, *The Civil Law Tradition* (Stanford: Stanford University Press, 1969), pp. 15–19.
36. Merryman and Clark, *Comparative Law*, pp. 187–188.
37. Mauro Cappelletti and William Cohen, *Comparative Constitutional Law* (Indianapolis: Bobbs-Merrill, 1979), pp. 9–11.

Chapter 3. The Appellate Idea in the United States

1. Julius Goebel, Jr., *Antecedents and Beginnings to 1801*, vol. 1 of *The Oliver Wendell Holmes Devise History of the Supreme Court of the United States* (New York: Macmillan, 1971), pp. 1–2. In the remaining part of this chapter, I shall lean heavily on Professor Goebel, drawing information bearing on colonial times from his Chapter I, on the Constitutional Convention from his Chapter V, and on the Judiciary Act of 1789 from his Chapter XI.
2. Ibid., p. 1.
3. Ibid., p. 5.
4. Ibid., p. 13.
5. Ibid., p. 18.
6. Ibid., p. 25.
7. Ibid.
8. Ibid., p. 207.
9. Ibid., p. 225.
10. Ibid., pp. 209–210 and 227–229.
11. Ibid., p. 239.
12. Ibid., p. 414.
13. Ibid., p. 473.
14. Ibid., p. 472.
15. Ibid., p. 554; Albert J. Beveridge, *Life of John Marshall* (Boston: Houghton Mifflin, 1919), vol. 1, p. 257.
16. Henry L. Hart, Jr., and Herbert Wechsler, *The Federal Courts and the Federal System*, second edition (New York: The Foundation Press, 1973), p. 36.
17. Views of the Minority, Senate Document 1571, Fifty-first Congress, first session, August 8, 1890 (to accompany H.R. 9014).
18. *Congressional Record*, vol. 21, Fifty-first Congress, first session, September 19, 1890, p. 10223.
19. Ibid., p. 10363.
20. Federal Judicial Workload Statistics During the Twelve-Month Period Ended December 31, 1979, Administrative Office of the United States Courts, Washington, D.C., pp. 5 and 15.
21. Law Enforcement Assistance Administration and National Criminal Justice Information and Statistics Service, State Court Caseload Statistics, Annual Report, 1976, Table 16, p. 61 (manuscript copy, October 12, 1979).
22. Federal Judicial Workload Statistics, p. 1.

23. Ibid., pp. 48–49.
24. Law Enforcement Assistance Administration, State Court Caseload, Ibid., p. 23.
25. 1979 Annual Report of the Director of the Administrative Office of the United States Courts, Washington, D.C., pp. 4 and 7.
26. Federal Judicial Workload Statistics, p. 2.
27. 1979 Annual Report, pp. 47–49.
28. Management Statistics for the United States Courts, 1978, Director of Administrative Office of the United States Courts, p. 13.
29. "The Supreme Court, 1977 Term," *Harvard Law Review*, vol. 92, no. 1, pp. 332–336.

Chapter 4. The Elements of Deciding Appeals

1. In *The Common Law Tradition: Deciding Appeals* (Boston: Little, Brown, 1960), Karl Llewellyn lists fourteen Major Steadying Factors in Our Appellate Courts, pp. 19–51. Six of these, and arguably others, are in my list, which I think is a bit more barebones.

Chapter 5. Place and Patterns of Work

1. Karl Llewellyn, *The Common Law Tradition*, p. 321.
2. Irving Stone, *The Agony and the Ecstasy* (New York: Doubleday, 1961), p. 27.

Chapter 6. Preparing for Argument

1. These cases are *United States* v. *Francomano*, 554 F.2d 483 (1977), and *United States* v. *Mehtala*, 578 F.2d 6 (1978).
2. *United States* v. *Belgodere Mora*, 598 F.2d 682 (1979).
3. 487 F.2d at 1284.
4. Id. at 1287.
5. 490 F.2d at 1217.

Chapter 7. A Term of Court

1. Quoted in Lloyd Paul Stryker, *The Art of Advocacy* (New York: Simon and Schuster, 1954), p. 229.
2. "The Judge as Advocate's Consumer: On Reading Briefs and Hearing Argument," Boalt Hall School of Law, University of California at Berkeley, February 27, 1979.

Chapter 8. The Creation of Opinions

1. 418 U.S. at 557.
2. Ibid.

Chapter 9. The Workings of Collegiality

1. 427 U.S. 215, p. 224.
2. Ibid.
3. Ibid., p. 228.
4. Ibid., p. 230.
5. Ibid., p. 233.
6. Ibid., p. 235.
7. 28 United States Code 332.

Chapter 10. Craft Skills and Social Values

1. Learned Hand, *The Spirit of Liberty: Papers and Addresses of Learned Hand*, collected by Irving Dilliard (New York: Alfred A. Knopf, 1952), p. 44.
2. Arthur E. Sutherland, *Constitutionalism in America* (New York: Blaisdell Publishing Company, 1965), p. 383.

Chapter 11. Loss of Innocence and the Quest for Legitimacy

1. G. Edward White, *The American Judicial Tradition* (New York: Oxford University Press, 1976), p. 2.
2. Arthur E. Sutherland, *The Law at Harvard* (Cambridge: The Belknap Press of Harvard University Press, 1967), pp. 175–176.
3. Oliver Wendell Holmes, Jr., *Collected Legal Papers* (New York: Harcourt, Brace, 1920), p. 239.
4. Oliver Wendell Holmes, Jr., *The Common Law* (Boston: Little, Brown, 1881), p. 35, quoted in Morton White, *Social Thought in America* (Boston: Beacon Press, 1970), p. 68.
5. J. B. Thayer, "The Origin and Scope of the American Doctrine of Constitutional Law," *Harvard Law Review*, vol. 7, no. 3, p. 148.
6. Ibid., p. 144.
7. G. Edward White, *American Judicial Tradition*, p. 252.
8. Felix Frankfurter, "John Marshall and the Judicial Function," *Harvard Law Review*, vol. 69, no. 2, pp. 217–238.
9. Learned Hand, *The Bill of Rights* (New York: Atheneum, 1968), p. 14.
10. Ibid., pp. 29–30.
11. Ibid., p. 55.
12. Herbert Wechsler, "Toward Neutral Principles of Constitutional Law," *Harvard Law Review*, vol. 73, no. 1, p. 19.
13. Alexander Bickel, *The Least Dangerous Branch* (Indianapolis: Bobbs-Merrill, 1962), p. 240.
14. Ibid., p. 244.
15. Ibid., p. 236.
16. Ibid., p. 237.

17. 354 U.S. at 266–267.
18. Bickel, *Least Dangerous Branch*, pp. 238–239.

Chapter 12. A Time for Reappraisal

1. A perceptive article on the phenomenon of structural litigation is Owen M. Fliss's foreword to "The Supreme Court 1978 Term," entitled "The Forms of Justice," *Harvard Law Review*, vol. 93, no. 1, pp. 1–58.
2. Frank M. Coffin, "The Frontier of Remedies: A Call for Exploration," *University of California Law Review*, vol. 67, no. 4, p. 989.
3. Robert E. Heilbroner, *An Inquiry into the Human Prospect* (New York: Norton, 1975), pp. 137–138.
4. Thomas S. Kuhn, *The Structure of Scientific Revolutions*, second edition (Chicago: University of Chicago Press, 1970).
5. Ibid., p. 92.

Chapter 13. A Judge Seeks His Bearings

1. J. B. Thayer, "The Origin and Scope of the American Doctrine of Constitutional Law," p. 157.
2. John Rawls, *Theory of Justice* (Cambridge: Harvard University Press, 1972), p. 14.
3. Ibid., p. 60.
4. Ronald Dworkin, *Taking Rights Seriously* (Cambridge: Harvard University Press, 1977), p. 205.
5. Ibid., p. 134.
6. Ibid.
7. Ibid., p. 136.
8. Ibid., p. 142.
9. Ibid., pp. 198–199.
10. See, for example, "Jurisprudence Symposium," *Georgia Law Review*, vol. 11, no. 5 (September 1977), pp. 969–1424.
11. Dworkin, *Taking Rights Seriously*, p. 149.
12. Philio Soper, "On the Relevance of Philosophy to Law: Reflections on Ackerman's *Private Property and the Constitution*," *Columbia Law Review*, vol. 79, no. 1, p. 64.
13. Rawls, *Theory of Justice*, p. 23.
14. Frank E. A. Sander, "Community Justice," *Harvard Law School Bulletin*, vol. 31, no. 2, pp. 18–19; Daniel McGillis, "The Quiet (R)Evolution in American Dispute Settlement," Ibid., pp. 20–25.
15. See A. D. Dick Howard, "State Courts and Constitutional Rights in the Day of the Burger Court," *Virginia Law Review*, vol. 62, no. 5, pp. 873–944. One stimulus for this movement was the article of Justice William Brennan, entitled "State Constitutions and the Protection of Individual Rights," *Harvard Law Review*, vol. 90, no. 3, pp. 489–504.

16. Frank M. Coffin, "Justice and Workability: Un Essai," *Suffolk University Law Review*, vol. 5, no. 2, part 2, p. 571.
17. I have tried to scratch the surface of this subject in "The Frontier of Remedies: A Call for Exploration."
18. Hand, *The Spirit of Liberty*, p. 130.
19. G. Edward White, *The American Judicial Tradition*, pp. 198–199.

Index

Individual rights (*cont.*)
  vs. state or majority, 213, 216,
    220, 232, 234–35, 243–44,
    249
  and "balancing interests,"
    239–40
  See also Civil rights/liberties
"Inferior" court, 25, 28
  colonial concept of, 34
  and court of first resort, 197–98
  disavowal of Supreme Court
    opinions by, 89
Intermediate court of appeal, 42.
  See also Court(s)

Jefferson, Thomas: quoted, 82n
"Jobbist," the judge as, 196–99
Johnson, Andrew, 37
Joinville, Jean, sire de: quoted,
  26
"Judges' Bill," 39
Judges' postargument conference, 63, 79, 110, 111,
  135–40, 197
  and decision-making, 111,
    138–40
  in sample cases, 118–19, 124,
    129
  and value judgments, 136,
    139–40, 201
  See also Collegiality
Judicial branch, 188–92
  Constitution and, 34–36
  and justice subsystems,
    242–43
  monitoring (of government in-
    stitutions) by, 9, 95,
    223–25
  public perception of, *see* Pub-
    lic perception and ex-
    pectations

relations of, with legislative
  branch/Congress, 8, 10, 34,
  36, 45, 60, 176, 188, 189,
  208, 209, 217, 224, 235–37
  (*see also* Law)
  See also Appellate judges; Ap-
    pellate system (state-
    federal)
Judicial combat, 25
Judicial conduct, 7–8, 189
  code of ethics and, 7–8, 12, 218
Judicial Conference of the United
  States, 189, 190–91
Judicial council (of circuit
  courts), 188–92
Judicial function, 9–11, 52
  defined (by Thayer), 208
  historical influences on, 28,
    248–49
  reappraisal of, 215–30
  See also Decision-making;
    Law
"Judicial nose," 103–5
Judiciary Act (1789), 35
Judiciary Committee (Senate),
  37
Jurisdiction:
  appellate, 35, 39, 100–101
  objection to, 76–77
  of circuit courts, 35–36
  "diversity," 45, 100, 101
  importance of, 156
Jury, 201–2
  and jury system in ancient
    Greece and Rome, 22, 23
Justice, U.S. Department of, 242
Justices of the peace, 33
Justice subsystems, 242–43. *See
  also* Judicial branch
Justinian, emperor of Byzantium: Digest or Code of, 24,
  26, 28

The Federal-

THE SUPREME COU

Created by the Constitution, Art
III: nine justices, appointed for l
by the President, with the "advi
and consent" of the Senate. Inte
prets and applies the Constitutio

THE INFERIOR FEDERAL COURTS

Created by Congress, Judiciary Act of
1789 pursuant to Article III of the
Constitution. Appointed for life by
the President, with the "advice and
consent" of the Senate.

Direct appeal from decisions
holding state laws unconstitutional

U.S. Statute;
U.S. a party

Four thousand req
for cert
70 percent from
circuit courts

Direct appeal

U.S. CIRCUIT COURTS OF APPEALS

Created by Congress in 1891 (Evarts Act).
Eleven circuits. Each court decides questions
of law on briefs and oral arguments.

SPECIALIZED COURTS

1. Court of Claims
2. Court of Customs and
Patent Appeals

U.S. DISTRICT COURTS

Ninety-five districts. Each district has from
1 judge (Wyoming) to over 25 judges
(Southern District of New York). Jurisdiction: law and equity; claims under federal
law; civil claims between citizens of different states, if over a fixed amount. Trial
with or without a jury.

FEDERAL AGENCIES

Interstate Commerce Com-
mission, Tax Court, Secu-
rities and Exchange Com-
mission, National Labor
Relations Board, Federal
Trade Commission, etc.

BANKRUPTCY JUDGES

Preside over bankrupt-
cies, reorganizations, ar-
rangements, wage-earner
plans.

ADMINISTRATIVE LAW
JUDGES

Civil-service positions.
Conduct hearings and sub-
mit reports and
recommendations to ad-
ministrative boards or
agencies.

U.S. MAGISTRATES

Conduct preliminary hearings;
determine bail; assist district
judges by serving as special mas-
ters and reporting suggested
findings to judge.